Industrial Policy in Developing Countries

Industrial Policy in Developing Countries

Failing Markets, Weak States

Tilman Altenburg

Head of Department, Sustainable Economic and Social Development, German Development Institute, Germany

Wilfried Lütkenhorst

Associate Fellow, German Development Institute, Germany and Jingshi Principal Professor, Beijing Normal University, China

Edward Elgar
PUBLISHING

Cheltenham, UK • Northampton, MA, USA

Published by
Edward Elgar Publishing Limited
The Lypiatts
15 Lansdown Road
Cheltenham
Glos GL50 2JA
UK

Edward Elgar Publishing, Inc.
William Pratt House
9 Dewey Court
Northampton
Massachusetts 01060
USA

A catalogue record for this book
is available from the British Library

Library of Congress Control Number: 2015938371

This book is available electronically in the **Elgar**online
Economics subject collection
DOI 10.4337/9781781000267

MIX
Paper from
responsible sources
FSC® C013056

ISBN   978 1 78100 025 0 (cased)
ISBN   978 1 78100 026 7 (eBook)

Typeset by Columns Design XML Ltd, Reading

Printed and bound in Great Britain by TJ International Ltd, Padstow

Contents

List of figures, tables and boxes

FIGURES

TABLES

BOXES

Foreword

This is a most timely book. While global attention is increasingly focused on the development dynamics in emerging countries, the policy challenges and tough choices for the vast majority of low- and middle-income countries are easily overlooked. Yet it is in these countries where the gap is greatest between what *needs* to be done and what *can* be achieved by structurally weak states, inexperienced policymakers and incipient institutions. As the authors argue convincingly, markets alone fail to deliver the results developing societies want to see – while their governments' capacities to design and push through effective policies are severely constrained.

Meanwhile, the task ahead is not getting any easier. Globalised markets demand the build-up of ever more competitive industries; new technological trajectories (robotics, artificial intelligence, digitalization) redefine international comparative advantages and the division of labour these in turn generate; poverty and inequality are anything but history; and the imperative of a rapid green transformation to fight climate change, resource depletion and environmental degradation raises hitherto unknown complexities. The authors deserve credit for developing a conceptual framework that allows for a holistic view of these interdependent dimensions of global and country-level development processes.

Against this backdrop, the level of ambition of this book is formidable. Fortunately, the authors are acutely aware of the associated risks. Arguing from a rich base of experience – Tilman Altenburg has engaged in policy-oriented development research for decades; Wilfried Lütkenhorst brings to bear a long career in UN development cooperation – they offer careful reflections and balanced assessments. The book is not about blueprints for action. Rather, it points to hard choices, identifies the limitations of policymakers facing an imperfect world and seeks to develop some signposts for development principles and pathways that may promise success. Above all, it is written in a spirit of modesty vis-à-vis the quest for solutions that are needed to advance developing societies in the direction they themselves want to take.

In addition, in terms of the long-standing industrial policy debate, I consider the more conceptual parts of the book as providing fresh and inspiring insights that go beyond the conventional *state vs market* discourse. Indeed, the authors move from a narrow notion of industrial sector policy to an understanding of industrial policy as driving broader economic and social transformation. The book should make for fascinating reading by development researchers and practitioners alike.

Dirk Messner
Director
German Development Institute

Acknowledgements

This book is the result of our long-standing engagement in empirical and conceptual research related to industrial policy in developing countries. As such, it draws on some elements of our earlier work, which have been incorporated here into a broader framework of the foundations of industrial policy and its impact on the multiple goals that societies need to pursue in today's development reality. In this, the challenge of making economic growth processes socially and environmentally sustainable takes centre stage.

This book would not have seen the light of day without intense discussions and advice to which many colleagues have contributed. We would like to thank in particular Ha-Joon Chang, Michele Clara, Mike Hobday, Dirk Messner, Kenichi Ohno, Philipp Neuerburg, Hubert Schmitz and Imme Scholz for their comments on earlier versions of some chapters of the text. We also acknowledge the contributions made by Anna Pegels and Georgeta Vidican through joint work on green industrial policy and by Steffen Erdle, Friedrich Kaufmann, Matthias Krause, Markus Loewe and Christina Rosendahl through earlier country studies. The assistance of Ina Klemke proved invaluable in knocking the manuscript into shape. Needless to add that all remaining errors and inaccuracies are entirely ours.

Abbreviations

BRAC	Bangladesh Rural Advancement Committee
BRICS	Brazil, Russia, India, China and South Africa
BTI	Bertelsmann Transformation Index
CCS	Carbon capture and storage
COMESA	Common Market for Eastern and Southern Africa
COP 21	21st session of the Conference of the Parties to the UNFCCC
CPI	Corruption Perception Index
DBI	Doing Business Index
EAC	East African Community
EHPEA	Ethiopian Horticulture Producers and Exporters Association
EPRDF	Ethiopian People's Revolutionary Democratic Front
EPZ	Export Processing Zone
ETS	Emissions trading system
FDI	Foreign direct investment
FRELIMO	The Mozambique Liberation Front
GCI	Global Competitiveness Index
GDP	Gross domestic product
GHG	Greenhouse gas
GIZ	Deutsche Gesellschaft für Internationale Zusammenarbeit
GNI	Gross national income
GTP	Growth and Transformation Plan
GTZ	Gesellschaft für Technische Zusammenarbeit, now: GIZ
IEA	International Energy Agency
IFC	International Finance Corporation
IPTT	Indigenous Plant Task Team
LED	Local economic development
LLMIC	Low- and lower-middle-income countries
MENA	Middle East and North Africa
MVA	Manufacturing value added
NASSCOM	National Association of Software Services Companies
NDP	National Development Plan
NGO	Non-governmental organization

ODA	Official Development Assistance
OECD	Organisation for Economic Co-operation and Development
PMN	National Upgrading Programme
R&D	Research and development
S&T	Science and technology
SACU	Southern African Customs Union
SADC	Southern African Development Community
SEZ	Special Economic Zone
SME	Small and medium enterprise
SWAPO	South West Africa People's Organization
TVET	Technical and vocational education and training
UN	United Nations
UNCTAD	United Nations Conference on Trade and Development
UNIDO	United Nations Industrial Development Organization
WEF	World Economic Forum
WGI	World Bank Worldwide Governance Indicators
WTO	World Trade Organization

1. Why this book?

Productivity growth is a precondition for increasing living standards and maintaining competitiveness in the globalised economy. Low total factor productivity is the key reason for persistent poverty in developing countries. Therefore, poor countries need to increase productivity to eradicate poverty. The challenge is not only to develop more productive ways of doing business in activities already established but also to accelerate the structural transformation from low productivity activities in agriculture, petty trade and skill-extensive services to new activities that are knowledge-intensive and exploit the advantages of inter-firm specialisation.

The role of industry and specifically manufacturing as the key driver of structural change, technological innovation and productivity increases has been at the centre of development economics from its inception: 'Generally, industrialization was viewed as equivalent to development' (Ranis 2004, p. 4). This is mirrored by the fact that *industrial* policy has become a synonym for policies seeking to influence the direction, structure and pace of economic growth and development.

Undoubtedly, the main driver of structural change is the private sector. Still, governments have an important role to play in setting policy frameworks that stimulate competition and encourage innovation and technological change, as well as in correcting market failure. For instance, it may be important to support activities that do not pay off immediately for an individual investor but are likely to trigger manifold linkages and spillovers in the future; or to encourage new activities that do not emerge spontaneously because several interrelated investments need to be made simultaneously that exceed the resources available to any individual entrepreneur. Such government interventions accelerate structural change towards more competitive and higher value activities. This is what industrial policy is about.

The above notwithstanding, the concept of industrial policy has remained a hotly debated and controversial subject in developed and developing countries alike. It is the territory on which many an ideological battle has been fought: the role of the state is juxtaposed with that of the market, intervention is contrasted with *laissez-faire*, technocrats are

confronted with entrepreneurs. The dissent regarding the role of industrial policy is also to some extent due to a lack of clarity about its
definition. According to most definitions,[1] industrial policy comprises
'any government measure, or set of measures, to promote or prevent
structural change' (Curzon Price 1981, p. 17). While industrial policies
are sometimes employed to preserve and protect existing industries or to
mitigate the effects of structural crises, their principal aim is to accelerate
structural change towards more productive and dynamic activities. These
activities need *not* be part of the industrial or manufacturing sector.
Industrial policies quite often target activities in other sectors in which
governments assume untapped growth potentials, such as non-traditional
agricultural exports or high-value service activities like software development and tourism. Importantly, industrial policies are always about
seeking to move towards a desired future state of the economy; they are
directional and normative in nature.

While the theoretical case for industrial policy is not in doubt, there is
no consensus about the most effective instruments and right degree of
intervention. The controversy is mainly about *selective* interventions that
favour some sectors over others and thus interfere with the price
mechanism, the main signalling device of market economies. Critics
argue that governments are usually not very good at identifying coordination failures or anticipating future knowledge spillovers, and their
decisions may well end up reducing allocative efficiency and creating
perverse incentives for investors and bureaucrats. However, proponents
rightly emphasise that industrial policy is a desirable response to pervasive market failures, particularly in development contexts calling for
fundamental normative decisions on future societal pathways.

It is now widely accepted that industrial policy *may* work well in
countries with strong meritocratic public services and political checks
and balances. These mainly include Organisation for Economic
Co-operation and Development (OECD) member states and some other
countries with high income levels. South Korea, Taiwan, Singapore,
Brazil and Chile are often mentioned as examples of countries that
successfully used industrial policies to catch up with the rich countries of
the OECD. More recently, the spectacular economic development success
of China in sustaining high growth rates, capturing global markets,
moving into high-technology sectors and, along the way, reducing
poverty levels has been attributed to its special industrial policy hybrid of
central control coupled with competitive markets.

Many observers, however, are quite sceptical when it comes to the role
of industrial policies in *low-income and most middle-income countries*.
According to all available governance indicators, these countries almost

without exception lag far behind with regard to government effectiveness, transparency and accountability. Hence, even though these countries obviously face particularly severe market failure, there is a big question mark as to the ability of their governments to intervene in markets in ways that increase public welfare.[2] In fact, economic history is full of failures of industrial policies. In any case, the appropriate policy mix is unlikely to be the same as in rich countries because both the *requirements* and the *capacity* for public intervention differ substantially. Yet, in stark contrast with the above-mentioned success cases of catch-up development, little is known about the quality and the outcomes of industrial policies in low- and middle-income countries.

This book focuses exactly on the latter group of relatively poor developing countries. There is a rich literature available on the development paths and policies of emerging economies both in terms of the first-generation newly industrialising countries in East Asia and, more recently, the BRICS countries (Brazil, Russia, India, China and South Africa). However, not much has been written so far on the industrial policy approaches and challenges of the vast majority of developing countries – which in Alice Amsden's typology are not even considered as the 'rising rest' but simply as the 'remainder'.[3] These countries are typically characterised by weak entrepreneurial dynamism, an incipient and small private sector, highly fragmented economic structures and a high degree of informality (with dominance of micro and small enterprises) – a scenario that, more often than not, is ignored in the mainstream industrial policy literature.

Moreover, today's poor countries are not only faced with a highly constrained development setting as characterised above but also with the formidable challenge of having to deliver results against a variety of economic, social and environmental objectives at the same time. This latter aspect of multiple and simultaneous policy goals is often overlooked, yet it is arguably the single most important feature determining today's development processes: while the industrialised countries enjoyed the luxury of being able to pursue growth and productivity objectives first, then dealing with the social implications by building up welfare institutions and, even later, starting to mitigate the environmental impact thus created, such a sequential approach is simply not available to poor countries today. Against the double pressure stemming from both their own populations (with rapidly rising expectations fuelled by modern global communication channels) and an impatient donor community, governments struggle to find pathways that build on synergies and avoid tough trade-offs between competing objectives. This predicament of having to address multiple goals is a recurring theme throughout this book. It is what makes rational and effective industrial policies so critically important in poor countries seeking to achieve long-term sustainable development.

Our book therefore addresses difficult questions that are particularly relevant for poor countries yet have often been overlooked in industrial policy analyses. Such questions prominently include:

- How can the industrial transformation be made socially inclusive, and what should industrial policies look like when the vast majority of the workforce are engaged in informal micro-enterprises?
- How can trends towards rising inequality and enclave economies be overcome?
- Is it preferable to promote local bottom-up economic development or to encourage growth poles and economies of scale?
- Is it realistic to expect welfare-oriented industrial policies to be adopted by regimes whose legitimacy rests largely on distributing favours among their political supporters?
- How can transformative structural change be promoted when governments are not subjected to the checks and balances of mature democracies?
- How relevant is the 'greening' of industries, and particularly decarbonisation for poor countries whose per capita CO_2 emissions are still negligible while poverty levels are high?

Our approach throughout this book is evidence-based and seeks to deliver a reality check. While dealing with a politically highly charged subject, we aim at providing a sober and balanced assessment of both the potentials and perils of industrial policy in a context where it matters most, that is, in shaping the development trajectory of economies seeking to overcome poverty and create wealth. Ultimately, we want to replace dogma with nuance, debunk some of the myths still prevailing and demonstrate that industrial policy needs to defy the twin challenge of failing markets *and* weak state capacities. Obviously, this does not render its proper design and implementation any easier. However, it also does not call into question the necessity to act.

The book is organised in the following manner. At the outset (Chapter 2), we develop our conceptual foundation and point of departure – the proposition that economic markets are subordinate to social norms and values and that industrial policy is faced with the reality of multiple societal goals that go beyond the realm of economic efficiency. More specifically, and placed in the context of emerging global sustainable development goals, chapters 3 and 4 address the challenges to promote inclusive growth patterns and to respond to the growing relevance of environmental concerns in industrial policymaking (green industrial policy).

This is followed in Chapter 5 by a review of the evolution of the industrial policy discourse, with emphasis on the need to develop systems and principles of governance that can balance market and state failure. This chapter also sums up key principles of smart industrial policy.

In Chapter 6, we focus on the context-specificity of industrial policy and try to distil the main elements that characterise the design and implementation of industrial policy in developing countries. We argue that these countries face the common challenge of latecomer development, which confers both advantages and disadvantages on them. Within an overall setting of severe and mutually reinforcing development constraints on the demand and the supply side, especially the poorest countries have to find ways to kick-start market-based economic development, to reduce persistently high poverty levels and to build up environmentally sustainable economic and technological capacities. This chapter also considers the political economy of developmental policymaking. It acknowledges the widespread existence of limited access orders (North et al. 2012), that is, regimes where political elites divide up control of the economy and stabilise their position through systems of clientelism, and industrial policy may be employed as one instrument for rewarding supporters. This is often coupled with weak policy management capabilities and a strong influence of external factors ranging from donor agencies to international trade agreements that may limit the range of available policy options.

In Chapter 7, we present five country case studies. By selecting Ethiopia, Mozambique, Namibia, Tunisia and Vietnam, we review the manifestation of industrial policy in countries at different income levels, with significant variations in their development strategies and with different political and institutional systems.

Chapter 8 pulls together the key insights from the case studies in a comparative perspective aimed at identifying critical determinants of policy success or failure. In doing so, it places particular emphasis on the way the interaction between public and private actors is organised, the importance of a long-term transformative vision as a national 'project', the policy implementation process within the broader space of planning and/or searching for solutions, and the specific challenges stemming from emerging planetary boundaries as epitomised by the threat of climate change.

The concluding Chapter 9 distils the main lessons of our study and offers an outlook on the key industrial policy challenges ahead for developing countries.

NOTES

1. See Aiginger (2007, p. 319 f.) for a compilation of definitions.
2. Chang (2006) and others point out that state bureaucracies of East Asian industrial latecomers (e.g. South Korea) were fairly ineffective at the beginning of their take-off. Thus, initial ineffectiveness obviously does not rule out the possibility of step-by-step improvements. Still, these bureaucracies obviously had the capacity to organise learning processes effectively, in a way that the vast majority of low- and lower-middle-income countries have not yet been able to replicate.
3. Based on a conceptual foundation related to manufacturing experience and industrial diversification, Amsden distinguishes the 'rising rest' (China, India, Indonesia, South Korea, Malaysia, Taiwan and Thailand in Asia; Argentina, Brazil, Chile and Mexico in Latin America; plus Turkey in the Middle East) from all other developing countries, which as the 'remainder' are considered as falling further behind in economic development (Amsden 2001).

2. Societal goals ruling markets

In this chapter, we will establish our point of departure for the remainder of the book. We will make three fundamental points. In Section 2.1 we argue that a conceptual approach that reduces industrial policy to the function of correcting exceptional and temporary market failures (externalities) is misleading. It does not do justice to the normative content of any industrial policy that seeks to chart the future course for economic and social development. Section 2.2 further substantiates this argument with an excursus into the ethical dimension of economics. On this basis, Section 2.3 elaborates on the policy challenge of having to address a multitude of societal goals, which – in the overall perspective of sustainable development – include the promotion of socially inclusive patterns of growth and the safeguarding of environmental resources.

2.1 EXTERNALITIES: A RED HERRING?[4]

At the outset, it is worth recalling that most of the arguments used to justify industrial policy evolve around various types of market failures, ranging from information shortcomings to spillovers of various types, imperfect capital markets, uncoordinated investment decisions, systemic infrastructure requirements, and so on – all of which are rooted in externalities that drive a wedge between private and social costs and benefits. Hence, so the argument goes, policy interventions are needed to take corrective action.

In fact, there are a number of valid theoretical arguments to justify industrial policy interventions (see Pack and Saggi 2006, pp. 268 ff.; Chang 2009, pp. 7 ff.):

- *Coordination failure.* Many investment projects require simultaneous investments in related activities to become viable. Assuming that these interlinked activities are not yet in place and that they are not tradable, entrepreneurs will not invest unless someone else at the same time undertakes the necessary related investments. Hence, considerable coordination is required.

- *Dynamic scale economies and knowledge spillovers*. Price signals help entrepreneurs identify where they can *currently* exploit comparative advantages; but they do not help to find future production possibilities if substantial learning-by-doing economies are involved. In other words, it may be desirable for society to invest in an emerging economic activity (such as the electronics industry), which has the potential to create manifold linkages and spillovers, even though the initial investments may not pay off for any individual entrepreneur. This is because individual investors cannot (a) anticipate the range of new technologies and markets that may develop at a later stage of maturity of this industry and (b) appropriate all the gains of those activities.
- *Informational externalities*. Information about lucrative business options may not be freely available. Developing a new business idea involves costs and risks of failure. When the idea materialises, however, competitors may quickly copy it and thus dissipate the *rents* (see definition in Box 2.1) that can be obtained from the business innovation. Due to this non-appropriability of some of the innovation rents, there is a case for governments to encourage the discovery of future business opportunities. As Hausmann and Rodrik (2002, p. 4) put it:

> … there is great social value to discovering that cut flowers, soccer balls, or computer software can be produced at low cost, because this knowledge can orient the investments of other entrepreneurs. But the initial entrepreneur who makes the 'discovery' can capture only a small part of the social value that this knowledge generates [… because] other entrepreneurs can quickly emulate such discoveries. Consequently, entrepreneurship of this type … will typically be undersupplied.

BOX 2.1   DEFINITION OF ECONOMIC RENTS

Economic rents are a key concept for understanding industrial policy. They are defined here as super-normal profits resulting from situations of imperfect competition. 'Economic rents' can be obtained through:

- innovation allowing investors to generate incomes greater than those from the next best risk-adjusted alternative (temporary innovation rents);
- payments received for non-produced inputs (resource rents);
- monopolies (monopoly rents); and
- policy measures that restrict competition, such as production licences or import taxes (policy rents).

- *Environmental externalities.* Many environmental public goods, such as clean air, clean water and biodiversity, are not sufficiently taken into account in private investments. Policies are therefore needed to gear the choice of technologies towards more environmentally sustainable development paths. Such policies include elements of command and control as well as a range of stimulus packages. Market-based instruments, for example the establishment of tradable emissions rights, are gaining importance. Due to the immediate threat of global warming, the internalisation of environmental costs, and decarbonisation of production in particular, is likely to become a major driver of industrial policy worldwide.

The theoretical case for the aforementioned market failures is undisputed. Controversy arises with regard to its practical relevance, particularly whether governments are well positioned to correct failure rather than further distorting markets. Light interventions following the logic of Hausmann and Rodrik (which is grounded on informational externalities) – that is, to subsidise search costs for innovative investors and phase them out once the business model has proven its viability – are now widely accepted. The much more controversial issue is linked to long-term strategic interventions that are justified on the grounds of coordination failures and assumed dynamic scale economies. To successfully build a globally competitive aircraft industry in Brazil or an automotive industry in South Korea would have been unthinkable without anticipatory and coordinated public support for a range of complementary activities. Betting on the success of an entirely new industry and sustaining it throughout its infant phase, however, is obviously risky.

This conventional externalities-based *raison d'être* of industrial policy as presented above is a necessary first step yet does not tell the whole story and cuts the argument far too short. This is not to say that this line of reasoning is irrelevant. However, we submit that the rationale and legitimation of industrial policy need to be framed in a broader normative context.

In reality, markets do not function according to the neoclassical paradigm (with *homo oeconomicus* acting rationally in a competitive space with full information, instant adjustment speed and absence of externalities). Furthermore, the question must be asked if the results of a pure market logic can stand the test of societal acceptance. Two simple examples can serve to illustrate this point:

- While a perfectly functioning market will generate a functional income distribution that responds to relative availabilities and prices of labour and capital as the main production factors, this income distribution may or may not be socially acceptable. Additional assessment dimensions will have to be factored in relating to the fundamental imperative of fairness and to aspects like regional distribution, gender equality, ethnic and cultural norms, and so on. For example, societies may wish to maintain a regionally balanced distribution of economic activities even when this implies sacrificing some allocative efficiency.

- The technology choices that will result from market allocation mechanisms can be expected to be most cost-efficient as assessed from the perspective of today's prices and their anticipated future trends. However, this does not account for possible societal preferences in favour of long-term technology diversification with a view to reducing future risks and dependencies in a broader national perspective.

Hence, relying on a purely market-based allocation of resources constitutes a partial economic logic that – within a hierarchical perspective – is subordinate to the realm of social norms and goals. Markets are all about allocative efficiency – and in this domain, they may arguably be the most effective coordination mechanism; however, additional societal preferences related to distribution, fairness, risk management and political prudence need to be factored in. The fact that market processes meet efficiency standards, cannot and must not be equated with their societal acceptability. In other words, markets represent a *process norm,* which must be subjected to *outcome norms* in terms of what a society considers as both necessary and desirable. For the latter assessment, non-market institutions (from informal social networks and non-profit community services to elected governments) need to assume responsibility by going beyond Pareto optimality as a framework and monetary demand as a yardstick.

Fundamental critique of the market failure concept comes also from evolutionary economists (including Stiglitz, Dosi, Freeman, Nelson, Cimoli and others) who dismiss the welfare theorems of neoclassical theory altogether as largely irrelevant. They argue that standard assumptions – such as perfect competition, tradability of knowledge and full rationality of decision-making – are highly unrealistic. Consequently, the concept of market failure is regarded to be useless as a yardstick for government interventions. According to Cimoli et al. 2006, pp. 20 f.):

> The whole world can be seen as a huge market failure ... non-market institutions (ranging from public agencies to professional associations, from

trade unions to community structures) are at the core of the very constitution of the whole socio-economic fabric. ... they offer the main governance structure in many activities where market exchanges are socially inappropriate or simply ineffective.

In this book we do not go that far, taking into account that the concept of market failure can be a useful starting point to assess the logic of government intervention in markets. There is little doubt that market failure is pervasive, particularly in many developing countries at low income levels. At the same time, despite all imperfections, markets are in most instances a more efficient mechanism for resource allocation than discrete government decisions. Hence, governments need an analytical tool that helps to decide when market processes should be relied upon and when intervention is needed. Evolutionary theory does not offer any alternative concept that might help to make this distinction.

However, as efficient as markets may be in terms of generating allocative efficiency, they cannot substitute for the responsibility of the state to set long-term development goals based on consulting and engaging all societal stakeholders. Economic development takes place within a framework of social values and norms that are superior to market mechanisms as an instrument.

Moreover, the accepted boundaries of markets are set within historical contexts and modified by social conventions. Markets are a social construct with delineations that have changed significantly over time – one example being the gradually tightening introduction of labour and health regulations (Chang 2001; Chang 2010). Particularly in developing economies, which almost by definition are characterised by a fuzzy and moving borderline separating their market and governance structures (Cimoli, Dosi and Stiglitz 2009), social conventions are rapidly changing. While the global community has adopted rules of the game banning slave trade and other forms of human trafficking, many countries still allow the crudest forms of environmental damage to happen, to travel down rivers and to cross borders.

The dividing lines between responsible, irresponsible and illegal behaviour are man-made and can be redrawn. At the same time, it needs to be recognised that 'markets are not mere mechanisms. They embody certain norms. They presuppose – and promote – certain ways of valuing the goods being exchanged' (Sandel 2012, p. 64). This recognition leads us straight into the relationship of economics and ethics.

2.2 ECONOMICS AND ETHICS

So far, we have emphasised the distinct role of social norms, goals and aspirations in shaping industrial policy. This opens up fundamental questions of value judgments and how they impact on economic theory and practice.

The conceptualisation and positioning of economics in the treacherous space between a positive (i.e. allegedly value-free) science and a normative 'moral science' has shaped methodological debates among economists, social scientists and philosophers for centuries. In particular, the evolution of welfare economics from its original utilitarian philosophical foundation into a highly technical discipline has marked this debate. At the same time, in the harsh opinion of Boulding (1969, pp. 5 f.):

> Welfare economics ... has been a failure, though a reasonably glorious one ... Many, if not most, economists accept the Pareto optimum as almost self-evident. Nevertheless, it rests on an extremely shaky foundation of ethical propositions ... It assumes selfishness ... such that it makes no difference to me whether I perceive you as either better off or worse off. Anything less descriptive of the human condition can hardly be imagined.

Value judgments thus can (and do) easily enter the realm of what is often portrayed as a technical, value-free economic analysis. A telling example are seemingly technical assumptions about discount rates, that is, introducing a mechanism into long-term modelling exercises that (de-)values future costs and benefits as compared to those occurring today. Any assumed discount rate is indeed a technically couched (i.e. disguised) value judgment built into policy advice. Famously, in the debate about climate change, two seminal studies (Nordhaus 1994; Stern et al. 2007) work with discount rates of 6.0 per cent and 1.4 per cent, respectively, thus taking radically different views on the present value of costs and benefits impacting future generations (Broome 2008). Indeed, it has been demonstrated that the drastically differing policy recommendations derived from both studies can be explained almost entirely by the diverging discount rate assumptions used (Weisbach and Sunstein 2008).

Similarly, and generally noticed to a lesser extent, the deeply entrenched approach of measuring national welfare through the gross domestic product (GDP) is based on hidden value judgments. While these are not of an inter-generational nature, the fundamental assumption is that each monetary unit has the same value regardless of whether it is earned and spent by a billionaire businessman or a person living in abject poverty. This example should suffice to dispel the notion that economic efficiency and growth objectives are of a technical nature while distributional objectives are about value judgments. In reality, both spaces are closely intertwined and the 'tendency to separate efficiency from ethics' (Crespo 1998, p. 201) can hardly be justified (see also Hausman and McPherson 1993).

Thus, one essential meeting point of economics and ethics has always been the question of whether or not economic efficiency yields results that from a broader societal and moral perspective can be considered as fair or just. In more technical terms, this is the debate around the distribution of goods and services, the absolute and relative incidence of poverty and the prevailing income inequality levels that result from market-based competitive allocation processes. In development economics, the controversy around inequality-inducing growth dynamics (as advocated by Hirschman's theory of unbalanced growth (1958) and epitomised by the Kuznets curve) and subsequent approaches arguing for redistribution with growth (Chenery et al. 1974) and the priority fulfilment of basic human needs (Streeten 1981) have been iconic concepts in this domain.

In parallel, concerns about the earth's limited endowment with natural resources and limited absorptive capacity for public bads like pollution triggered a new breed of global modelling exercises (Meadows et al. 1972, 'Limits of Growth') and the emergence of ecological steady-state growth theories (Daly 1977). More recently, mounting concerns about various types of planetary boundaries and the ultimate catastrophe possibly following from global climate change have lent renewed urgency to environmental and resource economics (Rockström et al. 2009, Nordhaus 2013).

There seems to be a strange paradox at play: while over decades a fierce debate has emphasised the normative implications of *positive* economics and its misguided attempts to claim value-free territory, today we witness *normative* economics (dealing with policy prescriptions) itself trying to steer clear of values and norms and to find a foundation in *positive* market failure reasoning. In the same vein, the ongoing debate on the sustainability transformation and the role of green industrial policies is primarily couched in Pigouvian terms (primarily justifying interventions as a means to increase allocative efficiency) or, at best, in Schumpeterian terms (creative destruction as a means to disrupt existing pathways and boost technological innovation), yet rarely with reference to societal norms and objectives.

We would argue that the normative content of industrial policy in general – and of the new breed of green industrial policy in particular – is high and pronounced. Green industrial policy (see Chapter 4) involves an exceedingly long-term transformation that is global in nature, requires the adoption of sustainability norms and standards for both production and consumption and has implications for both intra- and inter-generational distribution and equity. All the more so as irreversible tipping points of instability are not the monopoly of ecological systems. In view of widely rising levels of income inequality (not only for emerging economies but also for developed economies; OECD 2011), the danger of reaching also social tipping points is real. Against this backdrop, the triple challenge of maintaining economic growth, avoiding environmental disasters and keeping inequality and poverty levels in check, that is, to shape a green and inclusive future, is the defining element of the current industrial policy agenda.

However, in stark contrast to the need to bring various strands of economic research more closely together, there remains a noticeable gap between much of mainstream development economics on the one hand and research with an explicit sustainability focus on the other. While issues of factor costs, economic growth and trade dominate the former, it is the scarcity and waste of resources as well as the environmental impact of their exploitation that are emphasised in the latter. Similarly, in the industrial policy research community, a dividing line between more conventional approaches and innovative attempts to integrate sustainability goals into industrial policymaking has not disappeared.[5]

2.3 THE REALITY OF MULTIPLE SOCIETAL GOALS: SUSTAINABLE DEVELOPMENT AND INDUSTRIAL POLICY

As stressed above, industrial policy is a tool, an instrument to support societies in reaching agreed goals and objectives. These can be purely economic in nature, yet any economic efficiency agenda is closely intertwined with goals that address broader issues of social cohesion and environmental sustainability. Indeed, it is these three pillars – economic, social and environmental – of a multidimensional goal system that have come to be integrated in the notion of sustainable development. Let us take a brief look at this concept.

The most often quoted definition of sustainable development dates way back to 1987 and originates from the so-called Brundtland Commission: 'Sustainable development is development that meets the needs of the present without compromising the ability of future generations to meet their own needs' (World Commission on Environment and Development 1987, p. 43)

It is noteworthy that – starting from this definition more than 25 years ago – sustainable development has been conceptualised as a needs-based approach. This establishes an intrinsic link to the means available to satisfy needs, that is, to productive capacities and growth, as well as to questions of poverty, deprivation and distribution. From this perspective, it is only logical that later on – most pronounced in the Outcome Document of the 2005 World Summit – the so-called three pillar approach of sustainable development was postulated:

> We reaffirm our commitment to achieve the goal of sustainable development … To this end, we commit ourselves to undertaking concrete actions and measures at all levels and to enhancing international cooperation, taking into account the Rio principles. These efforts will also promote the integration of the three components of sustainable development – economic development, social development and environmental protection – as interdependent and mutually reinforcing pillars. (UNGA 2005, para. 48)

This reflects a fundamental recognition of sustainable development not being just about the environment, not being a mere afterthought to conventional economic reasoning, not being separate from economic growth but to be built into its very foundation and structure. The essence of the notion of sustainable development thus lies in its call for a full integration of economic efficiency with social stability and equity, and with the need to respect planetary boundaries, that is, the limitations of both natural resources and the absorptive capacity of our biosphere. Exactly this understanding was reiterated in 2012 at the Rio+20 Earth Summit. In its outcome document, 'The Future We Want', it is stated: 'We also reaffirm the need to achieve sustainable development by promoting sustained, inclusive and equitable economic growth, creating greater opportunities for all, reducing inequalities … and promoting integrated and sustainable management of natural resources and eco-systems' (UNCSD 2012, para. 4).

We put special emphasis here on the genesis and content of sustainable development not just because the concept has become a mantra of international declarations. More importantly, the intersection of eco-nomic, social and environmental targets is indeed the genuine locus of industrial policy decisions in real world scenarios. Whether China is hit hard by the environmental repercussions of its rapid growth and urban-isation, whether Germany is meeting resistance to its energy transition due to unforeseen distributional implications or whether civil society groups in Ethiopia protest against the impact of planned dams on indigenous population groups, there is powerful evidence that the pursuit of isolated and imbalanced goals breeds resistance. We are familiar with the notion of environmental tipping points but not sufficiently aware of the existence of social tipping points as well. Yet, in a bird's eye perspective, it seems that more often than not goals of social inclusiveness are marginalised at the cost of economic growth targets, which in turn are frequently set without proper regard for their environmental consequences.

Clearly, it is in the narrow *economic* domain where the theory of industrial policy has been developed and the practice of industrial policy has been predominantly applied so far. In this economic space, we are typically dealing with issues like raising productivity, enhancing competitiveness, creating employment, supporting enterprise development, capturing new export markets, stimulating technological innovation or promoting high-potential industrial sectors.

In this context, it is important to distinguish between two different sources of productivity growth – achieved either through better factor combinations within existing activities or through reallocation of economic activities across sectors, from low-productivity agriculture and petty trade to specialised manufacturing and services. The latter results in structural change and diversification and, as such, constitutes the core of industrial policy.

However, it is in the social and environmental dimensions – and in exploring the causal chains and avenues through which these are related to 'hard core' economic growth and diversification goals – that industrial policy will need to find convincing answers going forward. In chapters 3 and 4, we will thus concentrate on these two pillars of sustainable development.

NOTES

4. In parts of sections 2.1, 2.2 and 2.3, we draw heavily on reflections that were presented earlier in a discussion paper together with Anna Pegels and Georgeta Vidican. We are grateful for their agreement. See Lütkenhorst, Altenburg, Pegels and Vidican (2014).
5. The former is represented by Lin (2012a); Chang and Grabel (2014); and Salazar-Xirinachs, Nübler and Kozul-Wright (2014), while examples of the latter can be found in Hallegatte, Fay and Vogt-Schilb (2013); Schwarzer (2013); Rodrik (2013); Johnson, Altenburg and Schmitz (2014); and Pegels (2014).

3. Industrial policy for social inclusion

Achieving inclusive growth is a goal with various manifestations. On the one hand, there is the aspect of fostering a production system that is inclusive in the sense of being integrated and closely interlinked – as opposed to a dualistic (or otherwise fragmented) system with only very weak economic relations between large formal enterprises and small, often informal enterprises. On the other hand, inclusiveness refers to different dimensions in the distribution of economic gains, ranging from functional income distribution (between labour and capital) to distribution among different population groups (e.g. gender-related or based on ethnicity) and the extent of regional disparities.

Following a brief introduction on the current global concern about rising inequality levels (Section 3.1), we will explore two approaches that have been applied to achieve greater inclusiveness of economic development. Section 3.2 focuses on small and medium enterprises and labour-intensive production while Section 3.3 deals with spatial redistribution.

3.1 RISING INEQUALITY AS A GLOBAL CONCERN

Empirical evidence shows that in recent years levels of income inequality have been rising in the majority of countries worldwide. Between 1990 and 2008 (based on a sample of 141 countries), this is true for 90 per cent of high-income countries, 90 per cent of countries in Eastern Europe and Central Asia and two thirds of South and Southeast Asian countries (Ortiz and Cummins 2011). While sub-Saharan African countries have mostly seen decreasing inequality, most OECD countries exhibit rising Gini coefficients, including in traditionally low-inequality countries like Germany and the Nordic states (OECD 2011). The same applies to China, with one of the starkest urban–rural income gaps worldwide and a Gini coefficient of 0.42 that, in the view of some observers, has exceeded an internationally agreed warning line (Lin 2012, p. 248).[6]

This trend towards higher levels of inequality has coincided with accelerated globalisation. It would require further in-depth research to establish the complex causality flows connecting both phenomena. On the one hand, globalisation has increased the concentration of capital incomes, which have grown much faster than labour incomes (Piketty 2014). As a result, concentration at the top of the global income pyramid has increased dramatically. In 2014, the richest 85 people owned as much as the entire bottom half of the world's population (Oxfam 2014, p. 8). On the other hand, the globalisation of production networks has enabled many countries to reap the benefits of technological specialisation – with the effect of lifting large population segments in developing countries out of poverty within a global 'shifting wealth' (OECD 2010) scenario.

Global concentration of capital incomes and income inequality are likely to increase even further, and it is difficult to anticipate how this will affect the relative wealth of different world regions. There is a growing premium on highly developed skills required to master more sophisticated technologies, whereas readily available lower skill levels receive only subsistence wages. More specifically, it can be observed that the ongoing digitalisation of production has also moved design and innovation activities into the tradables sector thus exposing them as well to the forces of global competition. In view of this powerful trend, a recent study concludes:

> Globalization and technological change may increase the wealth and economic efficiency of nations and the world at large, but they will not work to everybody's advantage … This means that without further intervention, economic inequality is likely to continue to increase … Unequal incomes can lead to unequal opportunities, depriving nations of access to talent and undermining the social contract. (Brynjolfsson, McAfee and Spence 2014, p. 52)

Rising inequality levels are potentially explosive, in particular in national contexts of poverty and deprivation. They generate a whole range of negative secondary consequences not just in the economic domain (e.g. in terms of productivity losses) but also for education, health, social cohesion and trust (Wilkinson and Pickett 2009). High inequality levels put the limits of resilience of social systems to a dangerous test and can easily trigger a process moving from stability to fragility, unrest and civil strife. Moreover, there are obvious risks of small ultra-rich minorities building up enormous lobbying power, allowing them to bend rules in their favour. Industrial policy needs to use 'carrots and sticks' to influence resource allocation. If such policies are captured by small elites to appropriate subsidies, contracts or concessions, then inequality is not just an ethical issue but also a threat to welfare-oriented policymaking. It is remarkable that – after years of preoccupation with the collapse of financial asset prices – even a mainstream entity like the World Economic Forum (WEF) now identifies severe income disparity as the most critical global risk factor – as perceived by more than 1,000 experts from industry, governments, civil society and academia (WEF 2013).

In the same vein, the ongoing UN-led intergovernmental negotiation process that seeks to replace the Millennium Development Goals with a new set of Sustainable Development Goals for the post-2015 period is according high importance to inequality. The question of whether or not to establish a stand-alone goal committing countries to reducing inequality in all its dimensions has become one of the most contentious issues in the General Assembly's Open Working Group on Sustainable Development Goals.

3.2 INCLUSION VIA PROMOTING SMALL AND MEDIUM ENTERPRISES AND LABOUR-INTENSIVE PRODUCTION

A key challenge for industrial policy is to contain rising inequality *at source*. This implies deliberate attempts to build up balanced economic production structures rather than relying primarily on *ex post* redistributive measures. This would appear to put a premium on emphasising the promotion of small and medium enterprises (SMEs), a focus on sectors of economic activity that are based on labour-intensive production technologies and paying special attention to keeping regional imbalances in check. While the last aspect is addressed further below (see Section 3.3), we want to first ask the question if and how a special emphasis on SMEs and labour-intensive technologies can be justified.

While being important at all levels of development, empirical studies have clearly shown that at the lower income levels typical of most developing countries, the prevalence of SMEs is particularly pronounced. As average income increases, the size distribution of firms typically moves upward, with the share of micro and small enterprises (and that of the informal sector) moving down and that of more sophisticated medium enterprises rising (Snodgrass and Biggs 1996).

The promotion of SMEs, in particular in low-income, high-poverty contexts, has been a central industrial policy mantra in much of the economic development literature and practice. Yet the developmental impact of SMEs is ambivalent (Liedholm and Mead 1999). They represent the vast majority of enterprises in developed and developing countries alike, account for the bulk of formal employment, offer economic opportunities also to low-skilled workers, tend to be regionally more dispersed than large enterprises and are a breeding ground for private sector entrepreneurship. However, they also tend to exhibit below average productivity and offer comparatively low levels of salary and less secure employment than large enterprises. Strong trade-offs can thus exist between promoting the drivers of high-productivity growth vs holding such transformation back with the aim of conserving low-skilled jobs and maximising employment. The need to balance the promotion of technological progress (which by definition implies structural change at the level of both sectors and enterprises) with the social requirements of allowing a smooth reallocation of people and resources calls for a special focus on the implications for SMEs.

At the same time, it is critically important to be clear about the specific objectives behind the promotion of SMEs and to recognise the potential downsides such an approach may have. Simply postulating that SMEs are both efficient and inclusive is not enough. While there are well-known market failures working against SMEs (such as limited information about economic options and restricted access to finance, both in terms of loans and equity), empirical evidence also points to a generally higher productivity of large enterprises compared to SMEs. It is mainly large enterprises that can exploit economies of scale, invest resources into research and development (R&D), and develop new, more efficient technologies. Industrial policies in favour of SMEs may thus succeed in increasing the latter's productivity yet, at the same time, exert a negative influence on aggregate productivity levels by preserving a size composition of enterprises that is suboptimal from an economic growth perspective (Pagés-Serra 2010, p. 213). Again, this is not to be seen at all as an argument against policies in favour of SMEs. The point made here is simply that there may be economic opportunity costs for what is considered a socially desirable goal in terms of inclusiveness.

It is also frequently claimed that reliance on relatively labour-intensive technologies, particularly at early industrialisation stages, can make a strong contribution to creating jobs. This has been a central theme in the rise of the East Asian 'tigers', with labour-intensive export production leading to a rapid inclusion of the growing labour force and a broad-based income rise. However, whether this development model still holds in the future is subject to intense debate. The technologies underpinning the globalisation and outsourcing process are rapidly changing. Based on recent breakthroughs in a multitude of interconnected information technologies, we witness a new powerful wave of automated technologies becoming available at scale and potentially reshaping the global division of labour (see also Section 6.2 below with reference to the 'Second Machine Age'). There is thus a danger of countries locking themselves into labour-intensive, low-skill manufacturing operations that may soon be replaced by machines and become obsolete.

In this context, it bears mention that producing goods and services with labour-intensive technologies and producing them in small enterprises is distinctly not the same. Much of the labour-intensive export production in Asia and beyond takes place in large enterprises at significant scale. For instance, in garments exporting companies in China, economies of scale are a strong co-determinant of competitiveness and have led to single enterprises literally employing thousands of workers and in turn being part of even bigger export clusters (Liu and Shu 2001).

The above reflections lead to conclusions that call for differentiated and well-considered industrial policy responses. In essence, the case often made for a wholesale promotion of 'the SME sector' is not valid. When looking at long-term economic strategies (i.e. outside purely socially motivated job preservation objectives that may apply to certain locations) there is no compelling reason to promote SMEs for their own sake. Rather, the policy goal should be to create and sustain ecosystems of interconnected firms (foreign and domestic; large, medium and small), which can combine the scale advantages of large firms with the flexibility of a multitude of small, specialised firms. The latters' products and services can then feed into regional and global production networks led by large firms, which develop new technologies, breed new business ideas and challenge incumbent firms. In this 'ecology of firms' perspective (Klein and Hadjimichael 2003), it becomes essential to maintain the dynamism of smaller enterprises (which tend to be the fastest growing but are also subject to a high degree of market turbulence), not to prolong the economic life of individual SMEs.

Along similar lines, labour-intensive production activities need to be seen with their long-term potential and threats in mind. While many developing countries are in dire need to boost employment and income for low-skilled population groups, and some countries have made fast progress by channelling surplus labour into labour-intensive manufacturing and services, they need to monitor technological changes that could erode the advantages of such a strategy. Specialising on low labour costs may be a good strategy for entering into new activities and markets, yet should be seen as a temporary solution to be complemented with upgrading strategies.

3.3   INCLUSION VIA SPATIAL REDISTRIBUTION

The debate around the potential and the limitation of an active regional (and local) development approach has been at the centre of industrial policy research for quite some time. We will review below the key findings of this debate as one central aspect of seeking to make economic development more inclusive.

Economic activities are unevenly distributed geographically, that is, they have a spatial dimension. Any shift in resource allocation between sectors thus affects the regional pattern of the economy and impacts on the degree of inclusiveness of economic development. In particular, the transition from agriculture to manufacturing has far-reaching spatial consequences, as industrialisation requires and reinforces agglomeration economies. Even within sectors, a strong tendency towards the clustering of economic activities can be observed as they build on externalities often concentrated in specific regions. While some determinants (local availability of raw material inputs, strategic locations for trading, etc.) may be given, most externalities evolve as economic activities unfold. Certain initial activities attract related industries, which again reinforce the attractiveness of that location, that is, there are advantages of proximity at work. Pools of labour with specific skill sets are built up, the growing number of related enterprises increases the supply of complementary assets as well as the competitive pressure to improve them, and public agencies are set up to supply pre-competitive services. Agglomeration economies drive regional specialisation.

Deliberately or not, industrial policy always impacts on economic space. To the extent that it strengthens emerging clusters, or encourages spillovers from activities in one place that materialise in another, it becomes an element of regional policy. Policymakers should be aware of spatial effects and consider if and when there is a need to intervene. Increasing spatial imbalances, however, are not necessarily a cause for concern. On the contrary, spatial imbalances are necessary to exploit agglomeration economies and induce backward and forward linkages, thereby contributing to higher productivity and incomes (Hirschman 1958). Of course, there may be situations when agglomeration 'overshoots' and produces undesirable effects, such as damage to ecosystems in heavily populated and industrialised areas, or socially unacceptable levels of income disparity. Still, policymakers need to recognise that geographical concentration of people and wealth is a corollary of economic development. Neoclassical economists in particular are sceptical about governments trying to go against the agglomeration trends of markets. A World Development Report dedicated to economic geography gives a quite clear message in this regard: 'A rising concentration of people and production in some parts of a country has marked economic growth over the last two centuries. To fight this concentration is to fight growth itself' (World Bank 2008, p. 27).

The question whether, to what extent and how governments should encourage spatially more balanced patterns of development and seek proactively to achieve better living conditions for the inhabitants of lagging regions is therefore not a straightforward one. Irrespective of the ongoing academic debate, governments in both developing and developed countries often take measures to encourage a more balanced geographical distribution of economic activity. The European Regional Development Funds are the most prominent example. They encourage investments and local development initiatives in less favoured regions in order to reduce regional and social imbalances within the European Union (EU). Likewise, a wide range of policies has been tested in developing countries to persuade entrepreneurs to invest in backward regions, promote small industries in small towns and villages, and create new growth poles outside core economic regions. The popularity of such policies is in contrast to only limited evidence of success. Many academic reviews (e.g. Dewar 1998 for the US) come to rather critical conclusions regarding the effectiveness of regional economic policies.

However, policies for spatial balancing have a strong political rationale. For instance, from a normative perspective (i.e. not efficiency-driven), the German constitution posits, as a social norm, equitable living conditions in all of the country's regions. Furthermore, the overall trend towards decentralisation gives the political constituencies in less dynamic regions more political voice and thus creates incentives for politicians to set up programmes that promise more industrial activity and more jobs in those regions. In some countries, decentralisation has even made local economic development (LED) a mandatory task for local governments (Cunningham and Meyer-Stamer 2005, p. 4). Likewise, in the field of international development cooperation it is easier for donor agencies to gain political support for programmes that target the poor directly where they live and work, such as in lagging rural districts, than to strengthen emerging agglomerations where people are relatively better off. This has made LED programmes for lagging regions quite popular in development cooperation.

Policymakers basically face the choice between limiting themselves to 'spatially blind' (World Bank 2008) policies and trying to influence the choice of locations through private investments, in order to pursue a balanced growth strategy. The World Bank favours the former. It provides evidence that even when growth is unbalanced, development can still be inclusive because people migrate to places where they find more product-ive jobs, or because those who stay back home in lagging regions benefit from overall rising wage levels, remittances and greater financial scope for public service provision. The World Bank therefore suggests relying on 'spatially blind' institutional reforms to create a more investor-friendly business climate, ensure enforcement of property rights, and liberalise factor markets for labour and land to allow people, including the poor, to migrate to more prosperous regions. In countries where huge proportions of the population live far from the centres of economic dynamism, governments should also emphasise the improvement of connective infrastructure, including highways, railroads and telecommunications.

However, most of the literature on LED follows another paradigm. The focus here is on geographically targeted incentives to enhance the competitiveness of economic activities in lagging regions. It is hoped that the economy can be developed where the people live rather than forcing the inhabitants to migrate. The record of these efforts, however, has often been quite disappointing, forcing LED proponents to rethink their strategies. Rücker and Trah (2007, pp. 12 f.) identify three phases of LED policies, each with a different emphasis:

- During the first phase, governments mainly offered tax breaks or subsidised the cost of public services to encourage investors to move to lagging regions. In some countries, governments defined new growth poles in rural areas and small towns to encourage decentralised investments. Such efforts have mostly failed because entrepreneurs still preferred to invest in urban agglomerations where they could benefit from the proximity to markets and multiple externalities. Developing country examples of failure include Kenya (Ikiara, Olewe-Nyunya and Odhiambo 2004) and Zimbabwe (Zwizwai, Kambudzi and Mauwa 2004). The record in industrialised countries has not been much better. In general, agglomeration economies are strong drivers of locational choice. Subsidies can do little to compensate for them (Deichmann et al. 2008).
- In the second phase, attention shifted to promoting endogenous economic development efforts. Emphasis was given to supporting local entrepreneurship, enhancing specialisation within local clus-ters, strengthening social capital in communities, mobilising collective efficiency and setting up community-based enterprises to meet the development needs of local people. In contrast to the previous phase, decision-making shifted from the central to the

municipal level. Again, these efforts seem to have had relatively little success, which is hardly surprising in a globalising knowledge economy. Even in remote regions of developing countries, entrepreneurs nowadays compete against goods and services provided by leading international companies. It is hard to see opportunities for endogenous growth in lagging regions where firms cannot reap economies of scale and where the quality of almost any input factor is below international standards. Economic activities in these regions can only survive and thrive if they build on a specific comparative advantage. A review of experiences from local clusters in developing countries suggests that the most important development impulses come from outside the respective regions. Specialisation in value chains catering for global buyers or for urban demand is one important option, with opportunities existing in agriculture, manufacturing and services (from information technology to tourism). Linkages with internationally operating firms and demanding consumers are highly important for technological learning and can help to bring local productivity levels closer to international best practice (Schmitz and Knorringa 2000).[7]

- The third, and most recent, approach tries to go one step further and balance endogenous economic development and integration in wider markets. It recognises the limitations of earlier efforts to develop mainly 'from within'. This approach focuses on a competitive local business environment and measures to strengthen the supply side capacities of regions in order to make them more attractive for investment on a competitive basis. In addition, measures are taken to better exploit local spillovers from integration in national and international markets. Thus the focal point is still the region, but the strategy is to build on its comparative advantages in trading with other regions.

Although the debate is not settled, empirical evidence suggests that trying to work squarely against the agglomeration forces of markets is rarely successful and often not even desirable. Unbalanced growth may be inevitable, especially in early stages of transition from agrarian to industrial societies. Still, people tend to have manifold socio-cultural ties to their home region and may therefore have a preference to stay if they can make a decent living rather than migrating to unknown places – even if the latter would allow them to attain higher incomes and generate more growth for the national economy. Hence it may be desirable to undertake efforts to strengthen local economies in those regions where people live – rather than to strengthen the pull effects of the most dynamic economic centres. This option can also be justified on environmental grounds. Once environmental costs are fully internalised in economic calculations, it is likely that market processes will lead to less centralised spatial patterns that require less mobility of people and goods and better reflect the carrying capacity of local ecosystems.

Policymakers may choose to promote lagging regions for such reasons. Empirical evidence, however, suggests that regulations or subsidy schemes that try to channel investments towards places with strong locational disadvantages rarely ever achieve their objectives. Efforts to develop lagging regions 'from within' have equally shown poor results. The most promising way is to strengthen the local supply side to make the respective region more attractive to external investors and encourage regional learning through knowledge transfer and measures to enhance absorptive capacity for new technologies.

One industrial policy option is to create dedicated spaces, which provide especially favourable investment conditions in terms of stable and conducive incentive systems and the basic physical (transport, energy, water, etc.) infrastructure required. Such spatial approaches – whether in the form of Export Processing Zones (EPZs) or other Special Economic Zones (SEZs) – are increasingly adopted by a wide range of developing countries. Globally, the number of various types of special zones rose from 176 (in 47 countries) in 1986 to a staggering level of 3,500 (in 116 countries) in 2006 (WTO and IDE-JETRO 2011) and has been increasing further in recent years. While such zones can trigger technological, vocational and managerial learning and skills upgrading for firms located inside, they have also been shown in many cases to induce learning spillovers for firms located in the same region (UNIDO 2009), that is, from within the zone towards a clustering of economically linked firms in its surrounding areas.

Importantly, the concentration of firms in the same location also allows for collective experimentation with innovative industrial policy measures – either related to decent work conditions (health, safety, social security) or to environmental goals. Indeed, a variety of 'green zones' already exists – ranging from basic pollution control zones to eco-industrial parks and more ambitious low-carbon special economic zones – and several countries, including India and China, have adopted policy frameworks and guidelines for establishing such zones. They are increasingly considered as offering great potential for cost-effective promotion and adoption of energy-efficient technologies, renewable sources of energy and sustainable buildings as well as recycling and waste use/disposal systems (Yeo and Akinci 2011).

NOTES

6. The Deputy Governor at the People's Bank of China recently opined: 'The increase in inequality is the most serious challenge for the world. I don't think the world is paying enough attention.' And he added: 'It's not just about tax, we need to go further. We need to look back at how and where ... wealth is being created' (quoted in Aldrick 2011).
7. Bazan and Navas Alemán (2004) and Schmitz (2006) provide evidence that operating simultaneously as a global supplier and as a producer for local markets may be particularly successful because it makes it possible to learn from highly efficient global value chains and to employ the acquired capabilities in independent local market operations.

4. Industrial policy for a green transformation

While equitable, inclusive and regionally balanced economic develop-ment has long been a concern for industrial policy (despite its having been overshadowed by an often narrowly defined economic growth agenda), attempts to conceptualise green industrial policies[8] are of more recent origin. We will thus elaborate on this approach and its implications in greater detail below.

Given the expected drastic consequences of climate change and the increasingly rapid deterioration of other environmental resources, the development of resource-efficient, low-emission technologies is arguably the most important challenge for future industrial policy. While the current debate is focused on low-carbon technologies, scarcity of other finite resources – in particular water and fertile soils – will also soon become acute at the global level.

Today, climate change is the most burning issue. The looming danger of catastrophic climate change has given rise to concerns about economic development exceeding the earth's carrying capacity, that is, running against planetary boundaries and exiting our 'safe operating space' (Rockström et al. 2009). While the international community has acknow-ledged a 2°C global warming as a redline not to be crossed, according to the central scenario of the International Energy Agency's global forecast (IEA 2013), the world is currently moving along a path of a long-term average temperature increase of 3.6°C. Importantly, this scenario already accounts for all measures announced to date by national governments in the fields of promoting the use of renewables, pricing carbon, adjusting the energy subsidy systems and increasing energy efficiency. Given that about four fifths of the energy-related CO_2 emissions for the next two decades are already 'locked-in'[9] in terms of the existing capital stock (IEA 2011, p. 40), global warming can only be kept below the 2°C threshold if the carbon intensity (carbon emissions per unit of economic output) of the world economy is sharply reduced. Any additional warming would have dire impacts on global ecosystems, including severe droughts, floods, hurricanes and massive extinction of species.

4.1 SCOPE AND LIMITATIONS OF MARKET-BASED POLICY APPROACHES

The required decoupling of economic growth from resource consumption is a daunting task for industrial policy, as it calls for radical changes in entire socio-technical systems. To enhance carbon efficiency, for example, it is not sufficient to increase the energy efficiency of combustion in power plants and motors. The required levels of decarbonisation can only be achieved if new concepts of mobility are developed based on public transport and intelligent logistics; if patterns of urban development change; if new light and resilient materials are developed; and if farming systems drastically reduce energy inputs. The transition towards a resource-efficient economy requires a true paradigm shift rather than incremental improvements along established technological trajectories. New development pathways need to be defined, agreed upon and implemented through economically viable and scalable innovations.

The need to protect finite environmental resources adds a new rationale to industrial policy, requiring a more proactive government attitude and different policies. Given the pervasiveness of market failures in dealing with environmental challenges, the question arises as to how they can be effectively remedied. The orthodox economic response calls for the pricing (i.e. internalisation) of externalities. In the case of climate change – and, for the sake of the argument, just concentrating on CO_2 emissions as the main driver – the solution would thus appear to lie in the appropriate pricing of carbon. This in turn can be achieved either by introducing a (Pigouvian) carbon tax or by relying on a quota approach in terms of a cap-and-trade system.

Without any doubt, the underpricing of environmental assets has contributed significantly to the past growth of the world economy. This is true for developed and developing countries alike. Concurrently, it has generated the unsustainable ecological footprint, which we have locked ourselves into. Thus, there is a strong case for getting the prices right (prices of emitting carbon, of using material and energy resources, of generating pollution and waste) and have them reflect the prevailing scarcities. This would provide incentives to move from high-carbon to low-carbon technologies on the supply side and from unsustainable to sustainable consumption patterns on the demand side.

However, accurate pricing is not the end of the story and just serves as the point of departure for more ambitious green industrial policies. Apart from the ethical challenges of pricing immaterial values such as biodiversity, individual species or the aesthetic value of nature, *going beyond pricing* is necessary mainly for four different reasons:

- Prices can act as powerful incentives for technological and behavioural change, yet the resulting adjustment period remains beyond control. At the same time, there are products and processes, which, in view of their irreversible environmental consequences, may call for immediate and decisive action or outright banning. Non-degradable plastics, persistent organic pollutants and ozone-depleting substances are cases in point – and have indeed triggered international collective action towards their gradual phase-out.

- As the prices and markets for environmental goods are socially constructed, they depend on political decisions just as much as 'command-and-control' instruments, such as decisions legislating emissions limits. Also, pricing approaches have enormous implications for the creation and allocation of rents among firms, sectors and countries, and are therefore politically highly contested. While carbon taxes at the required scale are politically difficult to enforce, the existing cap-and trade systems are fraught with implementation problems. First, lobbyists have so far achieved very generous exemptions, which have largely undermined the instruments' effectiveness. For example, as a result of generous quota allocations the carbon price of the European emissions trading system (ETS) fell from a peak of €30 in 2006 to a level below €6 at the end of 2013. Second, a global agreement on emissions rights presupposes difficult international settlements (Green 2014), for example on how to value historical liabilities of early-industrialising nations or whether, in the case of global value chains, producing or consuming countries are accountable for emissions. For the foreseeable future, cap-and-trade systems are therefore likely to remain more a patchwork of national and regional initiatives than an instrument of global coverage (IEA 2010).

- The impact of setting appropriate prices may be restricted by other market imperfections (World Bank 2012), such as low price elasticities (limited consumer response to price signals e.g. due to lack of technological alternatives or due to behavioural inertia), principal–agent problems (e.g. in the case of tenants paying energy bills thus reducing energy-saving incentives for owners) or lack of confidence in the long-term stability of politically set prices.

- The introduction of environmentally sustainable technologies at the requisite scale and speed involves the breaking-up of entrenched development paths. It calls for institutional and technological innovation and learning, 'kicking old habits' of behaviour as well as the creation of a new low-carbon compatible infrastructure (Halle-gatte, Fay and Vogt-Schilb 2013). This massive challenge of societal adjustment coupled with the exceeding urgency of action thus requires more than simply getting the prices right. Regarding the latter point, that is, radical and systemic change requirements, the key task is to create incentives that push forward the develop-ment, testing, deployment and upscaling of sustainable tech-nologies.[10] This in turn presupposes the combination of smartly designed subsidies (like in the case of feed-in tariffs for renewable sources of energy) with incentives to encourage and steer R&D efforts in the desired direction as well as investments into dedicated infrastructure and multi-stakeholder partnerships, for example in the form of regional innovation clusters.

4.2 POLICY DIRECTION THROUGH GUIDED STRUCTURAL CHANGE

All in all, green investments are strongly guided by policy incentives that reflect political priorities rather than by prices resulting from unfettered supply and demand. In this context, market-based incentives have an important role in dealing with environmental externalities and public goods, but – as shown above – pricing is not sufficient and in many cases politically not even feasible. Hence policymakers need to combine different types of regulatory measures to achieve their objectives. How-ever, this opens up a new set of problems, as policy measures may be incompatible, such that one measure undercuts the effectiveness of another. In this context, the alignment of different policy instruments assumes crucial importance.

Traditionally, industrial policy has been pursued with the aim of increasing the productivity of capital and labour, with the private sector being the main driver of productivity growth. The public sector may have a supporting role in subsidising search processes, coordinating market actors, or protecting and encouraging newcomers, but it should normally avoid picking specific technologies, and it should not interfere in the deployment of mature technologies.

However, time is of the essence. Any delay in bringing emissions down would magnify environmental damages and increase the costs of adap-tation enormously. According to the German Advisory Council on Global Change (WBGU 2009, p. 2):

It is of paramount importance that the level of global emissions reaches its peak by the year 2020 at the latest because otherwise the reduction of emissions in the subsequent period would have to take place at a speed that would fully overstrain the technical, economical and social capacities of our societies.

In the case of industrial policy for climate change and other environmental goods, the *speed* of innovation thus becomes crucial. Therefore it may be necessary:

- to *select technology families* – such as second-generation biofuels, photovoltaics, wind power, carbon capture and storage (CCS), or battery-fuelled cars – and to push the multiple complementary investments needed for their success (Kramer and Haigh 2009). Betting on all potential technologies simultaneously would exceed the available resources even in the richest economies and would delay the commercial breakthrough of the first technology family.[11]
- to *subsidise the deployment* of environment-friendly technologies. Whereas technology diffusion is normally a market-driven process, public programmes may subsidise the introduction of new resource-saving technologies. In many cases such subsidies are needed only temporarily as technological learning curves and upscaling lead to rapid unit cost decreases as demonstrated powerfully in the case of wind energy and solar photovoltaics.

As Mazzucato (2014, p. 2) points out, 'unsurprisingly we find that across the globe the countries leading in the green revolution ... are those where the State is playing an active role beyond that which is typically attributed to market failure theory'. Again, this does not at all imply a winner-picking role for the state at micro level, but it does call for a public policy responsibility of defining desirable and often necessary technological development corridors or, as Mazzucato puts it, to ensure a sufficient degree of development 'directionality'.

Green industrial policy thus needs to rely on a variety of instruments. Market-based instruments – such as tradable emissions rights, taxes and other ecological charges that put a price on public goods – are the centrepiece. As has been shown, however, pricing environmental goods is not sufficient. There is also a need to use non-market mechanisms, such as outright prohibitions or bans, as well as other regulatory limitations in cases where future costs cannot be calculated or where monetisation would be unethical (such as for loss of biodiversity). In addition, green industrial policy needs to support research, increase the transparency of markets through standards and labels, encourage technology diffusion and seek to change consumption patterns. Box 4.1 summarises the key policy elements of what the German Environment Ministry calls 'ecological industrial policy' (BMU 2008).

In essence, industrial policies that aim to increase resource efficiency and reduce harmful emissions may require a more proactive and interventionist government role. The benefits vis-à-vis countries pursuing hands-off economic policies may be twofold: proactive governments may gain in terms of more sustainable resource management; and they may benefit from early mover advantages if they manage to trade goods and services more adapted to the resource-efficiency paradigm (Porter and van der Linde 1995).

BOX 4.1 KEY ELEMENTS OF GREEN INDUSTRIAL POLICY

Green industrial policy ...

- eliminates subsidies with harmful effects on the environment;
- levies ecological charges and taxes to internalise environmental costs;
- establishes emissions trading schemes to 'monetise' public goods;
- finances public and encourages private environmental research;
- provides financial instruments for environmental investments and business start-ups, including venture capital and leasing;
- sets ambitious environmental targets that are announced and calculable on a long-term basis in order to give markets time to develop commercial solutions. One solution is the 'top runner approach', under which the best product on the market in terms of environmental sustainability determines the standard that the other products within this product group have to reach within a specified period;
- uses public procurement to encourage environment-friendly products and processes;
- promotes different lifestyles and consumption patterns;
- supports eco-labels to enhance market transparency and mobilise consumer pressure in favour of better products;
- sets up market-incentive programmes to accelerate the diffusion of new environment-friendly technologies; and
- establishes public databases for environmental and efficiency technologies.

Source: Summarised from BMU (2008).

4.3 HIGH UNCERTAINTY AND LONG TIME HORIZONS

It must be emphasised though that green industrial policy takes place under great uncertainty and is dealing with exceedingly long causal chains and time horizons. While industrial policy in general is faced with the perils of uncertainty, and with the need to venture into assessments and judgments that try to anticipate and shape desired future scenarios, in the case of green industrial policy the dependence on evidence derived from a variety of basic and applied natural sciences (geology, biology, physics, climate science, engineering, systems analysis, etc.) is fundamental. While these may generate reliable knowledge in isolation, the variance of projections grows in proportion with the level of multi-disciplinarity, the size of the system and the time horizon considered.

Hence, policymakers are often in a quandary when having to take calculated risks that exhibit high and quantifiable immediate costs contrasting with uncertain future benefits. While the fact of discernible and significant man-made climate change is proven and potentially disastrous consequences are written on the wall, the lack of precision in long-term forecasts (coupled with short-term political mandates) leaves room for escapist positions held by powerful groups of vested interests. This is exacerbated by the often controversial nature of research findings, in particular when it comes to translating global climate models into regional and national scenarios, which involve higher levels of uncertainty. Against this backdrop, it is easy to find hired guns that provide elaborate justifications for any conceivable policy position. Indeed, evidence-based policymaking (necessary as it is) is often constrained by what has been termed 'policy-based evidence-making' (Geden and Fischer 2014).

Moreover, uncertainty stemming from the scientific modelling of climate change is compounded by further spheres of uncertainty, within which industrial policy has to operate:

- The *dynamics of complex ecosystems* are unpredictable and subject to erratic tipping points. There is already mounting evidence of catastrophic climate change, irreversible loss of biodiversity and risks of collapsing water systems due to increasingly anoxic conditions. If indeed 'our emotional apparatus is designed for linear causality' (Taleb 2008, p. 88) and most of our economic models are based on the notion of marginal variation rather than abrupt, discrete change, then we are ill equipped to deal with such non-linear events.

- The *technical feasibility and commercial applicability of new transformative technologies* (at the required scale and at affordable cost levels) is inherently doubtful. This applies equally to innovative energy storage technologies, different approaches to electric mobility or the future potential of CCS technologies. Furthermore, many technological solutions for one problem may create new problems in other domains – the use of biofuels as a low-carbon source of energy may threaten food security; nuclear energy as a low-carbon technology comes at high risks of radioactive emissions and security issues; the fracking of shale gas may pollute groundwater tables, and so on. Societies tend to assess such risks differently, as demonstrated by the diverging national responses to nuclear energy and fracking, which adds another layer of uncertainty: even when technological solutions are feasible and commercially viable, they may not be socially acceptable.

- *Global policy approaches* are both necessary and notoriously slow to emerge. International climate negotiations in the framework of the United Nations Framework Convention on Climate Change (UNFCCC) have delivered a series of disappointing outcomes. Whether or not this is bound to change at the next milestone (COP 21 at the end of 2015 in Paris) is anyone's guess. At the same time, supranational carbon markets remain in their infancy and – assuming they do not fail altogether – are likely to take many years to become politically and operationally stable. Investors and policymakers alike can therefore hardly anticipate which internationally agreed targets or which carbon offsetting costs they have to factor into their strategies.

- The *impact of innovative policy instruments* cannot be predicted with any reasonable level of precision. More often than not, unexpected and unintended consequences occur. For instance, a few years ago hardly any analyst predicted the breakdown of the European ETS market; Germany's feed-in tariff, in contrast, drastically overachieved its targets, such that the resulting electricity price hikes attracted massive criticism (Lütkenhorst and Pegels 2014).

4.4 DEALING WITH STRANDED ASSETS

So far, the debate and literature on green industrial policy has centred on *investment-encouraging* incentives, that is, those that seek to stimulate new economic activities that can underpin the required sustainability transformation and gradually lock in a new green trajectory. More specifically, this applies to, for example, promoting energy efficiency in buildings, subsidising the deployment and use of renewable energy, or initiating new systems of electric mobility.

However, the flip side of *investment-discouraging* incentives needs to be factored in as well. The issue at hand is how to deal with those fossil fuel investment assets that are on the losing side of long-term structural change and face the prospect of a massive devaluation. While a (sufficiently high) carbon tax would induce the early 'mothballing' of such 'brown' productive capacities, the resulting employment losses and intense pressure for structural change are politically unacceptable in most societies. Hence the preference for policy instruments that incentivise new green investments while allowing the 'brown' capital stock to complete its economic life span – a strategy that prolongs adjustment periods at the expense of long-term welfare losses (Rozenberg, Vogt-Schilb and Hallegatte 2013).

In the green industrial policy debate, attention to such sunset industries has generally been insufficient. More recently, however, this aspect has gained some prominence under the label of stranded assets. It is relevant due to two different reasons. From a political economy perspective, the powerful vested interests and lobbying groups connected to those stranded assets have the potential to derail – or at least significantly delay – the green transformation. In addition, from a more narrow financial perspective, the massive amounts of capital involved can have severe repercussions in terms of creating market instability.

In the relevant literature, the notion of unburnable carbon is gradually moving centre stage. Starting from the concept of a global carbon budget (Meinshausen et al. 2009), that is, the amount of carbon still available for release into the atmosphere under a 2°C scenario, the aim is to quantify the amount of carbon resources that, though existing, cannot be burnt any more. Based on quantitative modelling exercises, it is estimated that in a realistic scenario without widespread use of CCS technologies, approximately 45 per cent of all 'proved and probable' oil resources (equalling an amount of 600 Gb) must remain unexploited (McGlade and Ekins 2014). Concurrently – and somewhat paradoxically – massive exploration programmes are underway towards discovering and extracting new Arctic and deepwater oil resources.

As a consequence, there is a lingering fear that stock markets around the world may soon be faced with a huge 'carbon bubble' that is in danger of being abruptly deflated. According to the Carbon Tracker Initiative (2012), the world's known fossil fuel reserves (with a breakdown of 65 per cent coal, 22 per cent oil and 13 per cent gas) are tantamount to five times the world's carbon budget up to 2050. At the same time, many leading stock exchanges are heavily exposed to a fossil fuel based portfolio, with 20–30 per cent of their market capitalisation invested in fossil fuel assets. The resulting risk is immense given that the financial robustness of the companies concerned hinges on the ability to keep exploiting their carbon assets or, alternatively, effect a rapid transition to new business models.[12]

NOTES

8. The term 'green industrial policy' is rapidly gaining currency. In recent years, it has found its way into globally negotiated commitments (UNCSD 2012) and is being increasingly used by economic development and policy researchers as well as by international organisations.
9. For the concept of carbon lock-in, see Unruh (2000).
10. Nordhaus underlines that in fact two layers of externalities are involved: 'Investments in low-carbon technologies are depressed because the private returns on innovation are below the social returns, and private returns are further depressed because the market price of carbon is below its true social cost. The net effect is to doubly discourage profit-oriented R&D in low-carbon technologies' (Nordhaus 2013, p. 286).
11. Selection of technology families is also necessary because social consensus is needed for implementation; many new technology families – from offshore wind parks to biofuels and CCS – encounter fierce local resistance in many countries.
12. However, available evidence points in the direction of widespread business as usual. Between 2011 and 2013, the level of embedded carbon at the New York stock market increased by 37 per cent (mostly from oil companies) while at the London stock market it went up by 7 per cent (mostly coal-based) (Carbon Tracker Initiative 2013, p. 4).

5. Governance and governments: balancing market and state failure

In the preceding chapters, we dealt with the normative foundation of industrial policy and its principal function to contribute to the achievement of goals that societies consider worth striving for. We demonstrated that industrial policy is necessarily faced with multiple social goals, intrinsic uncertainty, long time horizons and complex trade-offs. As a result, the demands on government capabilities – and, in the first place, government willingness – to adopt rational and consistent policies are exceedingly high.

Now, in Chapter 5, we will first address *technical* questions of how specific approaches of industrial policy can be conceptualised and what this implies for the scope and depth of intervening in markets (Section 5.1). We will then take up the *political* dimension of industrial policy in terms of the motivations and drivers of government action (Section 5.2) and the capabilities required to ensure rational and effective policy-making (Section 5.3). We will conclude with developing a set of principles that need to govern the delivery of smart industrial policy (Section 5.4).

5.1 HOW MUCH INTERVENTION?

Recapitulating a Long Debate

There has been a protracted debate on the role of industrial policy, especially with regard to latecomer development. This debate goes back to Alexander Hamilton and Friedrich List, who both advocated measures to protect the emerging industries of their home countries (the US and Germany, respectively) against the more competitive industries of Britain.[13] Ever since, the rationale of intervening in markets with the aim of shifting resources into sectors that governments perceive to be important for public welfare and future economic growth has been hotly debated.

Ample empirical evidence has been gathered on both industrial policy success and failure. On the one hand, there is increasing evidence that governments have played an active supporting role in almost every case of successful latecomer industrialisation. This applies to the US, Germany and Japan in their early development as much as it does to the newly industrialised countries of Asia[14] and certain industries or regional clusters in other developing countries.[15] On the other hand, there is also abundant documentation of misguided government interventions that wasted scarce public resources and distorted markets without producing the desired effects.[16]

In most cases, however, it is difficult to judge whether government policies have been instrumental in achieving certain outcomes, especially due to attribution gaps and the problem of the counterfactual, that is, it is impossible to prove what would have happened had the respective government not intervened or had it taken different measures. The Indian software industry is often cited as an example of a subsector that succeeded with very little selective government support (Athreye and Hobday 2010; Pack and Saggi 2006, pp. 33 ff.). Singh (2009, pp. 284 ff.), in contrast, claims that this sector owes its emergence to strategic government action. Likewise, there is always a debate as to whether more active industrial policies would have achieved even better results. For example, it is generally agreed that Hong Kong developed rapidly on the basis of laissez-faire policies (Chiu 1996), but Tban and Ng (1995) also highlight the limitations of Hong Kong's passive policy. They show that achievements regarding technology-intensive and high-technology products were quite limited. Conversely, critics of industrial policy claim that even the most successful stories of technological catching-up do not prove a causal relationship; growth might have been even higher without industrial policy interventions (Pack and Saggi 2006).

Furthermore, if we understand industrial policy as a process of 'self-discovery' (Hausmann and Rodrik 2002), whereby governments encourage economic actors to search for new opportunities, this necessarily implies trial and error. Hence, the failure of some of the policy experiments induced by government does not discredit the search process per se. Governments may act appropriately if they encourage a range of potentially lucrative activities as long as they have good reasons to assume that some of these activities are likely to generate knowledge spillovers and dynamic scale economies. It is possible that several government-sponsored projects may fail before one becomes a success – one whose benefits (in terms of spillovers and dynamic scale effects) outweigh the cost of all previous projects. Moreover, incentives to stimulate the search for new products, processes or markets sometimes generate unintended innovations. Military and space research in particular have yielded unexpected commercial successes in a number of industries – such as in the case of DARPA (Defense Advanced Research Projects Agency) in the US with its massive spillovers into new areas of information technology (Mazzucato 2014, pp. 74 ff.)

Taking all this into account, it is difficult to establish, even *ex post*, when industrial policies can be considered a success or a failure. Moreover, industrial policies are not cost-free. Even if they prove successful for the targeted sector, such success may come at a high cost for taxpayers and/or for consumers, who have to bear higher prices for protected domestic goods. It is impossible to establish whether these resources would have been better invested in other activities. This is why the industrial policy debate is unlikely to be ever fully settled.

BOX 5.1 INDUSTRIAL POLICY: CHANGING PERCEPTIONS OVER THE COURSE OF TIME

Over time, the perception of industrial policy has experienced several pendulum swings, from widespread acceptance during phases of mercantilism in the 16th to 18th centuries and import-substituting industrialisation between the 1950s and 1970s to outright rejection during the 1980s and 1990s. Developed countries have usually adopted a pragmatic stance and maintained a certain level of proactive policies to foster the competitiveness of their industries, while seeking at the same time to avoid highly market-distorting bureaucratic interventions. In contrast, many developing countries have followed the respective ideological mainstream, adopting radical policy changes. In the 1950s and 1970s most developing country governments (especially in Africa, Latin America and South Asia) heavy-handedly intervened in markets with the aim of building national industries. The late 1980s and 1990s witnessed the dismantling of protective trade policies and selective economic promotion under the hegemony of neo-liberal orthodoxy.

These abrupt policy changes reflect the weakness of institutionalised systems of policy learning in many developing countries. The management of government programmes is rarely results-based with built-in feedback mechanisms; there is often no independent policy research; some countries do not encourage public debate about policy alternatives; and few consensus-building mechanisms are in place. Furthermore, international financial institutions and donor agencies have supported different policy concepts over time. In particular during the 1980s and 1990s, they interfered strongly in domestic policies, using conditionality to impose trade liberalisation and the downsizing of the state.

Given the success of some Asian economies that heavily governed their markets (Wade 1990) in pursuit of industrialisation, and the contrasting failure of neo-liberal policies in terms of creating new competitive advantages, many developing country governments are now turning back to a more proactive promotion of specific activities. The recent global economic crisis has accelerated this revival of selective interventions. It has revealed the extraordinary interconnectedness of the global economy, a factor that greatly enhances the risk of negative spillovers from bankruptcies of certain banks and, to a lesser extent, large firms in the real economy, such as General Motors. The need to protect systemic banks and manufacturing enterprises, now again accepted throughout all OECD countries, is nothing but a new variant of the old industrial policy argument of the need to strengthen strategic industries.

Source: Authors.

Adopting a Systemic Approach

With industrial policy defined so broadly, it is not possible to delineate its scope exactly. Changing the sectoral composition of an economy involves the development of new industries and steady renewal of their competitive advantages. This requires private and public action on several fronts. Firms rarely achieve competitiveness on their own, that is, without a supporting environment of suppliers, production-oriented services and pressure from strong competitors (Porter 1990). Once firms start to specialise and target more demanding new markets, they require new services that are not yet available and can sometimes not be provided by market actors, especially as long as the new activities are still nascent. Science and technology organisations then need to be set up and start developing new routines of interaction with private enterprises. Some government facilitation may even be needed to organise collective action among firms, which is important for small firms to achieve economies of scale (Schmitz 1999) and build trust among the actors involved. Increasing interactions among firms, in turn, may require improvements in corporate law to ensure that contracts can be enforced smoothly. Public–private dialogue on issues of legal reform or economic promotion may serve to build consensus among public and private actors, trigger policy learning and improve the ability to formulate and implement reasonable strategies.

In sum, as Freeman (2008) put it, building competitiveness requires co-evolutionary dynamics among firms and institutions in several domains. This implies that policy interventions of different kinds – regulatory and supportive, generic and specific, focused on the macro or the meso and micro levels – are required to develop competitive new activities. Hence, they are all part of a country's industrial policy.

The concept of *systemic competitiveness* developed by Esser et al. (1996) tries to capture this complexity. It proposes a framework to distinguish determinants of industrial competitiveness at four levels and highlights the existence of systemic interdependencies between them (Figure 5.1):

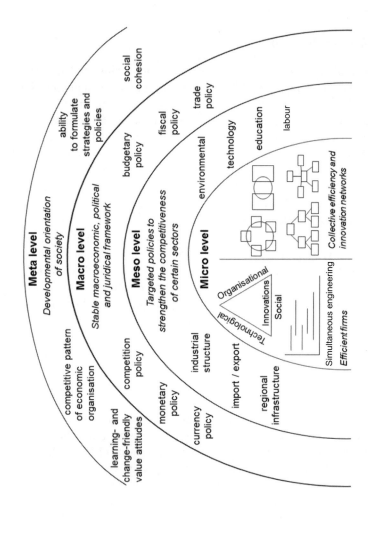

Source: Esser et al. (1996, p. 28).

Figure 5.1   Determinants of systemic competitiveness

42

- *At the meta level*, it is crucial that societies have development-oriented norms and values in place as the basis for a widely shared consensus on the necessity of industrial development and a competitive integration into the world market; this consensus is reflected by citizens' desire to invest in education and undertake efforts to accumulate wealth, firms' desire to upgrade technologically, and policymakers' willingness and ability to formulate visions and strategies and to implement policies.
- *At the macro level*, a stable macroeconomic framework is needed that is predictable and encourages learning and capabilities. This should include a realistic exchange-rate policy and general foreign-trade policy that challenges local industry to upgrade without discouraging and replacing it.
- *At the meso level*, manifold specific policies and institutions are needed to underpin a competitive advantage. These include technology institutes, training centres, export finance, etc. The meso level is also the world of local and regional industrial competitiveness initiatives to strengthen the firms' environment. Many of the institutions that act at the meso level are typically, or can in principle be, non-government entities, for example business associations, non-profit entities, or firms.
- *At the micro level*, capable and continuously improving firms are needed, as well as networks of firms with strong externalities.

All these levels are strongly interdependent, e.g. micro level dynamism depends on underlying norms and values as well as meso level support; likewise, macro and meso policies need to be aligned – e.g. export promotion programmes are unlikely to thrive if the national currency is grossly overvalued.

Functional and Selective Industrial Policies

Economic theory commonly distinguishes between 'functional' and 'selective' (sometimes called 'horizontal' and 'vertical') policies. *Functional* policies are those aimed at improving 'the framework in which firms and industries operate and where market mechanisms ultimately determine survival and prosperity' (EBRD 2008, p. 80). They include the provision of power supply, port facilities, improvement of the legal framework for business, and incentives for R&D. *Selective* policies, in contrast, favour certain activities over others. Such policies include trade protection and subsidies in the form of tax incentives or soft loans whenever these are targeted at specific firms, regions or sectors. Industrial policy involves both functional and selective measures.

Neoclassical economic theory is critical about selective industrial policies, arguing that differential support for activities distorts the allocative efficiency of markets. The key argument can be summed up like this: Markets encourage the creativity of individuals who take personal risks in the pursuit of profits. Competition among firms with different business concepts rewards efficient entrepreneurs and drives less efficient ones out of the market. It is this process of entry, innovation and exit in a competitive environment that drives productivity growth and determines where firms, regions, or countries have comparative advantages. Bureaucrats can hardly anticipate the outcome of this process. Attempts to channel resources into activities bureaucrats believe to be potentially competitive may therefore easily lead to less efficient resource allocation.

Others argue that selective policies are needed because market failure is pervasive. As a result, markets send out price signals that lead to less than socially optimal resource allocation. Many scholars of industrial development, including Amsden (1989), Wade (1990), Lall (2003), Chang (2009), Cimoli, Dosi and Stiglitz (2009) and others, have stressed that successful latecomer industrialisation has in most cases relied heavily on selective policies. These have included dedicated financial and non-financial support for industries considered to be strategic. Selectivity of support went far beyond tailoring incentives to specific sectors. In many cases, governments made rather arbitrary case-by-case deals with individual enterprises. Wade cites the example of the Taiwanese government deliberately delaying imports for certain firms to force them to source locally. He argues that such "'nudging" ... was going on in Taiwan all the time, week after week, decade after decade as Taiwan moved up the world technology ladder into the high tech sectors' (Wade 2007, p. 6). South Korea's early technological development largely built on imitation and reverse engineering of imported technologies (Kim and Nelson 2000, p. 3), even when that implied infringement of intellectual property rights. Similarly, the Malaysian government used tax exemptions and public procurement to reward or punish firms for their attitudes towards industrial development plans (Altenburg 1998, p. 5).

While such interventions seem to have produced good results in a number of countries (mostly in newly industrialising Asia), it is obvious that they come at a cost. First, picking winners by government bureaucrats may direct resource allocation to inefficient uses. Second, arbitrary interference in business is likely to discourage private investors from taking risks. Third, investors are encouraged to engage in rent-seeking activities. Selective measures are thus a double-edged sword, especially if they are not based on transparent rules.

To sum up, it is clear that there is a *normative* case for governments to act towards the achievement of agreed goals and a *theoretical* case for governments to intervene with a view to correcting and supplementing imperfect markets. The question is thus not whether industrial policies should be adopted or not but what the most appropriate policy mix is along the continuum between strict non-intervention and provision of preferential treatment for preselected firms or industries. Table 5.1 shows that governments have a range of options in terms of degree of selectivity and how selective support is allocated.

It should also be noted that the distinction between *functional* and *selective* policies, while theoretically attractive, is not clear-cut and does not provide much guidance for practitioners. Even those policies intended to be functional often indirectly influence the sector composition of the economy. Whether the exchange rate, for example, is overvalued or undervalued has a bearing on the relative profitability of export vs domestic market-oriented investments; whether governments favour primary or tertiary education influences the investment opportunities in more or less knowledge-intensive industries; and whether university education emphasises humanities or engineering sciences, and how many resources are devoted, say, to agricultural vs non-agricultural research all create differential conditions for industries. The same applies for the economic stimulus packages that many governments launched to ramp up consumption during the recent global economic crisis. Car-scrapping schemes, for example, benefited the automotive industry vis-à-vis competing transport technologies, and they encouraged producers of small, fuel-efficient cars more than those of luxury cars. Hence, even such stimulus packages imply a considerable degree of selectivity.

5.2 FROM PRETTY IDEALS TO UGLY REALITIES: THE POLITICS OF INDUSTRIAL POLICY

The mandate to translate societal norms and objectives into tangible and measurable results calls for an active state capable of formulating, implementing and – where and when necessary – correcting a set of mutually reinforcing industrial policy measures. An ideal industrial policy would build a societal consensus uniting all relevant stakeholders behind a national vision, translate this vision into coherent sectoral and technological priorities and thus move an economy along a desirable development path. This in turn presupposes a sufficient degree of

Table 5.1 Level of state intervention in markets

Low ➞ High

Strict non-intervention in markets	Market-enhancing policies	Reactive supply-side policies	Non-targeted proactive supply-side policies	Targeted proactive supply-side policies
Privatisation of public enterprises Reduction and equalisation of remaining trade barriers Labour market deregulation Simplification of firm entry & exit	Anti-trust policies Provision of business information systems Demand-side subsidies for the development of private service markets (voucher systems, etc.)	Trouble-shooting for investors in response to private sector demand	General export promotion Incentives for R&D, innovation Entrepreneurship development Promotion of resource efficiency	Promotion of *particular* activities or technologies (leather industry, solar energy, etc.), clusters or value chains: dedicated laboratories, skills development centres, etc.
				Strengthening existing activities ➞ Developing promising new activities
			Experimental design, performance-based, services delivered by public providers after competitive bidding ➞ Top-down selection; services delivered by public providers	Experimental design, performance-based, services delivered by public providers after competitive bidding; transparent criteria for selectivity ➞ Top-down selection; services delivered by public providers; discretionary case-by-case deals

Source: Authors.

political stability, the rule of law, transparency, a conducive legal and regulatory framework, and strong cooperation with the organised private sector and civil society.

Obviously, delivering on this ideal requires a couple of very demanding conditions to be met. These relate both to institutional and technical *capabilities* (which we address in Section 5.3. below) and to the *willingness* of governments to put the public good above their selfish interests, that is, to act according to the mandate received from their constituency as mostly derived from electoral processes (benevolence assumption). However, neither the capability nor the willingness of governments can be taken for granted. With regard to willingness, it would be naïve to assume that public actors always act as non-selfish welfare-maximisers. As Chang (1996, p. 18) states: 'The view that the state may act as an entity with its own will (and greed) is a useful antidote to the naïve assumption of welfare economics that it will correct market failures as soon as it finds them.'

This perspective is further substantiated when acknowledging that no state is a monolithic body. Fundamental policy decisions taken and concrete measures adopted are invariably implemented by – often powerful and deeply entrenched – bureaucracies, which are governed by their own set of rules and interests in support of their self-perpetuation. As a result, bureaucratic inertia and resistance can easily stifle even well-intentioned policies.

The broader topic of political or regulatory capture has accompanied the industrial policy debate from its inception. It is one of the essential building blocks of the claim that government failure is as great a risk and indeed a reality as market failure. In essence, it asserts that powerful interest groups – either embedded in state bureaucracies themselves or in the form of organised business groups – can influence the outcome of regulatory action by government agencies and counteract the intended purpose of incentive schemes (Laffont and Tirole 1991).

In this context, it is worth pointing out that, in mature democratic societies, the predominant form of political capture derives from lobbying rather than straightforward corruption. This distinction is important as it implies that the related activities are principally legal, legitimate, transparent, open to everybody and mostly in the broader interest of entire industrial sectors rather than being firm-specific (Boehm 2007). Hence, the issue is not primarily one of business 'purchasing' political decision-makers or specific pieces of legislation. Rather, it is the gradual dilution and diversion of policy measures away from their intended goals with a view to reducing their effectiveness and impact.

In fact, public actors are guided by a number of non-economic incentives, which may lead to unsustainable results. Politicians may want to demonstrate that they are taking action in order to satisfy their constituencies, regardless of outcomes. Rather than taking evidence-based decisions, it is in their interest to systematically overrate benefits and underrate costs. Lobbyists may reinforce such biased assessments to ensure continued flows of subsidies. In the same vein, implementing agencies have an interest in setting up new programmes or expanding them in order to increase their budgets and power. In general terms, bureaucrats face at best minor penalties if they misallocate resources. Politically backed industrial policy instruments may thus be kept in place far beyond the point where market actors would abandon a non-performing project.

Government intervention thus implies considerable political risks. It is crucial to anticipate where and when interventions are likely to mitigate an existing market failure and in which circumstances they may do more harm than good. To draw this line in practice – especially *ex ante* – is exceedingly difficult, given the huge number of potential direct and indirect, short-term and long-term effects of interventions, which explains why, despite a growing consensus on certain core principles of industrial policy, dissent still prevails with regard to the appropriate level of intervention in practice.

A lot of research has been conducted to identify elements of good governance relating to industrial policy. Three questions are at the centre of this research:

- Which *governance patterns* are suitable for dealing with the increasing technological complexity in open market economies? To what extent is hierarchical policymaking still appropriate, and in what situations do market-based or network-based forms of governance deliver better results?
- How intensely should *the state* network with *business*? To what extent is embeddedness in particular sectors important to ensure a thorough understanding of their particular needs and opportunities, and at what point do the risks of favouritism outweigh the benefits of tight collaboration?
- How can public *service providers be held accountable*?

Below, the state of the debate regarding these elements of good governance is summarised.

Governance Patterns: Markets, Hierarchies and Networks

With regard to the first question, studies on policymaking in hierarchies and networks help to understand how consensus is negotiated and decisions are taken in the face of increasingly complex technological challenges and more diversified constellations of actors. Scharpf (1993) distinguishes between

- the anonymous market as a means to coordinate production;
- hierarchical decision-making, through which high-level authorities make rules and impose them on subordinate actors; and
- networks as a form of governance between markets and hierarchies.

Industrial policy (like many other policy areas) is increasingly shaped by network-like forms of governance, which are based on self-organisation and voluntary horizontal coordination. Due to the growing complexity in terms of technologies as well as the number of actors and markets involved, central decision-making authorities are unable to obtain and process all the relevant information for policy decisions. Other actors, including firms, business associations and lower-level public agencies, need to be involved in searching for solutions and implementing them. Their involvement cannot rely on hierarchical decision-making alone. Modern industrial policy therefore combines the governance mechanisms of hierarchical decision-making (to enforce taxation, environmental standards, etc.), networks (to encourage voluntary industry standards, etc.) and markets (introducing voucher systems, subsidising demand for services and triggering the development of new markets). These governance forms are interdependent. Policy networks, for example, are sometimes established in the shadow of hierarchy, meaning that governments threaten industry with the enactment and enforcement of legal restrictions should voluntary solutions not produce the desired outcomes (Meyer-Stamer 2009).

For the state, the increasing range of possible governance mechanisms implies new roles. While the main role in the hierarchical mode was to set and enforce rules, public agencies increasingly also act as initiators, coordinators and facilitators. This also qualifies the standard critique of industrial policy that governments are not good at picking winners – modern industrial policy is about facilitating stakeholder dialogues to jointly identify challenges and constraints, and to define shared objectives rather than isolated bureaucracies arbitrarily devising and implementing sector strategies in a top-down manner.

State–Business Networks: Between Partnership and Favouritism

According to public-choice theory (e.g. Krueger 1974), businesses lobby for trade protection, administrative entry barriers and subsidies in order to reduce competitive pressure and obtain extra profits (rents). State–business relations are of a corporatist nature, whereby protected cartels of business insiders benefit from state protection, while the state gains support from the respective faction of the private sector. As these cartels are not subjected to market discipline, they tend to be inefficient and permanently extract surpluses from consumers and taxpayers. Market-oriented reforms are needed to break these corporatist alliances and create competitive pressure. But rent-seekers will lobby against such reforms. To bring about market-oriented reforms, governments thus need to be insulated from the rent-seeking interests of business.

Whereas the public-choice perspective calls for insulating government decision-making from business interest groups, the concept of embedded autonomy (Evans 1995) highlights the need for dense links between governments and industrial capital. Evans argues that governments must have a good understanding of the needs and the opportunities of the private sector to devise appropriate strategies. They need to know, for example, when infant-industry protection is needed and when it can be phased out. Governments should be 'embedded in a concrete set of social ties that binds the state to society and provides institutionalised channels for the continual negotiation and renegotiation of goals and policies' (Evans 1995, p. 12). Public–private policy networks are needed to ensure frequent meetings on particular policy issues, and repeated mutual exposure serves to build trust.

But – very much in line with scholars of public-choice theory – Evans also sees the risks of political capture. Therefore, he points to the need for autonomy in policymaking. Only autonomy enables the state to transcend the particularist interests of business groups and pursue a welfare-oriented strategy. As Rodrik (2004, p. 17) puts it,

> The critical institutional challenge therefore is to find an intermediate position between full autonomy and full embeddedness. Too much autonomy for the bureaucrats, and you have a system that minimizes corruption, but fails to provide the incentives that the private sector really needs. Too much embeddedness for the bureaucrats, and they end up in bed with (and in the pockets of) business interests.

Holding Service Providers Accountable

Principal–agent theory (Pratt and Zeckhauser 1985; World Bank 2004a) sheds further light on the question of how public service providers can be held accountable for providing necessary services and how political capture can be avoided. It addresses the problem that, when services are paid for not by the beneficiaries but by someone interested in certain outcomes (such as a government interested in industrial development), the service-providing unit may pursue interests that coincide neither with those of the funding agent nor the beneficiaries. Thus the 'principal' interested in achieving certain goals, in terms of industrial development in our case, faces the problem of devising incentive schemes to get the service-providing 'agent' to align with their goals.

In practice, this task is often difficult because the principal is not in close contact with the beneficiaries and thus lacks information. To deal with this dilemma, the principal needs a system of accountability that provides two elements: 'verifiable observation of performance and a system of rewards-penalties linked to the information so generated' (Collier 2007, p. 5). Like public-choice theory, principal–agent theory portrays bureaucrats as fully rational self-interested agents whose actions can only be directed towards the pursuit of welfare maximisation if they have the right economic incentives. This assumption has been criticised for ignoring that human actions are motivated multidimensionally. First, self-interest goes far beyond the immediate pursuit of material benefits. For instance, politicians and bureaucrats are usually interested in retaining legitimacy through the success of their policies. Second, human behaviour is always partly motivated by non-rational and non-economic considerations, including the desire for social recognition and sheer altruism. Fostering a culture of professional behaviour based on intrinsic motivation is thus an important complement to a system of material incentives.

5.3 POLICY CAPABILITIES REQUIRED

With regard to *capability*, it is by no means evident that public agencies are capable of identifying market failures correctly and adopting corrective measures that increase social welfare. Efforts to substitute for the market as an allocation mechanism may well reduce efficiency and, above all, create incentives for entrepreneurs to engage in lobbying and rent-seeking rather than productive investments. Empirically, efforts to define strategic industries with assumed spillover effects *ex ante* have often failed. In particular, top-down approaches adopted by socialist and developmental governments during the 1960s and 1970s to set up supposedly strategic industries (such as steel plants, cement factories, automotive assembly plants) under government ownership or public control have rarely been successful. As a consequence, governments nowadays see their role as facilitators and catalysts rather than as entrepreneurs. Modern industrial policy is more about creating an enabling environment for interaction and learning, targeting promising high-value activities in a joined-up manner with private sector stakeholders, encouraging innovations and facilitating synergies. Still, even such light-handed interventions require considerable competence on the part of governments.

Defining Industrial Policy Management Capability

The strands of the academic debate presented above are important, as they identify and explain significant facets of state–business relations. Against this backdrop, we can define more clearly what is required to make good industrial policies. We define industrial policy management capability as the ability of political leadership to influence structural change in a way that improves the competitive performance of the economy sustainably. This capability can be broken down into four major components:

- *Strategic capability* refers to the ability to design policies conducive to sustainable and inclusive productivity growth. This presupposes a good understanding of the changing requirements of the global economy as well as the ability to monitor industrial development at home; in addition, it assumes an analytical ability to translate the observed phenomena into a strategy of socio-economic transformation; to set targets and identify incremental steps towards their achievement; and to create a social contract in support of this strategy. Where external actors play key roles (large foreign investors, donor agencies, etc.), governments need savvy and political power to align them with the strategy.
- The *capability to establish clear rules* for market-based competition that facilitate contract enforcement and easy entry or exit for firms and provide safeguards against monopolies and cartels.
- The *capability to deliver services effectively*. Where markets fail to deliver the necessary services, governments must be able to set up service agencies and devise incentive schemes and verifiable performance measurement systems that ensure effective and customer-oriented service provision. Meritocratic recruitment and

promotion systems are key to ensure that the agency staff have a good understanding of the opportunities and constraints faced by the private sector. Close interaction and feedback loops between service providers and those affected by their decisions are important to maintain embedded relationships.

- The *capability to create or remove protection when needed, while avoiding political capture*. Certain levels of protection and other targeted support may need to be provided by the state to encourage economic diversification and upgrading, but they should be phased out as soon as these targets have been achieved. This requires close observation of learning processes and the independence to withdraw or reallocate rents before they become unproductive. The transparent, predictable and rules-based formulation and implementation of policies are important to prevent the abuse of incentive systems by politicians, bureaucrats or beneficiaries in industries. Governments must be held to account for their interventions, such as through general checks and balances in the political system – including electoral competition, an independent judiciary and critical feedback from independent media – as well as monitoring and evaluation mechanisms built into all major industrial policy programmes.

The appropriate degree of public intervention in any case depends strongly on the effectiveness of governments. As Lall (2004, p. 101) put it, 'if a rational choice of strategy differentiated by country were possible, the optimal one would take into account current and future government capabilities'. In practice, of course, strategies are not only decided upon on the basis of rational choices. Less efficient and accountable governments sometimes engage quite actively in selective policies as a vehicle for patronage. We will present some illustrative examples in Chapter 7.

5.4 PRINCIPLES OF SMART INDUSTRIAL POLICY

Industrial development is path-dependent. The most appropriate development strategy depends on manifold initial conditions, including the endowment of natural resources and labour, distance to major markets, population density, and many others. Once initial investment and policy decisions have been taken, countries start accumulating those specific capabilities, which are needed to advance the chosen sectors and technologies and neglect others. As Nelson (1994) shows, the choice of technological trajectories shapes national institutions, and vice versa. Industrial policies are thus contextual.

The above notwithstanding, the previous sections allow us to define some generally valid principles of effective policymaking.[17] Most of these principles aim to get the process right. They build on Rodrik's (2004) understanding of industrial policy as a search process, on elements of principal–agent theory, and lessons from different strands of management theory. As an example, the introduction of safeguards against political capture can be regarded as a generally valid principle of good industrial policy practice. *How* these safeguards are organised, however, is context-specific. In some countries, formalised auditing systems may be established, either within public administration or partly privatised; in others, community-based feedback mechanisms may be a more manageable and appropriate solution.

In addition to sound macroeconomic policies related to fiscal, financial and exchange-rate management (which we do not address specifically) we submit that the following five principles assume particular importance:

- Create a well-sequenced 'national project' to direct structural change.
- Combine an enabling environment with targeted interventions.
- Gradually prepare for global competition without overburdening local entrepreneurs.
- Adopt a business approach with competitive elements.
- Establish monitored learning processes.

Create a Well-Sequenced 'National Project' to Direct Structural Change

Arguably the most important precondition for industrial policy to be effective is the definition of a national project for socio-economic transformation and the political commitment to take measures to upgrade existing productive capacities step by step in the desired direction. This is not about picking winners or bureaucratic micro-management of markets. Yet governments have a role to play in creating and sustaining a societal consensus with regard to the broad direction of structural change, such as to:

- develop a market economy with social and environmental safeguards, that is, ensure a sustainable development path;
- enhance international competitiveness as a precondition for earning foreign exchange;
- strengthen the division of labour within the economy;

- experiment with new activities that create and expand the market for national producers and to support emerging competitive advantages proactively; and
- create the conditions for advancing from activities with low entry barriers and fierce price competition to knowledge-intensive activities that generate innovation rents.

As we underlined before, industrial policy needs to balance economic, social and environmental objectives. While competition is of the utmost importance as a driver of productivity growth, it can be harmful if strong (foreign) competitors massively crowd out local producers without providing alternative employment opportunities. Liberalisation should proceed at a pace that encourages technological learning among national actors rather than overstraining them in ways that leave only the option to exit the market. Temporary protective measures may be justified if they avoid creating rents that discourage technological learning; and if they do not foster activities and locations that are unlikely to become commercially viable in the foreseeable future.[18] Hence, the proper *timing* and *sequencing* of government intervention can be crucial success factors.

Obviously, structural change will also happen without proactive government support. Competitive markets drive productivity and income growth by themselves. As average productivity and income levels increase, comparative advantages will gradually shift towards activities of higher value. But relying on such 'natural' evolution may be too slow in a globalising world with many highly dynamic competitors. Strategic action, such as in the form of targeted human capital strategies or the setting of ambitious standards for the private sector, can accelerate the process.

The challenge for industrial policy thus is to identify the right level of government ambition and intervention. On the one hand, it is important to identify where economies may have 'latent' comparative advantages (Lin and Monga 2010; Lin 2012a) that private investors do not immediately recognise and develop due to existing market failures, and to create the conditions for their exploitation; on the other hand, it would be a waste of scarce resources if governments promoted industrial projects that fail to become economically viable or that move scarce capital or knowledge resources away from more productive uses. The difficulty is to assess in practice and *ex ante* what is potentially viable and constitutes a 'latent' advantage. This issue is at the heart of the debate between Justin Lin and Ha-Joon Chang (Lin and Chang 2009). It has been couched in technical terms by the latter as having to identify the turning point of an inverted U-shaped curve:

We could suppose some kind of inverted-U-shaped relationship between an economy's deviation from comparative advantage and its growth rate. If it deviates too little, it may be efficient in the short run, but its long-term growth is slowed down, as it is not upgrading. Up to a point, therefore, increasing deviation from comparative advantage will increase growth. After a point, negative effects of protection (for example excessive learning costs, rent-seeking) may overwhelm the acceleration in productivity growth that the 'infant' industries generate, resulting in negative growth overall. (Lin and Chang 2009, pp. 496 f.)

While targeting completely new industries that do not match a country's factor endowment and comparative advantages may easily fail, Chang is right in emphasising that it has proven successful in a number of cases, such as South Korea's deliberately ambitious move into steel and shipbuilding industry in the 1970s. However, the risks flagged by Lin are real and cannot be ignored: many countries – and certainly most developing countries – are ill equipped to implement a grand policy design of visionary dimensions.

Irrespective of the level of ambition, any effective national transformation project presupposes the willingness of governments to rely on inclusive stakeholder consultation processes. The challenge is to agree on a shared vision, identify realistic next steps for industrial upgrading and set incentives that push entrepreneurs to pursue those steps. Of course, governments cannot have all the relevant information about economic activities that might become viable in the near future and about the external effects these activities might eventually create. The technical tools that have been proposed to identify *promising activities* (or 'latent' comparative advantages)[19] and the *most binding constraints*[20] for their achievement are quite imprecise and offer little guidance for practical policymaking.

Hence, it is more promising to organise the search for next steps as a systematic and professionally moderated collaborative process between entrepreneurs, market analysts and government representatives. Appropriate formats include deliberation councils, supplier development forums, investment advisory councils, sector roundtables and private–public venture funds. Moreover, as strategies for industrial transformation necessarily cut across institutional boundaries, it is essential to coordinate activities of different line ministries, private sector associations and other organisations at different policy levels – macro, meso and micro. Coordination requires that mandates, competences and responsibilities be clearly defined.

Having collaborative and coordinating mechanisms in place is thus necessary but not sufficient. In fact, most countries have created public–

private forums and inter-ministerial task forces to deal with issues of competitiveness, but few have a clearly discernable national project. Ohno (2009, pp. 20 f.) therefore stresses the importance of a visionary top political leader who undertakes to galvanise such a national project with the support of a technocratic elite. The top leadership must be able to manage relations among ministries and agencies, between central and local government, between government and private sector, and, in the case of developing countries, between government and donors so that the national project is implemented even against the resistance of old elites. Ohno highlights the role of central policymaking bodies in Asian development, entrusted with the power to enact the pertinent changes across different ministries – such as Japan's super-ministry MITI (Ministry of International Trade and Industry), the Economic Planning Board in South Korea or the Economic Planning Unit in Malaysia (ibid., pp. 82 f.). He considers such top leadership as especially important in developing countries that do not have well-institutionalised systems of technological and policy learning in place. What this in turn implies for the prospects of industrial policy in countries with weak leadership, multi-party government coalitions and/or frequent changes of government remains open for debate.

Combine an Enabling Environment with Targeted Interventions

A key challenge of industrial policy is to balance (a) an enabling investment climate that encourages productive private investment and market-driven structural change with (b) targeted interventions that accelerate productivity growth inclusively and sustainably.

Creating an enabling *investment climate* calls for a reliable legal framework that protects property rights and ensures contract enforcement. It should be recognised, however, that the successful East Asian countries – from South Korea and Taiwan in the 1970s and 1980s to contemporary China – did not always fully respect the intellectual property rights of foreign investors. Reverse engineering of existing technologies was a key element in nurturing national firms. However, it is doubtful whether this can be a role model for today's latecomers. International regulations are now stricter (see also Section 6.7 below), and China is probably the only developing country that has enough bargaining power to press foreign investors to share technologies and protect local firms that copy designs or engage in reverse engineering without risking the former's massive exodus.

As another element of an enabling investment climate, it is important to eliminate unnecessary bureaucratic procedures. In particular, developing countries often have inappropriate regulations that impose a high burden on investors without creating any value in terms of technological learning. For instance, African economies impose far more requirements for licensing a firm than European countries do. Moreover, many regulations are not effectively enforced, thereby creating space for arbitrary application of rules and bribery (World Bank and IFC 2005). While many regulations are functional – and it is therefore misleading to benchmark countries against the least regulated economy[21] – a periodic revision of existing regulations in order to abolish unnecessary, and simplify overly burdensome, procedures is important to encourage investments. The challenge is to establish levels of regulation that are both functional for the particular national development agenda and enforceable.

Additional *targeted interventions* need to be carefully designed. They should challenge entrepreneurs and encourage learning and innovation rather than creating a protected environment that suffocates entrepreneurial dynamism and technological learning. The most serious error of past policies, in socialist countries and in many countries following the model of import-substituting industrialisation, was to focus on building physical industrial infrastructure, rather than creating a competitive environment and nurturing innovative entrepreneurship and institutional learning.

Gradually Prepare for Global Competition without Overburdening Local Entrepreneurs

With regard to trade and foreign direct investment (FDI) policy it is now widely accepted that policymakers should reduce red tape and implement transparent customs procedures, keep effective protection relatively low, avoid extreme variation of tariff rates, encourage competition, avoid anti-export biases, not impose high taxes on exports, allow exporters duty-free access to inputs, attract foreign investors and foster linkages with local producers. More open trade regimes encourage learning and innovation, but liberalisation should proceed at a pace that does not overburden and daunt local entrepreneurs. The best policy would be one that prompts entrepreneurs to improve continuously without overwhelming them, though that approach presupposes a good anticipation of local entrepreneurs' learning curves. It is therefore difficult to agree on the right timing and sequencing of trade liberalisation, especially with governments continuously lobbied by interest groups who try to push policy into different directions.

While export-oriented growth creates a variety of both positive and negative development effects, it has generally proven to be a powerful conduit for accelerating growth and diversifying economies. In 2008, the Commission on Growth and Development undertook extensive research into the main determinants of successful growth processes that were sustained over a longer period. Specifically, the Commission looked at 13 countries having achieved an average annual growth rate of at least 7 per cent over 25 years. It identified five common ingredients of success (among them also committed leadership and effective government), with a strong reliance on the competitive forces of the world economy considered to be the prime determinant:

> During their periods of fast growth, these 13 economies all made the most of the global economy. This is their most important shared characteristic and the central lesson of this report. Sustained growth at this pace was not possible before 1950. It became feasible only because the world economy became more open and more tightly integrated. (Commission on Growth and Development 2008, p. 21)

However, research by Fagerberg and Srholec (2005, p. 44) shows that it is not so much the degree of openness to trade and FDI that explains performance but the ability to take advantage of them in terms of technological learning. As a result, a skilful and well-calibrated policy mix is needed that combines increasing openness with measures to improve technology adoption. But again, this is where the consensus ends. Some emphasise the importance of local content and national ownership requirements or other trade-related investment measures, while others argue that such interventions have usually scared investors away rather than leading to accelerated technology transfer (e.g. Moran 1999). Lall (1995) suggests softer 'target and guide' instruments, that is, winning over firms to make investments that fit the country's upgrading strategy and to persuade them to engage in technology transfer. Few countries, however, have been successful in pursuing such a strategy.[22]

Adopt a Business Approach with Competitive Elements

With regard to policy implementation, incentives are needed to ensure that the service providing agent in fact aligns with the principal's goals rather than pursuing its own interests, such as increasing its own budgets, hiring more staff or increasing its salaries. Moreover, implementing agencies need to have a good understanding of markets and the way private enterprises operate. Agencies must be able to 'speak the language' of business people. To collaborate effectively with the private sector, customer orientation and business-like behaviour are essential. Many countries have successfully transferred some tasks of economic promotion to private or semi-public entities which have the necessary flexibility, for instance to set up meritocratic recruitment and promotion systems, which may also enhance competition. If users are able to choose between different providers, competition will press providers into good-quality services and promote more specialised services. Users will be able to demand the services that suit their needs best (Committee of Donor Agencies for Small Enterprise Development 2001). Contests that allow private sector firms to bid for public resources can be particularly useful. Another possibility is demand-side financing via grants or voucher systems.

Compulsory co-financing by customers ensures that they will only use services that they really need. In the case of poor beneficiaries, such as micro-entrepreneurs, participation may be made contingent upon non-financial efforts that involve a high opportunity cost of time, such as organising in groups. Programme beneficiaries thus self-select into participating. Also, precautionary incentives are often less costly and easier to handle than *ex post* corrections – in other words, incentives to avoid the externalisation of environmental costs in the first place rather than encouraging end-of-pipe solutions; competition can also be ensured from the beginning rather than trying to correct the abuse of monopolistic power at a later stage.

Support should only be provided on a temporary basis, as long as market actors need to adjust to a changing environment. Credible exit strategies need to be formulated early on to signal that support is given for adapting to new challenges – not as an indefinite subsidy for inefficient rent-seeking industries. In the same vein, clear provisions are needed to end policy experiments in case of failure. At the same time, policy changes should be communicated early on and executed slowly to allow firms to adjust their structures and strategies. Policy shocks, such as the brisk trade liberalisation of the 1990s in many Latin American and African countries, may interrupt national learning processes and have negative long-term effects.

Entrepreneurs – and small firm owners in developing countries in particular – operate in information-constrained environments. Industrial policy therefore has a role in creating an environment that systematically increases the options among which entrepreneurs may choose. Unless private agents provide such information, exposure to the newest market trends, demands of trend-setting consumers, advanced technologies and business concepts should therefore be facilitated and knowledge-sharing among firms encouraged.

Establish Monitored Learning Processes

Finally, industrial policy should be designed as a systematic process of experimental learning. For this purpose, independent monitoring and evaluation is essential. It serves the dual function of learning from trial and error and safeguarding against political capture. As a general principle, incentives for industrial development should be linked to performance; this linkage was probably the most important factor in explaining the success of East Asian latecomer development (Amsden 2001) and presupposes the existence of performance measurement as well as feedback loops to ensure that policies are adapted accordingly.

A good learning system also requires the unbundling of different roles of government, particularly as a target setter and regulator, as a funding agent, service provider and evaluator. Unbundling creates clearer lines of accountability and gives service providers the autonomy to choose the best way of achieving their targets without undue political interference in decisions (World Bank 2006, p. 51). Likewise, competition can be promoted for different functions in order to improve performance. All these provisions help to improve the flexibility and effectiveness of industrial policy and minimise the risks of political capture.

NOTES

13. Similarly, in the second half of the 19th century the Minister of Industry in Meiji Japan, Okubo Toshimichi, recognised the need for protection and state-led industrialisation as a precondition for catching up with the West.
14. The successful cases most often cited are South Korea and Taiwan (Amsden 1989; Wade 1990; Rodrik 1995; Westphal and Pack 2000; Chang 2010).
15. Successful sectors in other developing countries include non-traditional exports in Chile (Kurtz 2001) and the aircraft industry in Brazil (Goldstein and McGuire 2004); a well-documented case of regional industrial cluster development is Penang, Malaysia (Rasiah 1994).
16. The import-substitution policies of the 1960s and 1970s in many developed countries are often cited as failures of industrial policy because they imposed high costs on consumers; despite long periods of protection, most of the industries established were unable to catch up in terms of productivity and competitiveness, and many protected industries fared badly after liberalisation (e.g. Esser 1993; Taylor 1998). In the Soviet Union and other Council for Mutual Economic Assistance (COMECON) countries, the failure of heavy-handed industrial policy before 1991 became even more obvious. Di Maio (2009, p. 129) claims that export promotion programmes throughout Latin America have been 'highly disappointing as these activities did not generate the positive externalities and the spillovers they were supposed to produce'. Many evaluations of regional economic policies draw similar conclusions (see Section 3.3). Finally, there have been a number of very costly

large-scale industrial policy failures in developed countries, such as the Concorde project in France and the UK and the development of the fast breeder reactor in Germany and Japan.
17. See also Altenburg et al. (2008) for an overview of principles of industrial policy.
18. How long the time horizon of industrial policy should be is a matter of open debate. There are a few examples of complex industries (automotive and semiconductor in Korea; aeronautics in Brazil) that succeeded only after quite long periods of protection. However, there are probably many more examples of failure despite costly long-term support. Long-term support therefore only seems to be justified if the protected industry makes substantial progress towards international competitiveness.
19. The 'Framework for Growth Identification and Facilitation' proposed initially by Lin and Monga (2010) and subsequently developed by Lin (2012a) basically suggests to identify lists of tradable goods that have been produced for about 20 years in countries with similar endowment structures and twice the per capita income. However, products – and the related entry barriers for their production – in most cases change profoundly over 20 years; furthermore, per capita income does not tell much about the availability of entrepreneurial and technical skills or the government's capability to create the institutional foundations for the necessary transformation.
20. The 'Growth Diagnostics Framework' proposed by Hausmann, Rodrik and Velasco (2008) is based on a decision-tree methodology to identify which growth constraints are most binding and to start removing them. In doing so, however, it ignores the systemic nature of competitiveness and the complementarities between different constraints. Also, it is unable to capture differences between general constraints at the macro level and the much more specific constraints that may undermine the competitiveness of particular subsectors of the economy.
21. See Altenburg and von Drachenfels (2006) for a critique of regulatory minimalism.
22. Well-documented examples are Singapore (Battat, Frank and Shen 1996, pp. 28 f.) and Costa Rica (Rodríguez-Clare 2001).

6. What is special about industrial policy in developing countries?

As pointed out in Chapter 1, most of the empirical evidence on the effectiveness of industrial policies originates from OECD countries, from the first generation of newly industrialising countries in Asia – in particular South Korea (OECD member since 1996), Taiwan and Singapore – or from upper-middle-income countries such as Argentina, Brazil, Chile, Malaysia, Mexico (OECD member since 1994), South Africa and Turkey.[23] Industrialisation in these countries builds on political systems with relatively well-established rules and regulations, reasonable administrative capabilities and a substantial degree of private sector development.

Much less empirical literature is available for low- and lower-middle-income countries,[24] although most developing countries belong to these categories. According to the World Bank country classification, 34 countries are in the 'low-income' group (up to US$1,045 gross national income (GNI) per capita in 2013) and another 50 countries in the 'lower-middle-income' category (US$1,046–4,125) – while 55 countries are classified as having upper-middle-income status (US$4,126–12,745). Industrial development strategies of countries at relatively low income levels are often inspired by, or even modelled after, policies that have been applied in countries with higher income levels and rather mature institutions. However, a variety of contextual factors need to be taken into account, which call for a customisation of industrial policies to the particular conditions prevailing in comparatively poor countries.

This chapter starts with elaborating on the main dimensions of context-specificity (Section 6.1), which are then addressed more specifically in the sections that follow. Section 6.2 addresses the common challenge developing countries face in terms of growing and diversifying their economies under latecomer conditions. In Section 6.3 we then move on to discuss a range of structural supply- and demand-side constraints that – when considered in conjunction – present a strong case for a proactive government helping to kick-start economic development. Sections 6.4. and 6.5 hark back to the theme of multiple societal goals (as

generally introduced earlier in Section 2.3) and address social inclusiveness and green growth under conditions of widespread poverty. In
Section 6.6 we revert to the political economy discourse related to the
capabilities and willingness to implement rational and effective policies
and discuss its manifestation in societies that have been characterised as
representing limited access orders. Finally, Section 6.7 highlights the
strong influence of external policy factors on the development path of
poor economies.

6.1   WHY AND HOW CONTEXT MATTERS

Evolutionary economics has shown that countries develop along unique
trajectories. The appropriate degree of intervention in markets and the
proper mix of policy instruments are therefore necessarily context-
specific. Any analysis of country experiences must account for substantial differences which exist, for example, with regard to the following:

- *History*: development in some countries is able to build on a richer
  tradition in terms of skills development for industry and trade than
  in others. A considerable number of developing countries have
  experienced civil war or failed policy experiments that destroyed
  social capital and undermined the potential for entrepreneurial
  development. Others have developed peacefully and gradually have
  been able to build up an entrepreneurial and business culture.
- *Location*: land-locked countries, for example, are faced with a
  number of specific disadvantages, especially the high cost of
  international trade. Local small-scale producers may, on the other
  hand, benefit from lower levels of import penetration. Other countries may benefit from location-specific factors, such as proximity
  to major consumer markets or trading routes.
- *Endowment with natural resources*: some countries are much better
  endowed with agricultural or mineral resources than others.
  Resource-rich countries face specific challenges for industrialisation, such as the so-called Dutch disease effect and rent-seeking
  incentives (Auty 1993; Rosser 2006), whereas resource-poor countries often face severe budget constraints and need to focus on
  labour and knowledge as their main production factors.
- *Level of economic diversification*: some least developed countries
  are at the very beginning of industrialisation. Here, a key industrial
  policy challenge is usually to develop new opportunities for rural
  non-farm employment. Some lower-middle-income countries, in

contrast, may already be firmly embedded in global value chains and require specific policies to maintain their export competitiveness or try to advance towards higher-value activities within these chains.

- *Capabilities and development orientation of political actors*: some developmental governments are determined to lead their countries towards industrialisation and take action to make the state bureaucracy more efficient and accountable. At the other extreme, some states are predatory (Evans 1995, pp. 43 ff.) in the sense that they try to extract as much surplus as possible for the elite's private benefit, without making relevant investments in economic transformation. Some failed states have hardly any government capable of organising development processes. In some of those countries where governments have failed to foster entrepreneurial development, non-profit organisations and philanthropic business groups have partly filled the gap and supported development initiatives to unleash entrepreneurial innovation.

As a result of such different preconditions, policymaking is highly contextual. Furthermore, policymaking is a political process, with different groups of society voicing their interests and influencing politics and policies to varying degrees. Governments try to accommodate those interests. Their strategies thus reflect not only differences in terms of geography, history and economic structure but also distinct preferences and power constellations among interest groups.

Policymakers should thus be careful with generalisations and policy blueprints. National strategies need to build on country-specific opportunities and constraints. At the same time, many developing countries, in particular those at lower income levels, share a considerable number of characteristics with regard to economic structure and governance. These common features suggest that the rationale for industrial policy and the chances of success of such policies differ considerably from those in richer societies with more advanced political and administrative systems. Moreover, having to develop under latecomer conditions creates a unique set of both advantages and disadvantages, which we turn to in the next section.

6.2 ECONOMIC DEVELOPMENT UNDER LATECOMER CONDITIONS

The world economy has seen tectonic changes in recent years. A period of sustained rapid growth has led to the rise of the global South and, more specifically, the emergence of the BRICS countries as global players. Whereas the initial hype around their high growth rates and their potential evolution into a coherent economic policy grouping seems to be tapering off, new cohorts of rapidly growing countries are being identified and subsumed under fancy labels.[25]

Hence, while the notion of a monolithic or homogeneous group of developing countries was always flawed, it has become even less appropriate over time. Actually, we witness a process of increasing differentiation unfolding with some developing economies having become strong and dynamic economic powers in their own right, many other countries climbing up successfully into middle-income status – and possibly facing a middle-income trap – and a shrinking group of low-income and least developed countries still fighting to move out of abject poverty (the bottom billion according to Collier 2007a). It is this differentiation into waves of latecomer development that led an ex-World Bank president to declaring 'the end of the third world' (Zoellick 2010).

The reality of significant changes in the global economic power balance is beyond doubt. Since 2009, roughly 75 per cent of global GDP growth has been generated by emerging and developing countries (Lagarde 2014). Focusing on the industrial sector as the main driver of economic dynamism, the share of industrialised countries in global manufacturing value added (MVA) dropped from 78 per cent (2000) to just 65 per cent (2013), while that of all emerging and developing economies increased from 22 to 35 per cent – with the caveat that this is overwhelmingly due to the rise of China, whose share alone surged from 7 to 18 per cent (UNIDO 2014).

The World Economy Today: Driven by Manufacturing and Globalisation

In a highly stylised sectoral perspective, economic development proceeds from an initial dominance of agriculture to an increasing role of manufacturing industry (the Great Transformation according to Polanyi 1944) and ultimately services (the Post-Industrial Society according to Bell 1974). Recently, however, the crucial role of manufacturing in increasing productivity, stimulating innovation, developing new technologies, upgrading economic capabilities and driving catch-up processes is re-emphasised. The popular narrative of development being driven by a dynamic services sector is increasingly questioned, inter alia, in view of many services being industry-based and, due to their organisational outsourcing, to some extent being just a statistical artefact:

As for the idea that developing countries can largely skip industrialization and enter the post-industrial phase directly, it is a fantasy. Their limited scope for productivity growth makes services a poor engine of growth. The low tradability of services means that a more service-based economy will have a lower ability to export. (Chang 2010, p. 89)

Looking at data for 2012 on the share of MVA in GDP (down to 15 per cent for industrialised countries), what stands out is the exceedingly high importance of manufacturing in China (33 per cent – with a slight increase from 32 per cent in 2000) as well as in the dynamic economies of Southeast Asia where this share has remained constant at 27 per cent. This is in stark contrast to Latin America and South Asia (both at 15 per cent) and Africa (10 per cent). Interestingly, India, with a share of 15 per cent and a much-heralded services export strategy, has now adopted a new manufacturing policy setting a target of raising the MVA share to 25 per cent by 2025 (UNIDO 2014, 2014a).

Concurrently, the seminal process of economic globalisation is continuing. Following a short-term slump in the wake of the financial crisis, the export intensity of most economies is rising again. Between 2009 and 2012, the share of exports in GDP grew from 26.5 to 30.3 per cent worldwide, from 23.7 to 27.7 per cent for OECD countries, from 27.7 to 29.6 per cent for middle-income countries and from 22.2 to 24.8 per cent for low-income countries (UN database). Why is this relevant?

Significantly – and highly important for industrial policy choices – globalisation is pushed through the production networks and value chains organised by transnational corporations. More than half of the trade in goods (56 per cent) and almost three quarters of the trade in services are generated by intermediate inputs, that is, products not intended for final consumers but for serving as production input for further processing. As such intermediates often embody foreign technologies superior to what is available in the importing countries, they are also identified as a major contributor to productivity gains (Miroudot et al. 2009). If developing countries wish to exploit the benefits of international specialisation and trade, they need to understand what drives global production networks and value chains and find ways of insertion that allow for them to enhance productivity and the appropriation of rents.

Being a Latecomer: Advantages and Disadvantages

Against this backdrop, when it comes to international competitiveness, poor developing countries face a problem typical for any latecomer in global economic development. These countries try to start industrial development in a situation where international competitors are already technologically much more advanced and have established long-term relationships with suppliers, customers and other business partners; created pools of labour with the relevant skills; and in some cases built up a brand reputation. Newcomers, especially those from lagging world regions, have to compete on an uneven playing field. They lack comparable network externalities, and they compete with firms that have already captured most of the relevant markets and accordingly benefit from substantial economies of scale. Collier and Venables (2007, p. 1) summarise this dilemma with respect to the competitive disadvantage of Africa:

> Africa has lagged behind partly because its economic reforms lagged those of Asia. When export diversification started to boom in Asia in the 1980s, no mainland African country provided a comparable investment climate. Now a number of African cities ... offer reasonable investment climates, but they cannot compete with Asian cities that have comparable investment climates since the Asian cities have established clusters of firms in the new export sectors. Such clusters provide firms in the cluster with the advantages of shared knowledge, availability of specialist inputs and a developing pool of experienced labour. ... Until African cities can establish such clusters, firms located in Africa face costs that will be above those of Asian competitors, but because costs are currently higher individual firms have no incentive to relocate.

In addition, latecomers to a globalising market face competition from far superior rivals. Many traditional pathways to high productivity are practically closed for latecomers. Countries that industrialised at an earlier stage typically built up competitive advantages in certain industries (such as steel, textiles or garments for export) and subsequently exploited spillovers to diversify into new activities. Today, competitive pressure is enormous in any mature industry, and entering the market against the economies of scale of established producers and exporters is extremely difficult. Newcomers thus need to be very creative in developing innovative niche markets – as Chile did with commercial salmon farming (Paraskevopoulou 2013) and India with IT-enabled services (Dossani 2005). Also, not every country may have the opportunity to embark on export-led growth. Land-locked countries in particular need to look for other options.

For several reasons, the difficulties for building competitive industries in latecomer countries tend to increase even further:

- Markets are now much better integrated, in terms of trade and investment rules and in terms of the costs of information, communication and transportation. The most efficient competitors can offer their products on a global scale and even reach out to very remote markets. Isolation no longer protects less efficient producers.

- International trade increasingly takes place in governed value chains, which require compliance with increasingly sophisticated standards, implying higher entry barriers for newcomers (Gereffi 1999). Compliance entails a dedicated institutional infrastructure to harmonise national and international standards, test products and processes, ensure traceability, and so on.

- The unprecedented rise of China has cut off many of the remaining avenues for technological upgrading (Kaplinsky and Morris 2008). In the past three or four decades, many developing countries have been able to take advantage of lower labour costs vis-à-vis industrialised countries in order to propel export-oriented industrialisation. Some of these countries have been able to develop gradually more productive and knowledge-intensive industries, either upgrading within the same industries or shifting into more sophisticated new industries. More recently, however, China has been moving into most of the respective market segments at even lower costs. No other developing country can currently match China's advantages in terms of labour supply and market size. Chinese exports have therefore taken away many of the traditional export markets of other developing countries, such as for garments and shoes. Moreover, China is increasingly also capturing higher-end markets, where it combines labour cost advantages with technological competence. Last, but not least, Chinese producers are massively penetrating developing countries' domestic markets and substituting local production.

At the same time, when seen from a positive perspective, latecomers also have some advantages, as they can build on business models and technologies that have been developed and tested elsewhere, which has implications for industrial policy. While the key challenge for rich countries is to improve capacity for technology creation and push the technological frontier, poor countries can benefit from the technologies developed elsewhere without having to invest in their development. Industrial policy in poor countries can therefore focus on strengthening local capabilities for technology absorption and adaptation (Goel, Dahlman and Dutz 2007, p. 85), inter alia through linking FDI with domestic industries.

The Role of FDI

Many developing countries, in particular those at low levels of income, rely and depend strongly on foreign investment as a driver of growth and technology development. In recent years, the importance of private sector actors has grown sharply. First and foremost, this is reflected in the shifting balance between official development assistance (ODA) and FDI flows to developing countries. While total ODA grew from $54 billion (2000) to $127 billion (2012), in the same period FDI surged from $211 billion to $576 billion. In the five countries we will consider in greater detail in Chapter 7 below (Ethiopia, Mozambique, Namibia, Tunisia and Vietnam), the annual inflow of FDI increased more than sixfold – jumping up from $2.5 billion to $16 billion.[26]

These shifts in resource inflows have important implications for industrial policy. The intersection between complementary FDI and ODA inputs should receive heightened attention, in particular in view of the fact that bilateral donor interventions are increasingly focusing on private sector development. Industrial policies have to be geared towards maximising the benefits of foreign investment in terms of technology spillovers, skill enhancements and generally the promotion of linkages with domestic supporting industries (Altenburg 2000).

There is a shared interest on the part of both governments and foreign companies to develop local supply capacity: for the former from a perspective of creating productive employment and strengthening the 'missing middle' of the domestic economic fabric; for the latter from the perspective of creating viable local sourcing options for parts, components and services that otherwise need to be imported at high transport costs. This business interest is frequently at the heart of corporate social responsibility strategies of transnational corporations and can be capitalised upon to reach broader development goals (Lütkenhorst 2004). This calls for deliberate efforts to target those investors that can be expected to make positive and lasting development contributions, be it as part of their sourcing strategies or as an element of reputational branding; indeed, quite often, both aspects go hand in hand.[27] Foreign investment – rather than being considered as a force of exploiting or destroying domestic resources and entrepreneurial capacities – should be regarded as a potentially powerful mechanism to create broader developmental impact.

Lin (2011) has recently given a further spin to the latecomer debate and argued that, as a result of rapidly increasing labour costs, China will have to intensify its technological upgrading, and the country's labour-intensive industries may thus move to low-wage locations, including many African countries. Given the huge amounts involved, this would imply massive export and employment gains:

> Let's assume that as a result of rising wages, 1 percent of China's production of apparel is shifted to lower-wage African countries. All things equal, that alone would boost African production and exports of apparel by 47 percent. A 5 percent shift of Chinese export-related investments in the industry could translate into $5.4 billion in additional exports – a 233 percent increase. (Lin 2011, p. 30)

So far, however, Chinese investments in Africa have focused on the mining and construction sectors. Also, the question must be asked if more than a handful of African countries can presently offer the infrastructural conditions (energy, transport, water) to allow for reliable, large-scale manufacturing export operations. While China is investing heavily into establishing special economic zones in various African countries, including in low-income countries like Ethiopia, Mozambique and Zambia, so as to alleviate infrastructural bottlenecks, the final jury on the success of these operations is still out. It seems, however, that for reasons related both to internal policy and management deficiencies and a challenging external environment (having to compete against 'factory Asia'), so far 'most African zones have failed to attract significant investment, promote exports, or create sustainable employment' (Dinh et al. 2012, pp. 73 f.).

At a more fundamental level, there is an intensifying debate regarding the impact of new automation technologies (including robotics and 3D-printing) on global sourcing patterns in both manufacturing and tradable services:

> In the long run, the biggest effect of automation is likely to be on workers not in America and other developed nations, but rather in developing countries that currently rely on low-cost labour for their competitive advantage. If you take most of the costs of labour out of the equation by installing robots and other types of automation, then the competitive advantage of low wages largely disappears. (Brynjolfsson and McAfee 2014, p. 184)

The result would be a growing trend towards 'reshoring' of previously outsourced labour-intensive operations and thus significantly reduced scope for one of the most powerful avenues of latecomer development in recent decades.

Generally, it can be observed that the labour absorption capacity of the manufacturing sector is shrinking over time and that the point of beginning de-industrialisation (measured in terms of the MVA/GDP share) is moving to earlier stages of the development process – a phenomenon referred to as 'premature de-industrialization' by Rodrik (2015). On the other hand, a growing globalisation of services may offer new chances to use specialised services as growth accelerators and sources of employment. This is the thesis put forward by Ghani and O'Connell (2014). Whether it holds, remains to be seen. We would caution against an overly optimistic view. Many of the new tradable services (e.g. in various forms of information processing) are themselves based on using low-skilled labour and may thus also be subject to automation in the near future.

6.3 THE NEED TO KICK-START DEVELOPMENT

The initial conditions for dynamic private sector based development in poor countries are generally less favourable than in richer societies. On the supply side, technical and entrepreneurial skills tend to be scarce. The lack of specialised and efficient firms in complementary activities further increases costs and often reduces quality. On the demand side, low incomes and little diversification of consumer demand severely restrict available business opportunities. Deficient infrastructure and insecure framework conditions for private transactions further add to the segmentation of markets and create diseconomies of scale. Also, productivity levels tend to be far below international standards. As a result, foreign competitors who build on economies of scale and systemic competitiveness in their home countries often crowd out local producers of tradable goods and services.

Mutually Reinforcing Demand- and Supply-Side Constraints

In poor countries, industrial policy faces the particular challenge of deficiencies on the demand side and the supply side reinforcing each other – a classical example of *coordination failure*.

On the demand side, the small size of markets, lack of diversification and consumer acceptance of low quality standards substantially constrain the opportunities for the development of a competitive private sector. Markets are small due to a combination of low incomes and, in most cases, small populations. Many low- and lower-middle-income countries belong to the 'bottom billion' countries, which typically have less than 20 million people with low average levels of income: 'Per capita income, even measured at purchasing power parity (PPP) prices, is less than $2,000 per year, so that the typical economy has a size of less than $40 billion and more often around \$20 billion' (UNIDO 2009, p. 9) – half the size of Luxembourg's.

Moreover, the cost of trading across borders tends to be high compared to developed countries. On average, developing countries impose much higher restrictions on the cross-border flow of goods, capital, people and ideas (World Bank 2008, pp. 97 ff.). Enterprises thus find it difficult to expand their markets through exports. Due to poor transport infrastructure and inefficient transport systems, trading is costly even within countries, which further adds to the segmentation of markets and diseconomies of scale. Bigsten and Söderbom (2006) argue that this segmentation explains the prevalence of small manufacturing firms in Africa. Likewise, Sleuwaegen and Goedhuys (2003) show that most firms in Côte d'Ivoire are technically inefficient because they produce far below the maximum attainable output level.

Furthermore, poor consumers demand a very limited range of products, and they are rarely able and willing to pay a price premium for high quality or fashionable design. Unless export markets can be targeted, local production is therefore largely confined to simple and homogeneous products for low-end markets, which further narrows the scope for product innovations and new business concepts. According to an argument put forward by Porter (1990), non-demanding domestic markets weaken the competitive advantages of firms because they discourage innovation.

On the supply side, there is underinvestment in pre-competitive areas such as education, vocational training, research, roads and electricity. With the exception of a few rent-based economies, very few developing countries can afford the necessary pre-competitive investments. As a result, companies in low-income countries are on average much less able to develop, and even to absorb, new technology than those in middle- or high-income countries. Also, very few companies in poor countries conduct formal research in order to pioneer their own new products and processes (WEF 2009, tables 9.03 and 12.01).

Moreover, as pointed out at the beginning of this section, the economies of low- and lower-middle-income countries tend to be much less diversified. Manufacturing accounts for only a small part of GDP and, within the manufacturing sector, the bulk of activities tends to be concentrated in a few branches with low entry barriers and mostly operating within the informal sector. This reflects both the limited capabilities for developing new business models and the narrow demand base. As regards levels of informality, a recent study addressing the long-term challenge of youth unemployment in sub-Saharan Africa arrives at quite dramatic conclusions. Even under optimistic assumptions of a 5–6 per cent growth rate over the next ten years, it is forecast that

> ... at best only one in four of Sub-Saharan Africa's youth will find a wage job, and only a small fraction of those jobs will be 'formal' jobs in modern enterprises ... The employment challenge is therefore not just to create jobs in the formal sector, important as that may be, but to increase the productivity of the almost 80 percent of the workforce who will be in the informal sector. (Agence Francaise de Développement and The World Bank 2014, p. 5)

In general, the low degree of economic diversification has two negative effects. First, limited availability of specialised inputs obligates downstream industries to import at higher prices or produce inputs of all kinds in-house at suboptimal scales without special expertise. Second, dependence on a limited number of industries, often related to natural resource extraction, increases economic vulnerability.

Given the limited technological capabilities and competitiveness of the private sector, few companies are able to compete in exports or in large-scale production for the domestic market. Enterprise structures are therefore typically highly polarised, with a small number of foreign and/or state-owned enterprises accounting for a considerable share of total output, and a myriad of micro and small enterprises creating low-productivity employment, but contributing little to GDP – a phenomenon known as 'structural heterogeneity' (Cimoli 2005). The lack of productive medium-sized firms is particularly problematic as it hampers efforts to create ecosystems of interconnected firms that would allow exploiting both flexibility and economies of scale. The weakness of the indigenous business sector is further reflected in the fact that, in poor countries, foreign investors usually account for a high proportion of total investment (Bell 2007) and have few local business linkages.

Productivity Gap between Small and Large Firms

Compared to high-income countries, the productivity gap between small and large firms is much more pronounced, and the overwhelming majority of firms are clustered at the lower end of the distribution of productivity (see Pagés-Serra 2010, pp. 75 ff. for Latin America). Conventional wisdom suggests that unproductive firms exit the market; labour and capital are then reallocated to more productive firms. Especially in poor countries, however, the tail end of least productive firms does not disappear. Instead, extraordinary productivity disparities persist, and the share of the labour force engaged in informal low-productivity micro-enterprises even increases (OECD 2009). Mead (1994) attributes this increase to a surplus of labour; when economic growth does not absorb the growing workforce, many unskilled unemployed people become self-employed or create informal micro-enterprises.[28] Micro-enterprise formation is thus driven by lack of dependent employment rather than perceived business opportunities. Such 'necessity entrepreneurship' is typically confined to simple activities with low entry barriers in terms of skills and capital requirements. In most developing countries these activities are overcrowded and profits correspondingly low. Nevertheless, the number of micro-firms and persons employed does not decrease as long as opportunity costs of labour are almost zero.

The depth of the productivity gap limits the scope for inter-firm specialisation and interactive technological learning. Few modern large firms source from domestic suppliers or sell through independent distributors because local firms rarely meet their quantitative and qualitative requirements. As a result, little knowledge is transferred. Low initial productivity and exclusion from the benefits of inter-firm specialisation and learning are mutually reinforcing. Empirical evidence from poor countries consistently confirms that enterprises that start small tend to stay small and fail to improve their productivity significantly. Very few grow into the segment of specialist medium-sized firms (Liedholm 2002; van Biesebroeck 2005; Hampel-Milagrosa, Loewe and Reeg 2015).[29] Due to this combination of low productivity and lack of specialisation, micro and small firms in these countries contribute very little to industrial development. For African countries, Morch von der Fehr (2005) and Eifert, Gelb and Ramachandran (2005) show that this is particularly true for firms operated by owners of African ethnic origin, whereas firms operated by other ethnic groups are less constrained. There may be different reasons, ranging from access to market information to cultural factors, such as different valuation of entrepreneurship or profit-sharing obligations that make it difficult to accumulate capital.

Taking all the above factors together, productivity growth at the firm level is seriously hampered (Table 6.1). The left column of Table 6.1 presents the most important drivers of productivity growth at the firm level, all of which play important roles in mature economies. Productivity gains are achieved via increased allocative efficiency, systematic R&D-based learning, and learning-by-doing in routine operations. The right column highlights that in low-income countries, two of these mechanisms do not play a major role. Entry and exit of firms have little impact on productivity growth, because the vast majority of new firms tend to be created by necessity entrepreneurs who merely replicate standard local business models, which is reflected in the observation that the productivity of new firms does not exceed that of exiting firms (Tybout 2000,

p. 28). Innovative firms are few and mostly come from different milieus. Firm-level R&D is also negligible. Learning-by-doing in routine operations – typically using imported standard technology – is the most important driver. Knowledge is incorporated in firms via purchase of new machines and licensed technology, or via interaction with customers. These mechanisms, however, are path-dependent and therefore rarely sufficient for creating competitive advantages at an international level.

Table 6.1   Drivers of productivity growth at the firm level

Type	Characteristics	Relevance in low-income compared to high-income countries
1	Productivity growth via increased allocative efficiency: new entrants challenge incumbents, the most productive challengers survive; entry and exit lead to more efficient allocation.	Relatively weak, despite considerable 'churning'. Most micro and small firms are necessity entrepreneurs, new firms enter at the same low level of productivity as incumbents and exiting firms. Certain firms (FDI, ethnic minorities) enter at much higher levels of productivity, but there is very little factor mobility between these and local firms.
2	Productivity growth through systematic, R&D-based learning within firms or in collaborative agreements between firms and S&T organisations.	Less relevant, as few firms perform systematic R&D and linkages with S&T organisations are weak.
3	Incremental productivity growth through learning-by-doing in routine operations within firms. Incorporation of knowledge via purchase of new machines, technology licensing, customers relations (esp. with lead firms in value chains), etc.	Most important form of technological learning in low-income countries, but highly path-dependent.

Source: Authors, building on Hobday and Perini (2009) and Altenburg and Eckhardt (2006).

Considering the multitude of prevailing demand-side and supply-side constraints, market failures are far more pervasive in poor countries. The industrial policy challenge thus is not just to ensure incremental adjustments in markets that otherwise function rather smoothly. Rather, the challenge is to *kick-start market development* in a situation where indigenous entrepreneurship is incipient and supply-side and demand-side constraints reinforce each other in various ways. Dinh et al. (2012, p. 47) underline this fact strongly for sub-Saharan African countries:

> The wide range of constraints indicates, first, that the solution to light manufacturing problems cuts across many sectors and does not lie just in manufacturing. Solving the problems of manufacturing inputs requires solving issues in agriculture, education, and infrastructure. Second, precisely because of these links, developing countries cannot afford to wait until the problems across sectors are resolved.

At the same time, they provide empirical evidence that firm-level technical and managerial support can have great bottom-up developmental impact (Dinh et al. 2012, p. 15) and can thus serve to underpin and complement the necessary broader kick-starting of market-based economic development.

6.4 THE CONTEXT OF PERSISTENT POVERTY

We have argued so far that industrial policy is strongly embedded in societal forces of divergent stakeholder interests, conflict, negotiation and ultimately consensus building. As a direct result, policy design and implementation must respond to a multitude of objectives, which at times can be reconciled while often trade-offs persist and need to be acknowledged. More specifically, objectives range from employment creation to food and energy security, reduction of regional and income inequalities, stimulation of growth and competitiveness, productivity enhancement, promotion of innovation and entrepreneurship, increases in domestic and foreign investment, fostering of technology transfer and spillovers, reduction of environmentally harmful emissions, encouraging resource efficiency, and so on.

While all of these multiple objectives are addressed at varying degrees of detail throughout this book, in this section and in Section 6.5 below, we want to concentrate on two goals of overriding importance: the fact that in most developing countries the pursuit of economic growth continues to take place under conditions of widespread poverty while, at the same time, new demands and imperatives of resource efficiency and decarbonisation – conveniently summed up as the green transformation – are emerging. In doing so, we pick up the thread initially developed in Section 2.3 above, which dealt with social inclusiveness and environmental sustainability as part of the overall industrial policy discourse, but this time zooming into their implications for low- and lower-middle-income countries.

The persistence of widespread poverty presents a compelling case for developing countries to put poverty reduction first. Industrial policy can make important contributions to reaching this goal. In view of widespread poverty, *inclusive* industrial policies are needed that prioritise employment and income opportunities for the poor and improve the provision of affordable services. Industrial policies need to account for specific trade-offs that exist between creating an investor-friendly business climate and protecting the livelihoods of the poor.

The core intention of industrial policy is to enhance economic growth, both via improvements within existing economic sectors and via structural change. It is now generally accepted that economic growth is a precondition for poverty reduction. The poor typically share the benefits of growth and, conversely, see their incomes reduced during recessions, even though the growth elasticity of poverty varies considerably from country to country (Ravallion 2001). Put simply, two countries may have the same rate of economic growth, but in country A the incomes of the poor may increase more than proportionally, whereas in country B their incomes may rise more slowly than average incomes or even shrink in absolute terms.[30] There are even a few cases of prolonged economic growth with rising poverty levels, because poor people often lack education, access to land and capital, and empowerment. Bhagwati (1958) coined the term 'immiserising growth' for this phenomenon, which he linked specifically to export-oriented growth under conditions of falling terms of trade (see also Kaplinsky 1993). In essence, not only the *rate* of GDP growth matters for poverty reduction but also the *pattern* of growth.

In order to be poverty-reducing, industrial policy should thus enhance development patterns that are both growth-oriented *and* provide opportunities for the poor to benefit from this growth. In principle, it is of course possible to devise industrial policies only with a view to enhancing competitiveness and productivity growth and to use the financial resources obtained from economic growth to finance welfare policies. However, there are good reasons to integrate pro-poor considerations in any policy choice in the first place, for instance because integrating poor people as producers and consumers may be conducive for equity *and* economic growth. Furthermore, the distinction between growth and welfare policies is somewhat artificial. In real life, almost any policy decision involves trade-offs between productivity and equity concerns and thus requires careful consideration of policy targets, such as:

- whether liberalisation is pursued rapidly to achieve quick productivity gains or slowly in order to allow poor producers to adapt;
- whether government resources are channelled towards resource-based or labour-intensive industries; or
- whether land use rights are granted to foreign investors or poor farmers.

To design industrial policies without accounting for their distributive and poverty impact – and welfare policies without anticipating their implications for growth and competitiveness – is likely to result in incoherent policies. If, for example, an industrial policy measure leads to the rapid crowding out of non-competitive jobs, the country will face increased poverty or have to incur high costs of corrective social policies. In such cases, it may be more effective, and preferable from an ethical point of view, to adopt a policy of slower adaptation plus retraining of workers.[31]

We use the term *inclusive industrial policy* to characterise policies that aim to shape structural change in a way that enhances competitiveness and productivity growth while increasing the incomes of the poor more than proportionally. What then are the key elements of inclusive industrial policy?

The Importance of Safeguards

First, certain safeguards may be required to protect the most vulnerable groups. On the one hand, there is considerable evidence that a liberal business climate that spurs competition is good for innovation and growth. Competition allows for easy entry and exit of firms, and the quick adjustment of labour to market requirements drives productivity growth *in the long run*. On the other hand, it is also evident that poor people displaced from one activity cannot easily switch to another more productive one, which is especially problematic for those who lack education and information about alternative opportunities. Likewise, gender, ethnic or class barriers may restrict their freedom to seize alternative opportunities. In sum, while 'creative destruction' (Schumpeter 1962) is generally a driver of productivity and income growth, it may aggravate poverty in marginalised groups of society. When foreign competitors suddenly engage in developing country markets, using far more advanced technologies and building on enormous economies of scale and scope in international markets, their competitive advantage will frequently leave local entrepreneurs without any chance to adapt, which may rapidly undermine the incipient development of local entrepreneurship. Footwear and garment imports from China have had such effects on local producers in some African and Latin American countries (see Gebre-Egziabher 2007 for Ethiopia). Similarly, the rapid rise of global retail chains in poor countries has crowded out many traditional retailers and small-scale producers in local supply chains (Reardon et al. 2003).

To avoid devastating social consequences, it may therefore be necessary to limit the economic freedom of commercial investors. It may, for example, in certain conditions be reasonable to:

- restrict foreign trade at least temporarily when economic activities crucial for the livelihood of poor people are heavily threatened or when countries face critical balance of payments problems and shortages of essential supplies (especially food and energy). Such emergency provisions are permitted under World Trade Organization (WTO) regulations. When the government of Ethiopia, for example, faced a severe foreign exchange shortage in 2009, they obligated coffee exporters to sell their stocks within a given time after the harvest, regardless of world market prices. Although such measures are obviously harmful for the country's reputation as a location for private investment, and may encourage illegal trade, they may in some cases be inevitable.
- restrict FDI if rapid market penetration is likely to have unacceptable social consequences. Vietnam, for example, carries out economic needs tests on a case-by-case basis to determine if, where and when outlets of international retailers receive an operating licence, depending on the local retail situation. These tests are in line with the WTO accession treaty as long as they follow a transparent procedure (see also Section 6.7 below).
- impose ceilings on land ownership to protect small-scale agriculture when large population groups depend on access to land to secure their livelihoods, which is especially likely where other forms of social security are unavailable. In fact, most poor countries have established such land ceilings.
- regulate land use in order to avoid crowding out of food production by non-food agro-industrial projects (biofuel, cotton, etc.). India, for example, restricts the processing of edible oils and sugar cane for the production of biofuels, fearing that high fuel prices would lead to food scarcity.
- establish public trading facilities and market data systems, promote agricultural cooperatives and set up public warehouses in order to reduce the power of local traders. In particular, small-scale producers in remote areas often lack information and are left at the mercy

of merchants who are much better informed and often have full control of prices.

All these interventions come at a considerable cost. They are likely to hold back private investments, not only in the sectors directly affected but also in the economy in general, because they may raise doubts among investors about the reliability of the general business environment. The negative effects in terms of forgone investments may outweigh the intended pro-poor outcomes. Policymakers need to take those unintended effects into account. Still, there are good reasons to consider imposing restrictions on certain markets that are critical for the livelihoods of the poor. Balancing the pros and cons of such interventions is one of the most difficult challenges for policymakers in poor developing countries.

Pro-Poor Employment and Income Generation

Second, industrial policies in developing countries need to respond to the urgent need for additional and more productive income and employment opportunities for the poor. The following patterns of industrialisation can be highlighted as potentially pro-poor:

- Promoting manufacturing activities that absorb large quantities of low-skilled workers, such as garment assembly for export (through duty drawback regimes, etc.). Poverty has been rapidly reduced in Asian low-cost, export-oriented countries like Vietnam largely because such industries demand significant amounts of unskilled workers. Similarly, Walker (1995) shows poverty-reducing effects of garment exports in Honduras.
- Policies that increase female participation in the workforce, such as by promoting industrial activities that have a preference for hiring women and by promoting women entrepreneurship. Policies that increase gender equality have consistently been found to also enhance economic growth (Klasen 2006).
- Policies that improve the access of the poor to rural non-farm employment. Poverty is especially persistent in rural areas. Non-farm activities help to diversify rural economies and relax the frequently observed oversupply of labour in agriculture, thereby increasing rural salaries. They may be promoted by improving access to infrastructure and rural finance or by promoting non-traditional exports. However, non-farm activities are not easily accessible for the poor, and the effects of non-farm employment on rural income inequality appear to be mixed (Reardon et al. 2000). A

range of targeted policies may be adopted to lower the barriers to the entry of the poor into the sector, including group approaches and the promotion of fair-trade initiatives (Harper 2009).

- Policies to stimulate productivity development in micro-enterprises. Such enterprises are often caught in vicious circles of low productivity and low investment. Helping promising firms to improve production and grow may increase incomes and create a number of positive externalities. Some governments, for instance, promote clustering of small firms to mobilise collective efficiency and increase their specialisation (Nadvi and Schmitz 1994). Others use public procurement to encourage upgrading of micro and small enterprises, such as by placing orders for school uniforms and furniture with those firms (Tendler and Amorim 1996).

On the other hand, not every industrial policy measure that targets needy producers is necessarily beneficial. As pointed out before (in Section 3.2), SME policies may actually reduce aggregate productivity by distorting the allocation of resources, especially if they support firms with weak business models and create incentives to stay small and informal. Trade-offs between growth and distribution thus need to be balanced carefully.

Innovative Ways to Serve the Poor

Third, products and services on the market sometimes do not cater to the needs of the poor. Demand is often too low, the cost of serving dispersed customers, especially in rural areas, too high, and the transaction costs involved in service delivery and enforcing payments prohibitive. Products and services are therefore designed for the needs of wealthier households or firms, which often creates a vicious circle: inappropriate service supply further reduces demand and leaves poor groups undersupplied, constraining their ability to increase their productivity and their scope for purchasing efficiency-enhancing services. Also, poor consumers often have to pay more than rich people for the same services. This 'poverty penalty' (Mendoza 2008) applies to credit, electricity, training, business development services and other inputs crucial for the competitiveness of firms.

There may be different reasons for the poverty penalty. First, cost per unit increases with the geographical or social fragmentation of markets. Second, poor customers tend to have little political voice, and many public service providers are not held accountable for the services they should be delivering to the poor (World Bank 2004a). Hence, there is a need to adapt services to the needs of the poor and reduce the poverty penalty. Microfinance provides the most prominent example of how a whole system of service provision can be redesigned to this end. Building on local social capital rather than collateral requirements, markets for small loans have unfolded rapidly. Innovative pro-poor banking techniques (such as solidarity lending, mobile banking and village banking) have greatly improved the credit access of poor population groups (González and Rosenberg 2006).[32] Similar social innovations have effectively been implemented with regard to group certification, which reduces the cost of certification of quality standards for small producers and thereby helps to use standards as an enabling mechanism rather than as a technical barrier to market access and trade. In other fields, market failure may be more difficult to overcome, and a higher degree of subsidy may be required. With regard to developing new production technologies, for example, Utz and Dahlman (2007, p. 108) recommend setting up professional bodies 'entrusted with in-field trial and demonstration of diffusion, adaptation, and assimilation of formal sector technologies'. Likewise, Altenburg and Stamm (2004) show that non-financial business services for SMEs are usually undersupplied in developing countries, especially strategic services that enable firms to switch to more efficient business models. Public sector programmes may be needed to fill such gaps. The key here would be to design incentive systems that encourage competition among service providers and hold them accountable for results.

The Importance of Opportunity Costs

Fourth, the opportunity costs of industrial policy experiments need to be considered with particular care. As long as poor countries are faced with huge deficits with regard to basic social services for health, education, water and sanitation, governments should ask themselves if and when industrial development programmes are justified. Investing in competitiveness is essential for creating the basis for sustainable productivity and income growth, but subsidies for industry imply a burden on taxpayers and/or consumers. When industrialisation projects are costly and create few opportunities for the poor – such as the Indian space programme or the nuclear programmes in North Korea and Iran – they can hardly be justified from a pro-poor policy perspective. Unfortunately, it is impossible to measure knowledge spillovers and dynamic scale effects in order to establish opportunity costs exactly.

In sum, widespread poverty and the backwardness of local small-scale producers justify a number of particular government interventions to protect vulnerable population groups and provide space for gradual adaptation. Policymakers should avoid pursuing one-dimensional growth and modernisation strategies. The challenge for inclusive industrial policymaking is to find an appropriate balance between encouraging productivity growth through competition, on the one side, and providing space for learning and the *gradual* adaptation of the workforce according to its capabilities and initial conditions, on the other.

6.5 GREEN TRANSFORMATION FROM A DEVELOPING COUNTRY PERSPECTIVE

It is stating the obvious that structural change – in developed and developing economies alike – has far-reaching implications for the environment. Specifically in low-income countries, the aim of structural change is to diversify and enhance the sources of economic growth, which in turn tends to damage the natural environment and deplete natural resources, such as energy reserves, clean water, soil and biodiversity. Rapid urbanisation, the dissemination of mechanised agriculture and the rise of modern manufacturing with enhanced division of labour and increasing economies of scale – all imply more intensive use of inputs, and often also transport over longer distances.

On the other hand, a structural shift away from agriculture to manufacturing and services, and from decentralised small-scale to centralised large-scale production, may alleviate pressure on resources, because

- many new forms of value creation are less directly linked to resource consumption;
- greater efficiency of the national economy frees up human and financial resources for investment in more environmentally friendly technologies;
- economies of scale in production may reduce the resource intensity of production. For example, agricultural production on larger farms is often more energy-efficient per unit than small-scale production, even if the large-farm product is then traded over larger distances (Schröder 2007; Reinhardt et al. 2007);
- structural change usually implies increasing involvement of producers in international value chains, where stricter product and process standards apply. As a consequence, suppliers in global value chains have to comply with more demanding environmental standards than producers serving local markets.

The relationship between growth and environmental damage is therefore not linear. Developing countries can try to actively decouple growth from resource depletion. For this to happen, appropriate industrial policies that incentivise the internalisation of environmental costs can play a crucial role.

Whereas the poverty reduction goal has always been germane to the industrial policy discourse in developing countries, debates on the challenge of green growth are of relatively recent origin, in particular in terms of the arguments derived from global climate change. At the same time, there are a number of reasons in favour of an early green transformation also in low-income countries.[33] These – as elaborated in greater detail below – include a whole range of economic and social co-benefits, the need to avoid being locked into unsustainable technologies without future prospects and the anticipation of stringent environmental standards (including carbon footprints) in global value chains. Neglecting in particular these new parameters of global trade would come at the risk of being excluded from rapidly growing world markets.

Implications of Climate Change

At the global level, there are complex normative issues involved in relation to *historical* responsibilities for climate change, which has been caused primarily by CO_2 emissions of today's industrialised countries. While the principle of 'common but differentiated responsibilities' has been universally accepted in climate policy negotiations, its concrete manifestation remains subject to heated debates. Indeed, even the *current* global distribution of CO_2 emissions is exceedingly skewed. In per capita terms, the range extends from 40.3 metric tons in the case of Qatar to 17.6 for the US, 9.1 for Germany, 6.2 for China and less than 0.1 for most least developed countries (2010 World Bank data). As can be seen from Table 6.2, the 37 countries with the lowest income levels generate less than 1 per cent – and the following 35 low-income countries less than 10 per cent – of all CO_2 emissions worldwide.

Global climate change, in particular, is likely to create new challenges and opportunities for developing countries. Global warming will influence agricultural productivity, leading to severe problems in some countries, especially those affected by drought and water scarcity, and to higher productivity in some temperate regions. Many poor developing countries are particularly vulnerable to the impacts of climate change. Coastal lowlands – such as the densely populated delta regions of the Ganges, the Nile and the Mekong – will be affected by rising sea levels.

Table 6.2   Global distribution of CO_2 emissions by country income level*

Country group	Lower limit of per capita income (2005 US$)	Cumulative share of global CO_2 emissions (%)	Number of countries
High income	20,000	46.3	35
Middle income	10,000	60.8	30
Low-middle income	5,000	89.9	30
Low income	2,000	99.1	35
Lowest income	280	100.0	37

Note: * Latest available years based on World Development Indicators database.

Source: Nordhaus (2013, p. 253).

For sub-Saharan Africa, climate change is expected to reduce the carrying capacity of rural ecosystems quite drastically (Collier, Conway and Venables 2008, pp. 340–43). According to the WBGU (2009), water scarcity will soon become a critical growth constraint in many countries which have not had severe water problems in the past, for instance as a consequence of melting glaciers in the Andes and Himalayas or of droughts, which are expected even in the Amazon basin. At the same time, agriculture, fishery, tourism and other economic activities dependent directly on the sustainable use of natural resources account for a relatively large part of GDP in poor countries, and the livelihoods of the rural poor may be affected in particular.

This fact has significant ramifications for industrial policy. Since many traditional activities may become less productive or even unviable, the shift towards less vulnerable economic activities needs to be accelerated, both within and across sectors. In agriculture, for example, there is a need to develop new crops and agricultural techniques. Outside agriculture, it is necessary to strengthen competitive advantages in manufacturing and services in order to cope with an accelerated exodus from rural areas. Also, energy conservation and efficiency measures can help save costs for companies and enhance their competitiveness.

Against this backdrop, any discussion of green growth in poor developing countries has two interlinked dimensions. On the one hand, the question of financial burden sharing arises. As shown above, there can be no doubt that developing countries bear a limited responsibility – both presently and historically – for the progressive exhaustion of the available global carbon budget. Hence, they have a legitimate claim on financial support for adopting green technologies, some of which are currently more costly than conventional brown technologies. The additional costs, however, are frontloaded, which makes it imperative for green funding facilities to be in place before investments actually have to be made (Bowen and Fankhauser 2011).

Co-Benefits of Green Growth

On the other hand, the greening of growth may be desirable in its own right also from the perspective of developing countries, that is, it may generate broader benefits that outweigh the additional costs. Indeed, possible co-benefits of green growth – beyond facilitating access to dedicated green donor funds based on verifiable roadmaps – are manifold and involve more than the obvious points of acquiring technological skills, triggering innovation, enhancing competitiveness and creating green jobs (Byrne, de Coninck and Sagar 2014; for a comprehensive account of the 'climate bonus', see Smith 2013). Co-benefits can be grouped into economic (e.g. energy security, local employment or water availability), social (e.g. contribution to energy access, health impacts) and environmental (e.g. decrease in air pollution and water use). Other ways in which co-benefits could manifest themselves, especially relevant for developing countries, are technology transfer, upgrading of domestic technological capabilities, reduced vulnerability to the price of fossil fuels, and improved livelihood conditions at the household level. Particularly for least developed countries from sub-Saharan Africa and parts of Asia, with limited access to fossil-based electricity, large-scale deployment of off-grid solutions based on clean energy technologies is critical for fuelling their development process and shifting to more sustainable agriculture (Guruswamy 2011). Rural electrification, in turn, can generate other benefits, such as educational improvements (Kanagawa and Nakata 2008).

At a more fundamental level, the critical challenge for low-income countries is to avoid the build-up of high-carbon economic capacities that rely on unsustainable technologies and create technological lock-in for decades to come. Above all, this relates to energy generation and consumption, transport systems and urban buildings infrastructure. Taking the right policy decisions under high uncertainty is a highly complex task. The cost–benefit profile of different technologies varies significantly in accordance with the time horizon considered. In the case of energy generation, in some cases, even today the lifecycle costs of coal-based power plants can be higher than those based on renewables such as onshore wind power. With further rapid cost decreases for renewables to be expected, the business case for conventional power plants is weakening fast. Moreover, a scenario of certain technologies being banned in future cannot be ruled out.

Increasing Pressure on Exporting Countries

Even though environmental challenges are not yet a top priority on the agenda of industrial policymaking in many poor countries, this is likely to change, particularly when exporting developing countries face the need to comply with environmental standards, including the growing number of private standards. Non-traditional export products with promising market potential, such as fish, shrimps or cut flowers, are often cultivated in environmentally unsustainable ways that conflict with sanitary or phytosanitary standards of import markets and may lead to import bans or rejection of lots. The same applies to the use of harmful substances in the fabrication of toys, garments or leather products. To ensure that products are exportable, it is therefore important to build efficient *and* environmentally sustainable production systems and set up quality assurance schemes, which may be quite complicated because it not only implies a need to set up laboratories and traceability systems – which commercial exporters are often able to manage – but also to build trust, sensitise and train smallholders, support collective action among producers, launch campaigns to regain consumer confidence and negotiate with the authorities of importing countries. These activities usually take place in the public domain.

Furthermore, as some countries, or groups of countries, introduce carbon taxes or carbon trading systems, international trade will be affected in a number of ways. If some countries do not participate, investors will have an incentive to shift investments to other destinations and to import goods, rather than producing them in markets with high carbon costs. On the one hand, given their much lower per capita emissions, poor countries will benefit from supplying emission allowances. Even now, developing countries can benefit from the Clean Development Mechanism – although few low-income countries are actually able to implement credible proposals (for Africa, see Collier, Conway and Venables 2008, p. 350). On the other hand, developed countries may put trade policy measures in place to penalise free riders who do not tax carbon emissions, such as border tax adjustments, food miles, carbon standards and labelling. This may adversely affect developing countries (UNCTAD 2009, p.v); for instance, these countries may have to introduce costly certification systems to document the carbon footprint of production and eventually pay taxes for exports to countries that tax their own carbon emitters.

In Table 6.3 we provide a synoptic overview of the main considerations relevant for developing countries in assessing the case for the adoption of low-carbon industrial policies from a climate change mitigation perspective.

Table 6.3   Adopting low-carbon development strategies in developing countries

Potential pros*	Potential cons*
Early acquisition of technological and managerial capabilities and skills related to sustainable technologies that will dominate in future	Overall scenario of tough trade-offs and exceedingly high opportunity costs (e.g. originating from critical investment needs in health, education, etc.)
Investment into future export potentials: access to stringently regulated markets in terms of carbon footprints and various sustainability labels that increasingly govern global value chains	Widespread poverty and high wealth aspirations of population put premium on growth objectives; widening access to energy valued higher than decarbonisation
Access to dedicated green donor funds (bilaterally and in terms of global climate finance facilities)	High upfront investment costs coupled with backloaded and often uncertain benefits; limited green donor funding available
Avoiding early lock-in of technologies that will decline and possibly be banned while new ones are rapidly phased in and becoming cost-effective	Awaiting impact of technological learning and cost curves to make new low-carbon technologies economically more attractive
Significant co-benefits (e.g. health benefits from clean air and water as well as resource efficiency) that are key for policy management	Lack of green awareness among private sector players focusing on quick profits

Note: * The table contains just a listing of relevant considerations on both sides. The arguments are *not* meant to be horizontally linked.

In sum, environmental concerns, and climate change in particular, will definitely become a major driver of change in global economic relations. Hence, this will also affect developing countries. As with any driver of global change, it is important to anticipate the manifold opportunities and risks for national development, and to take action at an early stage: first, because delayed action increases mitigation and adaptation costs; second, because countries may benefit from a first-mover advantage if they start seizing emerging opportunities now. Developing countries may take advantage of huge financial transfers, but only if the capacity needed is developed to be able to absorb investments in credible and certified low-carbon projects. Moreover, many countries will need to invest in climate change adaptation, such as enhancing agricultural research for new (drought-resistant, etc.) varieties to help protect national natural resources and – importantly from an industrial policy perspective – to exploit new market opportunities and prevent the loss of markets that might result if producers do not adapt early enough to changing international demand conditions.

6.6 INDUSTRIAL POLICY IN LIMITED ACCESS ORDERS

It is widely held that industrial policy may work if, and only if, the state is strong and builds on well-trained civil servants employed under merit-based incentive schemes and subject to political checks and balances. Soludo, Ogbu and Chang (2004, p. 27), for example, state that 'only when the state is capable and developmental, and has a vibrant capitalist class can industrial policies be effective'.

Let us briefly sum up what 'capable and developmental' implies, that is, what characteristics governments need to have in order to design and implement good industrial policies (in accordance with the principles outlined in Section 5.4). As argued above, political leadership should be able not only to establish and enforce clear rules for market-based competition but also to formulate, in close collaboration with the private sector and other stakeholders, a strategy of socio-economic transformation; to create a social contract in support of this strategy; and to implement the strategy effectively, which in turn presupposes institutional reforms that encourage efficiency, transparency and accountability.

One may doubt whether many poor developing countries can meet these criteria. To begin with, these countries usually lack financial resources and tend to have only a small pool of highly competent, well-paid cadres. Many industrial policies are costly – not only in terms of subsidies and investment in infrastructure but also in terms of investing in administrative capabilities, organising dialogue with civil society, monitoring results and creating other checks and balances. Financial and administrative skill constraints obviously limit the scope for proactive support and call for simple and inexpensive instruments.

The Political Logic of Limited Access Orders

Even more importantly, the political will to use available resources in a way that leads to a rise in public welfare cannot be taken for granted. The political systems of most poor countries can be characterised as neo-patrimonial regimes (e.g. Bratton and van de Walle 1997), which have a formally established legal-rational system that builds on codified and actionable rules and, in principle, clearly separates the private from the public realm. However, overlying this *formal* system is an *informal* one driven by personal relations, where individual favours are awarded in exchange for political support. Rulers favour members of the political elite to hold key positions in the bureaucracy and the state economy. These in turn assign positions or give other favours to their personal clients and so on, thus creating a cascading system of patron–client relationships that ensures loyalty with the political elite.

North, Wallis and Weingast (2009) extended this analytical perspective by including the idea of several elite factions competing for access to rents. In their framework of limited access orders, these elite groups strive for extraordinary profits to be obtained from privileged access to natural resources (e.g. mining concessions) or interference with markets with the aim of creating and exploiting trade and investment privileges. To protect their privileged positions, elites would typically do two things: first, they invest in patron–client relations as described above ('vertical' relations); second, they seek political settlements with elite groups that compete for the available privileges and rents ('horizontal' relations). The latter is considered necessary whenever other elite groups are able to credibly threaten to capture part of the rent or even overthrow the established elite. Access to the ruling elite is thus limited to those who, in the authors' terms, possess sufficient 'violence potential'. When several factions possess violence potential, they need to make informal deals dividing the rents proportional to their respective power resources; each group has an interest in demonstrating its violence potential to improve its bargaining power but also to avoid violent confrontations that might destroy the sources of rents or risks losing the privileged access.

In limited access orders, public (including industrial) policies are, to a greater or lesser extent, employed to support own clients or co-opt potential opponents and competitors; network insiders benefit from discretionary awards of contracts, jobs, and so on, whereas access of outsiders is informally restricted, even if the formally established legal-rational system stipulates transparent open tenders. In ethnically hetero-geneous societies, ruling elites sometimes seek legitimacy by supporting patron–client relationships along ethnic lines (Ikpeze, Soludo and Elekwa 2004, p. 345).

It goes without saying that such practices contradict the principles of effective industrial policy. Selective support may be provided for rent-seeking activities rather than on the basis of rational criteria, and government authorities may recruit and promote their staff on the basis of favouritism rather than merit. The practice of dispensing jobs in the public sector in return for political support has two negative consequences. First, it is likely to lead to overstaffed public agencies; second, and more importantly, if there is a tacit understanding that public positions are a kind of government award, while a government is unable to afford to pay attractive salaries, bribery may be tolerated. This is one explanation for the fact that low-income countries tend, on average, to regulate more despite their limited ability to enforce regulations: each regulatory procedure creates an additional opportunity for bribery (Djankov et al. 2002; World Bank and IFC 2005). The lack of checks and balances – such as the virtual absence of any independent monitoring of industrial policy programmes in most developing countries – is thus not only a matter of limited resources; it also reflects the logic of limited access orders.

Corruption on the part of some economic agents may easily lead to a vicious circle. As Tirole (1996) has shown, the reputation of individual entrepreneurs and bureaucrats is affected not only by their own past behaviour but also by the behaviour of their peers. When a broader group is known as being fraudulent, it will be difficult for individuals to establish a reputation for integrity, which lowers the barrier for dishonest behaviour and in turn is likely to reinforce the bad reputation of the group.

Weak Industrial Policy Management Capabilities

As a result of both scarce public resources and the political logic of limited access orders, the governments of most developing countries tend to be weak in terms of their industrial policy management capability. In Table 6.4, we have consolidated data from a number of different policy capability indicators and have selected low- and lower-middle-income countries (based on the World Bank typology) as a proxy for the group of poorer developing economies. The typology of capabilities used is based on the four dimensions introduced in Section 5.3 above.

With regard to *strategic capability*, the Bertelsmann Transformation Index (BTI) ranks countries according to their 'steering capability', that is, their capability to define strategic priorities and to implement them effectively. Moreover, the Index measures the ability of political leaders to create a broad consensus among social actors regarding political reforms without sacrificing their reform agenda ('consensus building'). While the Index does not appraise *industrial policy* reforms explicitly, it can be used as a proxy. As Table 6.4 shows, of all low- and lower-middle-income countries in the sample, about one third belong to the worst-performing quartile; two thirds are found in the two lower quartiles. Note that the BTI sample only includes transformation countries; had the mature industrialised countries been included, the performance gap would have been even starker.

With regard to the capability to establish *clear rules of the game for market-based competition*, the picture is similar. The Global Competitiveness Index (GCI; WEF) assesses the transparency of government policymaking, and the Doing Business Index (World Bank) measures the procedures, time and cost involved in resolving a commercial dispute. Again, low- and lower-middle-income countries are clustered in the lower quartiles, showing that policymaking lacks transparent rules, and that most of these countries fail to ensure enforcement of business contracts.

With regard to the capability to *deliver services effectively*, the World Bank Worldwide indicators for government effectiveness (WGI) can be taken as a proxy. The results are even worse for low and lower-middle-income countries. Eighty-nine per cent of these countries fall within the two lowest quartiles of all countries covered. The GCI's measure of 'wastefulness of government spending' turns out to be more favourable, but it does confirm again that poor countries are over-represented among the mediocre performers.

Finally, different sources confirm that low and lower-middle-income countries are mostly weak in terms of *avoiding political capture*. Transparency International's Corruption Perception Index (CPI) ranks around 180 countries. Although nearly half of them are low and lower-middle-income countries, the best performer in this group ranks only 31st. Only 12 per cent of these countries are found in the upper half. The GCI provides similar figures for 'favouritism in decisions of government officials' and 'judicial independence'.

In sum, even if such indicators are fraught with methodological problems,[34] and the numbers in Table 6.4 are not directly comparable due to the different size and composition of the samples, the overall picture is clear. *On average*, the industrial policy management capabilities of low- and lower-middle-income countries are rather weak. At the same time, there is considerable *variance* within the group. In fact, some low- and lower-middle-income countries rank quite high on different governance

*Table 6.4   Indicators of industrial policy management capability in low-
and lower-middle-income countries (LLMIC)*

Indicators of …	Source	% of LLMIC in lowest quartile	% of LLMIC in lower two quartiles
Strategic capability			
Steering capability	BTI	35	60
Consensus building	BTI	29	62
Capability to establish clear rules of the game			
Transparency of government policymaking	GCI	33	72
Contract enforcement	DBI	43	65
Capability to deliver services effectively			
Government effectiveness	WGI	51	89
Wastefulness of government spending	GCI	32	56
Capability to create/remove protection when needed and avoid political capture			
Control of corruption	CPI	51	88
Judicial independence	GCI	38	75
Favouritism in decisions of government officials	GCI	32	68

Sources: BTI: Bertelsmann Transformation Index, 2013 (n=129, incl. 68 LLMIC); CPI: Corruption Perception Index, 2013 (n=177, incl. 78 LLMIC); DBI: Doing Business Index, 2013 (n=189, incl. 82 LLMIC); GCI: Global Competitiveness Index, 2013 (n=148, incl. 60 LLMIC); WGI: World Bank Worldwide Governance Indicators, 2012 (n= 210, incl. 84 LLMIC).

indicators. Bhutan, Namibia and Cape Verde, for example, rank between 67 and 56 (out of 100 for best performers) on the World Bank Governance Indicator for government effectiveness – a ranking similar to that of some OECD countries;[35] the Bertelsmann Index ranks Ghana, Namibia and India high with regard to management capabilities, and Rwanda is given an exceedingly high ranking (rank 8 – in between Luxembourg and Sweden) with regard to transparency of policymaking.

Bad governance is especially common in resource-rich countries (see Box 6.1), which is consistent with the observation that the opportunity to extract large rents favours corruption, patronage politics and autocracy (Collier 2007a).

BOX 6.1 THE INDUSTRIAL POLICY CHALLENGE OF RESOURCE-RICH COUNTRIES WITH LIMITED ACCESS ORDERS

Since the early 2000s, prices for oil and gas, metals and ores have more than tripled (Morris, Kaplinsky and Kaplan 2012, p. 2). Sub-Saharan exports of those commodities increased from US$56 billion in 2002 to US$288 billion in 2012 (World Bank 2013a, p. 9). Moreover, high prices triggered mineral and oil prospection, leading to huge new discoveries in different parts of the developing world, with the effect that many countries that had until recently been classified as 'resource-poor' are now heavily dependent on commodities.

Extraction of subsoil resources often allows for abnormal super profits – primarily for those who can access oil pits and mines, but many others benefit indirectly through privileged access to, for example, real estate, construction and legal services. These opportunities create strong disincentives for diversification and structural change.

Economically, opportunities to pocket resource rents undermine incentives to undertake risky long-term investments in tradable goods and services that have to compete internationally, because competition tends to bring profits down to the average. Moreover, commodity booms produce capital inflows leading to currency appreciation, which in turn undermines export competitiveness ('Dutch disease'). Especially those economic activities that are commonly associated with technological learning and knowledge spillovers are strongly discouraged. Also, commodity price fluctuations have a big impact on public revenues and on fiscal and trade balances, thus making the affected economies highly volatile. *Politically*, societal groups may try to capture politics in order to access the sources of rents, either through legal or extralegal means. The latter may range from the use of clientelism to circumvent formal procedures, to outright corruption and violence.

Industrial policy can, in principle, adopt measures to counter these *economic* disincentives. Governments would need to increase savings and use long-term funds to avoid an oversupply of financial liquidity; channel investments into general capabilities and infrastructure that help to create new competitive advantages, and subsidise the search for new market opportunities; put pressure on international investors to share technologies and allow for technological learning; and foster economic forward and backward linkages from the resource sectors.

All these policies, however, are at odds with the political logic of limited access orders. Elite groups with access to resource rents have strong incentives to scale up spending to 'fuel' their clientelist networks – which increases the appreciation pressure; they have little reason to invest in diversification, which would nurture new elite groups with whom new elites settlements would have to be sought; they will oppose policy reforms that might constrain their scope for closing discretionary deals with investors. Hence, strong tensions exist between the policies required for mitigating the built-in disincentives of resource abundant economies and the political logic of limited access orders. In limited access orders, industrial policies which, in principle, are useful and even necessary tools for technological learning, such as national co-ownership or domestic content requirements, are likely to be used as vehicles that enable elite circles to capture resource rents.

Source: Altenburg and Melia (2014).

Ways Out of the 'Weak Capabilities Dilemma'

The weakness of governments in low- and lower-middle-income countries with regard to industrial policy management capabilities creates a dilemma. In the previous chapter, we argued that it is particularly the poor countries that need an active industrial policy. We have also argued that – given all the difficulties of mediating the interests of many stakeholders and the risks of misallocation and political capture – effective industrial policymaking is challenging. Few governments in the world are able to design and effectively implement comprehensive long-term strategies. Even in countries with strong institutions, policymaking is in most cases an incremental process of 'muddling through', whereby small reform steps are implemented, revised and adapted as intended and unintended results, support and resistance become visible. How, then, can we expect sound industrial policies in countries with typically weak implementing capacity and informal power groups able to capture and divert industrial policymaking?

The good news is that there is evidence of effective industrial policymaking in developing countries. While informal institutions whose functions are to allocate resources via neopatrimonial patron–client relations or to distribute economic power among competing elite factions are pervasive, there is also a high degree of variation in the way these institutions are organised across countries, and, in some of them, institutional arrangements have developed which do enable growth and structural change.

With regard to industrial policy management *capabilities,* scholars of South Korea's and Taiwan's industrial development argued that these governments' management capabilities were rather weak when they embarked on their enormously successful catch-up strategies in the 1960s (e.g. Chang 2006). Thus even weak governments may in certain conditions trigger successful industrial policy initiatives and improve their management capability over time.

Regarding the *willingness* of political elites to support policies of structural change rather than their immediate and narrow self-interests, research conducted by Khan (Khan 2010; Khan and Jomo 2000) in several Asian countries shows that ruling coalitions are composed and organised in diverse ways and have very different relationships to the productive sector. Khan identified groups within the political elite, within the enterprise sector and within the bureaucracy, which expect to gain more from enhancing economic growth and building competitive industries than from the sole redistribution of existing rents. His finding that informal institutional settlements do not necessarily preclude the successful implementation of policies for growth, structural change and industrial development is supported by a number of recent case studies.

These studies highlight different agents of change. Ohno (2009), for example, underlines the important role of the top political leadership in this triangle. Based mainly on Asian examples, he argues that leadership with a clear vision and commitment to modernisation and industrial development made the difference in successfully industrialising Asian countries. For sub-Saharan Africa, Kelsall and Booth's (2010) work on 'developmental patrimonialism' similarly emphasises the role of strongly committed presidents during growth and change-enhancing governance periods – with the downside that such phases typically ended with the demise of those developmental leaders. Similar evidence is presented by Altenburg (2013), but – not surprisingly – most case studies refer to resource-poor countries where the size of the rents to be extracted is much smaller than, for example, in oil-rich economies.

Other authors emphasise the role of 'pockets of efficiency' (Whitfield et al. 2015) or 'pockets of effectiveness' (Hout 2013) in the bureaucracy as promoters of structural change. In fact, pockets of efficiency have been identified in many empirical studies, even under quite adverse overall conditions. They can take different forms, including the following:

- *Government entities*, such as Ethiopia's Horticultural Development Agency, which proved to be far more effective and customer-oriented than most other government entities with comparable sector-specific mandates (see Section 7.1 below).
- *Business associations and chambers*, such as the National Association of Software Services Companies (NASSCOM), a chamber of commerce of the information technology and business process outsourcing industries in India. NASSCOM facilitates business and trade in software and services, encourages research in software technology, organises training, promotes inter-industry linkages and collaboration between industry and universities, provides market intelligence services and organises dialogue. India's international success in information technology services and business process outsourcing has been attributed to NASSCOM's proactive role at times when the Indian government created many obstacles for the industry (Athreye and Hobday 2010).

- *Non-governmental entities*, such as Bangladesh-based BRAC (Bangladesh Rural Advancement Committee), the world's largest non-governmental development organisation. BRAC promotes projects for rural employment creation, including, for example, agro-industries, handicraft production and marketing, and a vegetable export programme.
- *Non-profit corporations*, such as Fundación Chile, which played an important role in developing Chile's salmon farming industry.

Whitfield et al. (2015) developed a broader framework, which puts political settlements between three actor groups at the centre of analysis: political elites, the bureaucracy and entrepreneurs. In certain situations, elite factions and industries may be interested in developing competitive industries and promoting structural change (be it for altruistic developmental motivations or considerations of political power), and they may support pockets of efficiency in the bureaucracy to pursue their aspirations. Positive feedback loops between the three groups of actors may lead to growth-enhancing virtuous circles. Conversely, of course, the relationship may also be vicious, with collusive behaviour between self-interested actors groups. From a political economy perspective, it is thus imperative to recognise the particular interests of, and relationships between, the three groups of actors as a key to understanding whether structural change is likely to be supported or not.

6.7   STRONG ROLE OF EXTERNAL POLICY FACTORS

Industrial policy in developing countries is highly determined and circumscribed by external factors that are largely beyond the control of domestic decision-makers. The most important external factors relate to the provision of ODA by bilateral and multilateral donor agencies, and the existing international trade and investment rules.

Official Development Assistance (ODA)

In many poor countries, industrial policy programmes are almost entirely donor-financed. Donors thus need to be taken into account as important political actors in efforts to shape and implement policies. Their role, however, is ambivalent. On the one hand, donor engagement creates additional opportunities for governments to implement industrial policies, both in terms of funding and institutional capacity building. On the other hand, donor dependence may undermine the industrial policy management capabilities of the host country.

On the positive side, few industrial policy projects in poor developing countries would have been feasible without the financial or technical support of donors. Most activities aimed at boosting supply-side capacity, such as upgrading of technical and vocational training systems, cluster and value chain initiatives or building trade capacity, are heavily reliant on international support.

Even more importantly, donor engagement is often for the long haul and offers a welcome commitment to the support of capacity building and thus the quality of institutions. In most cases, partner institutions are encouraged to make policy formulation and service delivery more participatory and inclusive, which tends to promote better standards in terms of customer orientation, outreach, and monitoring and evaluation.

On the negative side, four issues are a matter of concern.

First, donors may try to impose ideological concepts that undercut the acceptance of active industrial policies. In particular, the structural adjustment programmes of the 1980s imposed neo-liberal conditionality upon recipients. More specifically, many scholars from developing countries criticise the Bretton Woods institutions for weakening the governance capacity of developing states by systematically stripping them of their assets, such as by reducing public sector remuneration and triggering the exodus of personnel from the public sector, substituting foreign advisors for the decision-making role of national bureaucracies, de-legitimising developmental visions, undermining the morale of national bureaucrats and privatising strategic functions of the state (Olukoshi 2004, p. 66). This critique may be biased inasmuch as it does not acknowledge the widespread domestic abuse of state functions. However, it rightly challenges the unrealistic assumption that latecomer development is possible without a strong and capable national bureaucracy.

However, with few exceptions – the International Finance Corporation's (IFC's) Doing Business agenda being the most notable one[36] – donors seem largely to have left behind their anti-statist attitude towards proactive private sector development policies and many donors are now supporting heterodox approaches. Nevertheless, they may still send biased messages. Following the structural adjustment programmes, donors encouraged recipient countries to draft Poverty Reduction Strategy Papers that were clearly biased towards social sector spending at the expense of investment in infrastructure, productive capacities and enterprise development (Hewitt and Gillson 2003; World Bank 2004, p. 9). Again, this new 'fashion' among donors turned a blind eye to the need for investments in productive assets and failed to encourage targeted private sector initiatives.

Second, large inflows of aid – relative to GDP – may reduce the competitiveness of domestic productive sectors in poor countries. These inflows lead to currency appreciation if they generate additional imports or increased domestic demand. Currency appreciation may crowd out productive investments and reduce export competitiveness (Dutch disease effect). Aid inflows can also drive inflation if the government spends these funds locally (Birdsall 2007, p. 13).

Third, the most talented and entrepreneurial people may prefer to work for aid institutions rather than to engage in domestic public institutions or private business. Especially in highly aid-dependent countries, donors and international organisations often attract a huge percentage of the available highly skilled workforce. According to Knack and Rahman (2004), a high number of donor organisations in a country correlates with declines in the quality of bureaucracy.

Fourth, donor fragmentation and non-alignment with national strategies may undermine the industrial policy management capabilities of recipient countries. Currently, this appears to be the most worrying by-product of foreign aid – despite the international agreements on 'aid effectiveness' (or in the new terminology 'development effectiveness') of Paris, Accra and Busan, which involve commitments to support country-driven strategies. The idea is that recipient countries set their own economic strategies for economic growth, poverty reduction and sustainability, define targets and improve their institutions, especially with a view to making them more accountable. Donors should align with these objectives. Moreover, they should use local systems for planning, service delivery, monitoring and evaluation whenever possible, and they should simplify procedures and coordinate with other donors to avoid duplication and reduce the transaction costs imposed on their partners.

Many donors, however, remain reluctant to harmonise with other donors and align with country strategies. Quite often they set up new implementation units that, even if they are located in the relevant counterpart organisation, operate de facto as independent entities.[37] While donors supply funds and technical expertise to implement industrial polices and build institutional capacity, they sometimes also contribute to policy fragmentation, overburden local administrations and tie up scarce professional resources. To some extent, this also reflects a weakness on the part of the host country. Governments obviously often lack the capacity to develop operational national strategies and to ensure that all donors are aligned with these strategies. In fact, it is common to observe several donors engaging in similar activities, setting up their own specialised institutions and applying their own methodologies for analysis, implementation and monitoring.

In Ethiopia, for example, about ten donors were involved in supporting the development of value chains according to an internal report by the Development Assistance Group (a platform to coordinate donor activities). The Development Assistance Group did not try to harmonise the different methodologies, nor were there any discernible efforts by the Ethiopian government to develop a 'country-owned' value chain approach and align donor contributions with it.

In the case of Vietnam, there has been a strong government drive to make the UN system's development cooperation programmes more coherent and synergetic (see also Section 7.5 below). However, while these efforts caused exceedingly high transaction costs in terms of a heavy and time-consuming coordination machinery, they covered just 2 per cent of the country's ODA inflows and left the bulk of bilaterally delivered ODA largely untouched.

Overall, the readiness and ability of governments to manage donor contributions consistently, and to impose the discipline necessary for donor harmonisation and alignment with country strategies, remains an important determinant of the success or failure of industrial policy in poor countries. The challenge faced by governments is aggravated by the high profile recently gained by philanthropic actors, which has further fragmented the donor landscape. Already in 2009, a multitude of philanthropic initiatives – led by new vertical, single-purpose institutions, such as the Gates Foundation – delivered development support amounting to 44 per cent of total ODA from OECD-DAC (OECD Development Assistance Committee) countries (calculated from UNDP 2011, p. 150). Today, these actors combine massive financial clout with strong advocacy and convening power and have become a force for developing country governments to reckon with.

International Trade and Investment Rules

International trade and investment rules can reduce the scope for domestic industrial policy. For members of the WTO, the use of certain policy instruments widely used by Western countries when they started to industrialise – and by successful Asian latecomers – is no longer permitted; mostly, the changes affect quantitative import restrictions, differential treatment of foreign and local firms, national ownership requirements and local content requirements. Export subsidies are banned for all but the least developed countries. Protection of intellectual property rights makes it illegal to imitate foreign technologies and engage in 'reverse engineering' to attain technological mastery of imported products. Additional restrictions may be included in bilateral trade agreements.

Some authors therefore argue that trade and investment rules exclude important policy options which countries need to climb the ladder from low-cost to sophisticated knowledge-based competitive advantages:

> When they were trying to catch up with the frontier economies, the NDCs [now-developed countries] used interventionist industrial, trade and tech-nology policies in order to promote their infant industries. ... In relative terms ... many of them actually protected their industries a lot more than the currently developing countries. If this is the case, the currently recommended package of 'good policies', emphasizing the benefits of free trade and other laissez-faire ITT [industrial, trade and technological] policies, seems at odds with historical experience, and the NDCs seem to be indeed 'kicking away the ladder' that they used in order to climb up to where they are now. (Chang 2003, p. 28)

However, three arguments qualify the relevance of this point.

First, those industrial policies that have been banned have often done more harm than good. While infant-industry protection through trade and trade-related investment measures (such as local content and trade-balancing requirements) *can* be helpful to nurture competitive infant industries, few countries have made good use of them. Import restrictions have arguably been important in East Asia, yet the respective rents created for local incumbents have in most cases not been used produc-tively. Likewise, restrictions on foreign ownership and local content requirements often scared investors away and undercut the competitive-ness of local products (Moran 1999). Import restrictions have arguably led to losses in economic welfare in most of the cases concerned.

Second, even under WTO rules, countries – and developing countries in particular – are still allowed to protect their industries to a consider-able degree. While tariffs have to be reduced, and can in most cases not be raised again, a good number of tariffs can still be retained. In addition, several provisions are still in effect, which allow countries to impose import surcharges when imports threaten to destabilise the balance of payments or when sudden import surges emerge that may jeopardise local industries. Protective measures can also be taken to ensure food security, although all these safeguards are limited to a maximum of eight years. With regard to foreign investments, governments are allowed to carry out Economic Needs Tests and deny investment licences if they expect, for example, negative employment effects. They can require investors to use local labour and to transfer technology. Certain subsidies, credits and infrastructure investments can be specifically targeted to attract 'developmental' industries (Chang 2009, p. 19). Moreover, governments are still allowed to offer subsidies for R&D, regional development and environment-friendly activities as well as incentives for firms to locate in science parks (Di Maio 2009, p. 127). Least developed countries are furthermore allowed to make use of export subsidies and benefit from a number of preferential trade agreements. The fact that only few poor developing countries have been able to take advantage of preferential trade agreements and other special provisions suggests that the binding constraints are not international trade and investment rules but supply-side constraints and structural problems, such as the increasing economies of scale required for exports.

Third, failure to comply with WTO commitments almost never leads to legal enforcement against poor, and especially least developed, countries. Bown and Hoekman show that 'of the more than 350 formal WTO dispute settlement cases through 2006, none of the 32 WTO Members classified by the United Nations as LDCs [least developed countries] have been challenged' (Bown and Hoekman 2008, p. 178). There are three main reasons: litigation is expensive; action against poor countries is politically sensitive; and these countries can fall back on special provisions that offer them special and differential treatment (ibid., p. 179).

In conclusion, even if certain policy instruments are no longer available for developing countries, their remaining policy space is still considerable. Poor countries still have many industrial policy tools at their disposal, which they can use legally, and they can even use policies that, while not in compliance with WTO agreements, are de facto tolerated, given that other countries rarely initiate dispute settlement procedures against poor countries. Especially for modern industrial policy that encourages search processes rather than protecting incumbents, the field is wide open. Lack of policy space does not seem to be a major problem; the main constraint is the ability to make reasonable and creative use of the tools that remain available.

However, while WTO membership is not a critical problem for industrial policy, two other developments are reducing developing countries' policy space.

First, industrialised countries now negotiate individual agreements with developing countries or groups of countries and may impose less favourable conditions on poor countries, even restricting their policy space. Poor countries would probably be much better off with a reliable multilateral trade regime than having to negotiate bilateral and regional free trade agreements on a case-by-case basis.

Second, private standards are gaining importance. These standards can be imposed by lead firms in global value chains or by strong industry associations. Poor countries are typically standard-takers (Nadvi and Wältring 2002). They have to ensure compliance if they want to trade with partners who adhere to certain standards without, however, having any effective means to participate in their formulation.

In sum, the economic, social and political conditions in poor developing countries are fundamentally different from those prevailing in mature developed countries. A combination of latecomer conditions, multiple goals involving significant trade-offs and structural weaknesses on both the demand and the supply side require an industrial policy that is *more active* and has a *different focus* than the policies applied in rich countries. However, it is not necessarily wise for governments to engage in each and every field where markets do not work properly. Even when market failure is obvious, well-intentioned interventions may do more harm than good when coupled with weak implementation skills. The key problem of industrial policy in poor developing countries is that, while the *need* to correct market failure is much greater than it is in highly developed societies, the *ability* of the public sector to tackle such failures is also much more limited: 'The competencies of government should affect the choice of instruments, and perhaps the "ambition" of industrial policy' (Stiglitz, Lin and Monga 2013, p. 9).

Besides the question of opportunity costs – which weighs heavily in a context of high and persistent poverty – there is thus the general question of limitations in terms of capabilities to manage industrial policy effectively. Moreover, most developing countries can be characterised as limited access orders where elites systematically use public spending to buy political support rather than to achieve long-term welfare gains and where few institutions exist to hold governments accountable for their policies. In such cases, policies can easily be captured by particular interest groups. Thus there is a special need to build political coalitions committed to inclusive and sustainable economic transformation and to design effective and simple policies that cannot be easily exploited by private interests. The following chapter will present five illustrative case studies that demonstrate how developing countries at different levels of income and economic diversification are trying to cope with these challenges.

NOTES

23. See e.g. Amsden (2001); Di Maio (2009); Stiglitz (1996).
24. Among the laudable exceptions are Soludo, Ogbu and Chang (2004); UNCTAD (2007); UNIDO (2009); and UNECA (2014).
25. For instance, the Next-11 (Bangladesh, Egypt, Indonesia, Iran, Mexico, Nigeria, Pakistan, the Philippines, Turkey, South Korea and Vietnam) or the MIST countries (Mexico, Indonesia, South Korea and Turkey).
26. Data are in current US$ and based on OECD statistics for ODA flows and on UNCTAD statistics for FDI flows.
27. Overall, the governance of economic development (understood as the public, commercial and civil society structures and networks shaping economic development decisions) has become more complex, hybrid and multidimensional. This is particularly true for trade-intensive economies, which are increasingly dependent on global value chains, trans-national corporations and, thus, to a growing extent, on private sector norms and standards.
28. Low demand for labour in modern formal enterprises may be partly due to rigid labour market policies, but the fact that micro-firm employment increases across all developing regions suggests that other factors are more important. Most importantly, standard manufacturing technologies require increasingly less labour. Only very few countries have GDP growth rates that compensate for the combined effect of the increase of the labour force *plus* enhanced labour productivity in firms using standard technologies.
29. See Hampel-Milagrosa, Loewe and Reeg (2015) for an interesting analysis of those exceptional firms that managed to grow from informal micro to medium-sized firms.
30. Evidence shows that growth fuelled by resource extraction and resource-based industrialisation tends to produce more inequality than growth based on labour-intensive manufacturing. This difference affects gender inequality in particular, because labour-intensive manufacturing provides opportunities for women to shift from extremely low-productivity self-employment or informal jobs to wage employment. Women's opportunities to benefit from resource extraction are considerably smaller (UNIDO 2009, p. 6).
31. Drawing on the work of Tom Kochan, Brynjolfsson and McAfee argue that high levels of employment indeed have public good characteristics: 'The benefits of increasing employment – reduced crime, greater investment, and stronger communities – extend to people throughout society, not just the employer or employee who are party to the employment contract. If unemployment creates negative externalities, then we should reward employment instead of taxing it' (Brynjolfsson and McAfee 2014, p. 239)
32. It should be noted that the sustainability of microfinance provision relies on interest rates that are far too high for long-term investments in technology and human capital. Microfinance thus has a positive effect on employment generation in petty trade and services, but contributes little to industrial development and structural change. For a critical perspective on microfinance, see Chowdhury (2009).
33. Here again, the focus of attention has been on the large emerging economies, which – in addition to the OECD countries – account for the lion's share of global greenhouse gas (GHG) emissions in general and CO_2 emissions in particular. In comparison, there has been widespread neglect of the determinants and potential drivers of green growth in low-income countries. Also, low-income countries do not command an effective voice in global climate negotiations and do not benefit much from climate finance facilities, which are concentrated on financing mitigation action in large, economically advanced developing countries (Boyle et al. 2013).
34. See, for example, Ravallion (2010) for a critical discussion of the methodological foundations of composite indicators in general and Arndt and Oman (2006) for the WGI in particular. For our project, a comparison of country indicators including sub-indicators of the Index of Economic Freedom, the DBI, the WGI and the BTI revealed several cases where country rankings diverged considerably although the respective indicators were similarly defined, hence suggesting quite severe data problems and perception biases.

35. Loewe et al. (2007, pp. 43 f.) argue that perception-based indicators may be systematically biased because respondents tend to rate a country implicitly against the countries of its region, leading to overly optimistic ratings for countries.
36. See Altenburg and Von Drachenfels (2006) as well as the World Bank's internal evaluation (WB-IEG 2008) for a critique of the market fundamentalism underlying the reports.
37. In Mozambique, the World Bank recently set up a new Competitiveness and Private Sector Development Project with a volume that far exceeds that of the technical counterpart, the Ministry of Industry and Commerce (MIC). Project content and design are mainly defined by the World Bank. Implementation will be done through a Project Implementation Unit located within the Ministry and headed by the former National Director for Industry of MIC, who left MIC for this purpose. The tasks of the Project overlap with those of a newly founded National SME Institute, and it is not clear to what extent the project will operate as a parallel agency (Krause and Kaufmann 2011).

7. Selected developing country case studies

So far, we have reviewed the general evolution of the debate around industrial policy and its more specific contextualisation under the conditions typically prevailing in most developing countries. We now turn to a select number of country cases and focus on how the concrete manifestation of industrial policy measures has shaped their development trajectories and contributed to their economic and social performance.

The countries under consideration are predominantly located in Africa – from Tunisia in Northern Africa to Ethiopia, Mozambique and Namibia in sub-Saharan Africa. In addition, Vietnam, as a fast growing Southeast Asian country, is included in the sample. In terms of their level of economic development, and in accordance with the World Bank income-based typology, we cover:

- two low-income countries (Ethiopia and Mozambique);
- one lower-middle-income country (Vietnam); and
- two upper-middle-income countries (Namibia and Tunisia)

At the beginning of each country section, we present an aggregated, standardised table with basic data. These are drawn from international sources so as to ensure comparability. National providers, such as Statistical Offices, may in some cases have more recent data available, which are not included in our standardised tables. However, the sections themselves reflect more recent developments, are tailored to the characteristic features of each individual case and develop a specific country narrative. Comparative insights and conclusions on success and failure of the chosen development paths and policies will be put forward in Chapter 8.

The brief country cases presented here build on extensive earlier studies and expert interviews in the field. With the exception of Vietnam, these were separately published (Altenburg 2010; Rosendahl 2010; Erdle 2011; Krause and Kaufmann 2011). While these studies have been updated and expanded significantly for the purpose of this publication, we thank the authors for allowing us to draw on their original work.

A caveat is necessary at this point. It should be noted that the following observations are mostly qualitative in nature. Data on policy implementation are not easily available. Costing of programmes is usually not transparent, and, even more importantly, the impact of policies is hardly ever evaluated. Our country case studies thus largely build on visible evidence, qualitative information gathered from experts, published case studies and grey literature. Judgments on the quality of programmes and perceived policy gaps are therefore somewhat subjective. Moreover, some of the sample countries have recently undergone major transitions of their economic and political systems, and the quality of institutions may therefore change considerably within short periods of time.

7.1 ETHIOPIA: KICK-STARTING STRUCTURAL CHANGE IN AN AGRARIAN SOCIETY

Economic Structure and Performance

With close to 97 million people, Ethiopia is one of Africa's most populous countries and at the same time one of the world's poorest, with a per capita income of US$470 (2013). Ethiopia is still an agrarian country whose potential for agricultural productivity growth has so far been severely constrained by irregular rainfalls, lack of irrigation and a very poor rural road network. From 1974 until 1991, the country was ruled by a pro-Soviet military junta that nationalised most industries and private urban real-estate holdings and tried to force farmers into production collectives. Mismanagement and the junta's violent rule provoked a long period of civil war, which ended when the Ethiopian People's Revolutionary Democratic Front (EPRDF), led by Meles Zenawi, took power in 1991. The EPRDF has been in power ever since, with Meles Zenawi as president until he passed away in 2012.

Since the war ended, development trends in Ethiopia have been among the most promising in sub-Saharan Africa, with an economy that has been constantly growing. Growth accelerated after 2005, reaching an annual average of 10.7 per cent in the period 2005–2013. This is twice the rate of the rest of sub-Saharan Africa – despite the fact that Ethiopia is relatively poor in subsoil resources. Moreover, growth was pro-poor in the sense that the poor benefited more than proportionally from this boom. As a result, the proportion of people living below the national poverty line declined significantly to 30 per cent (2011). Likewise, within three decades (1980–2012) 'life expectancy at birth increased by

Table 7.1   Ethiopia – basic data

Surface area (square kilometres)	1,104,300 (2014)
Population (thousand)	96,509 (2014)
● Share of urban population (per cent)	19 (2014)
● Share of population below national poverty line (per cent)	30 (2011)
● Gini coefficient	0.34 (2011)
GDP (current US$ million)	47,525
GDP per capita (current US$)	470
GDP growth (per cent)	10.5
Average GDP growth 2005–2013 (per cent)	10.7
Competitiveness rank (WEF)*	118 (2014–2015)
Sector composition of GDP (per cent)	
● Agriculture & mining	45
● Industry	12
● (thereof: Manufacturing)	(4) (2011)
● Services	43
Exports/GDP (per cent)	12
Net ODA received (per cent of GNI)	11.8 (2012)
FDI inflow (current US$ million)	953
FDI inflow per capita (current US$)	10
Manufactured exports/total exports (per cent)	87.1 (2011)
Medium- and high-tech activities in total MVA (per cent)	9.4 (2011)
Energy consumption per capita (kilograms oil equivalent)	381 (2011)
CO_2 emissions (thousand metric tons and metric tons per capita)	6,494 / 0.1

Notes: Unless otherwise specified, data refer to 2013.
* Out of a total of 144 countries covered.

Sources: World Bank (data.worldbank.org/indicator); UNIDO (2013, Annex 3); UNCTAD (unctadstat.unctad.org/wds/ReportFolders/reportFolders.aspx); WEF (2014).

15.8 years, mean years of schooling increased by 0.7 years and expected years of schooling increased by 6.3 years' (UNDP 2013, p. 2).

These impressive achievements are due to the return to political stability, devolution of collectivised farmland to smallholders and substantial investments in infrastructure, such as increased use of irrigation and public investment in marketing facilities; they also include the construction of the Grand Ethiopian Renaissance Dam, a hydropower mega-project that will allow Ethiopia to export electricity in the future. At the same time, big efforts were undertaken to improve education and vocational training at all levels.

The structure of the Ethiopian economy, however, has remained largely unchanged. Ethiopia's economy is still predominantly agrarian, with almost 85 per cent of the workforce engaged in the rural economy. Manufacturing industry's meagre 4 per cent (2011) contribution to GDP is one of the lowest globally, and it has even slightly declined over the last decade. The small manufacturing industry produces mainly basic food products and beverages (sugar, flour, beer), garments, leather and cement for domestic consumption. Many basic consumer goods, such as canned fruit, remain to be fully imported. Garment production was a fairly important part of Ethiopia's industry but has recently declined strongly due to imports from Asia as well as second-hand garments from OECD countries. The vast majority of firms are in the micro and small-scale category and dedicated to grain milling as well as fabrication of simple furniture and fabricated metal. Huge labour productivity gaps exist between the few dozen medium and large scale manufacturing firms and the (mainly informal) cottage industries (Gebreeyesus 2013).

The Ethiopian economy's extremely low productivity and lack of competitiveness are also reflected in its poor export performance. Exports have increased significantly, but this rise has almost exclusively been achieved through unprocessed and undifferentiated bulk products (coffee, gold, oilseeds, leather, pulses) and is subject to enormous fluctuations (World Bank Group 2014a). From 2001 to 2011, agricultural exports grew about eightfold, but manufacturing exports only threefold (Gebreeyesus 2013), even though the latter started from an extremely low basis. Industrial zones only attracted a handful of companies, creating employment for a few thousand garment assembly workers – compared to one million in Vietnam (Dinh et al. 2012, p. 116). In 2009, garment export accounted for US$8 million, 'a thousandth of the US$8 billion in exports for Vietnam, which has a similar population' (ibid.). A study of Ethiopia's medium and large-sized firms revealed that in 2010 exports on average only accounted for 3 per cent of their total sales, and this figure had even been declining over the years (Gebreeyesus 2013).

Only two competitive and internationally successful industries stand out in terms of export performance: First, air traffic, led by government-owned Ethiopian Airlines, which has grown and modernised rapidly over the last two decades to become one of Africa's largest airlines and 'Ethiopia's biggest export earner – three times as big as coffee' (World Bank Group 2014a, p. 21). This has also established Addis Ababa as a major hub for international air traffic. Second, cut flowers have become one of the top five export items, and the only one that can be considered a knowledge-intensive high-value product.

In a nutshell, Ethiopia's economic performance has been one of the most impressive examples of pro-poor growth globally – but this has been accompanied by *negative structural change* in the sense that growth has been driven by bulk agricultural products and some services rather than manufacturing and other knowledge-intensive industries, which implies that labour tends to move from potentially high- to low-productivity sectors (McMillan and Rodrik 2012). This is a counter-intuitive finding, given the Ethiopian government's commitment to follow the lessons of East Asian export-led industrialisation. The subsequent section therefore explores Ethiopia's industrial policy in detail.

Industrial Policy: Ideology and Practice

When President Meles Zenawi took office in 1991, he was confronted with a situation of multiple market failure. While the EPRDF recognised the private sector as the main driver of economic growth and started to dismantle the state-owned enterprises inherited from the past, there was very little private sector to build upon. The vast majority of the population were peasants and pastoralists without any entrepreneurial tradition and skills. The better educated and entrepreneurial persons had mostly fled the country during the years of socialist dictatorship and civil war. Even today, Ethiopia has an extremely low percentage of business registrations per 1,000 inhabitants, far below those of most other sub-Saharan countries (World Bank Group 2014a, p. 25). Moreover, the new regime distrusted the old elites, which it regarded as rent-seekers. The distinction between *rent-seeking* capitalists interested in making quick money from trade and financial transactions and *developmental* capitalists who invest in industrial infrastructure, technological capabilities and value creation is a key element of the EPRDF's ideology. Creating a new class of developmental capitalists virtually from scratch while restricting the exploitative rent-seekers was seen as the main challenge (Altenburg 2010; Gebreeyesus 2013). Rather than following the neo-liberal spirit of the time, Meles Zenawi amalgamated his own version of African latecomer development, which combines efforts to nurture basic entre-preneurship in an agrarian subsistence economy with elements of a carrot-and-stick approach borrowed from South Korea and Japan. The government's first full-fledged Industrial Development Strategy dates from 2002/03. Subsequent strategies modified this strategy slightly, with the Growth and Transformation Plan 2010/11–2014/15 (GTP) being the most recent strategy document. Key elements of these policies include the following (Altenburg 2010):

- A big-push strategy to build the human capital needed for industrial development: around twenty (mainly technical) new universities were founded and a system of technical and vocational education and training (TVET) was set up which, by 2010, had 815,000 enrolled students. The public sector-led TVET is regarded 'as the key in improving the productivity of the enterprises and increasing their competitiveness in the global market' (Krishnan and Shaorshadze 2013, p. 5).
- Nurturing of a new class of 'developmental capitalists': after the revolution, political parties under the EPRDF coalition created endowment funds, and the government allowed those funds to invest in business. The party-affiliated funds were among the first to invest in the country's reconstruction after the civil war and thereby gained some early mover advantages. The EPRDF uses its influence on those enterprises to advance its industrialisation agenda, for example the endowment firms are nudged to offer apprenticeships under dual vocational training initiatives. Moreover, a number of other firms were selected on the basis of technical criteria in order to make them ready for exports.
- Agricultural demand-led industrialisation: productivity growth in agriculture was seen as a precondition not only for poverty alleviation but also for industrial development. Agro-based industrialisation was seen as the natural avenue to industrial development. Also, the EPRDF had its strongest political backing among the peasantry, with some four million members, mostly among the better educated and more successful farmers. The party structure is considered as a driver to educate and organise farmers in order to enhance their productivity and link them to modern markets.
- Targeting of priority industries: preferential treatment is given to certain industries, which build on the country's (potential) comparative advantages in agriculture and labour cost-intensive industries. The textile and garment, meat, leather and leather products, other agro-processing industries (e.g. sugar and sugar related industries) and the construction industry were singled out as priority industries (Gebreeyesus 2013).
- Export promotion: domestic firms were pushed to become exporters, assuming that this would force them to focus on competitiveness rather than rent-seeking. In addition, industrial zones were

established to attract foreign investment in labour-intensive export industries. Originally, export industries were clearly favoured as drivers of industrial development, but this export bias has been relaxed, and the most recent GTP acknowledges the importance of industrial development for the home market as another important pillar.

• Restrictions imposed on 'rent-seekers', especially trade and financial services: in 2009, the government accused 94 coffee export warehouses of hoarding, revoked their licences and shut them down (Gebreeyesus 2013, p. 21). Likewise, the government employed price caps and export bans in an effort to control inflation. In addition, the private financial sector is heavily regulated, with the aim of channelling credit into productive activities and limiting the extraction of rents.

In sum, industrial policy has been quite heavy-handed, with the government deciding which sectors and even which firms are good for development and which ones not. This attitude, however, has changed in the case of the cut flower industry, where modern investors are operating. The following section briefly compares two sectors – leather and cut flowers – with very different industrial policy approaches and explores the reasons for this.

A Tale of Two Sectors: Heavy-Handed vs Light-Handed Industrial Policies

The leather/leather products industry and the cut flower industry exemplify distinctly different patterns of public policymaking. While the former can be regarded as a traditional, technologically backward branch with many Ethiopian small firms involved, the latter emerged spontaneously, driven mainly by entrepreneurial foreign firms. While the government's attitude to the leather industry is one of educating, nurturing and handholding, its support for the cut flower industry is one of removing hurdles on request of the private industry and its association.

Leather and leather products: Ethiopia has one of the world's largest livestock populations, consisting of cattle, sheep and goats. It produces 2.7 million hides and 15.6 million skins per year, which are also one of the country's most important export products, accounting for 3.7 per cent in 2012 (World Bank Group 2014a, p. 58). Adding value to this resource base by producing finished leather products, such as shoes and bags, has been a long-time aspiration of Ethiopian governments. In fact, the country's first tannery and shoe factory was established as early as 1928.

The pro-Soviet military junta banned the export of raw skins and hides to encourage national value addition, and the EPRDF also declared leather processing a priority industry.

During the last two decades, a range of fiscal incentives and supply-side measures were provided to build the necessary capabilities, including the formation of the Leather Industry Development Institute for research, standard-setting and consultancy, the launch of several value chain and cluster initiatives as well as specialised trade fairs and matchmaking programmes, the creation of dedicated university-level and vocational training programmes and, last but not least, comprehensive firm-level coaching to improve design, marketing and factory management. Temporarily, the export of unprocessed hides was banned to encourage local value addition. Until about a decade ago, foreign investment in the industry was not allowed, with the aim of creating a protected learning space for domestic manufacturing capabilities.

However, none of these measures have been successful. Actual exports fell far short of the government's target to generate US$500 million from the export of leather products by the end of 2015, with the bulk (360 million) supposed to be coming from leather shoes. Shoe exports remained at a marginal level of around 70 million per year,[38] accounting for only 0.3 per cent of Ethiopia's exports. Moreover, most export production stems from a handful of foreign firms, which entered the market when ownership restrictions were lifted. None of the handpicked Ethiopian companies that had received all-round public support for years achieved a major breakthrough.

Cut flower industry: The above failure is in stark contrast with the emergence of the cut flower business. The flower industry is particularly interesting as it represents a private sector-led initiative with the government as a facilitator rather than an initiator and all-round service provider. When the government listed its priority sectors for the 2002/03 Industrial Development Strategy, cut flower production had not even been recognised as a promising industry.

Ethiopia's highlands offer very good agro-climatic conditions for the cultivation of flowers. In the early 2000s, some foreign investors set up the first successful flower farms. They grew roses, which are still the main export item, but later some diversified into new products. When the success of pioneering firms became evident, the Ethiopian Horticulture Producers and Exporters Association (EHPEA) was formed to address common problems and lobby the government for support. Initial problems included the difficulty to get land lease rights, uncompetitive air freight rates and lack of specialised support services. President Meles Zenawi recognised the new activity as an important contributor to export-led growth and engaged personally to remove any hurdles to the sector's development, for example setting land aside for new farm projects and ensuring that Ethiopian Airlines offer lower freight tariffs. Also, a fiscal incentive was offered to mitigate the investment risks of flower production. Furthermore, the Ethiopian Horticulture Development Agency was created as a responsive business-oriented service provider outside the bureaucratic structures of the line ministries. All these measures were developed in collaboration with the industry association EHPEA.

With these conditions in place, the industry evolved favourably. In 2013/14, about 120 farms accounted for the country's US$245 million exports.[39] Most producers are foreign investors, but about one quarter are Ethiopian firms that succeeded in emulating the pioneering investors' business models. Flower production is a risky and knowledge-intensive business, which only specialised firms are able to handle. The main tasks of public policy here are to remove specific obstacles that are beyond the reach of individual firms. Moreover, the Ethiopian government is supporting training and research to support the development of specialised capabilities with regard to flower cultivation techniques and to facilitate technology adoption among national firms.

Lessons and Challenges Ahead

In terms of economic growth and social development, Ethiopia's post-civil war performance has been extraordinary. But despite a strong developmental orientation, almost no structural change and no improvement of the country's trade position has been achieved. This is particularly remarkable as the government undertook an ambitious industrial policy programme that was fully endorsed by the top leadership. What explains this finding?

First, this may partly be a matter of time. After the civil war, trying to build a prosperous economy within a semi-feudal agrarian society without any entrepreneurial skills and traditions was a formidable challenge. Against this backdrop, any assumption that it would basically suffice to deregulate the business environment – as many advisors suggested in the 1990s – would have been highly unrealistic. The EPRDF's basic idea to invest in creating and nurturing a domestic entrepreneurial class was therefore quite plausible. This, however, obviously takes time, because it requires changing fundamental societal norms and attitudes. To expect major success stories after one or two decades of active industrial policy and export promotion may be asking too much.

Second, political interference may in some cases reduce allocative efficiency. The way party structures are used to nurture entrepreneurship implies considerable risks of arrangements remaining socially exclusive, thereby perpetuating the structural deficits of limited access orders. Using party-affiliated endowment funds to reach industrial policy objectives, using party cadres among the peasantry for agricultural modernisation, and handpicking sectors and even individual firms for support programmes may easily encourage favouritism and collusion. There are, however, clear indications that this is currently not common practice in Ethiopia. Our research suggests that there is no systematic favouritism when it comes to public procurement; the government, for example, deliberately transferred large construction works to international donors and subscribed to international codes of conduct to ensure open and transparent implementation; likewise, firm-level coaching programmes involved only a few party-affiliated endowment companies (see Altenburg 2010 for details). Also, the fact that Ethiopia stands out for its growth record with improved income distribution demonstrates that exclusion has at least not been a general characteristic of the development model. Hence the Ethiopian government is walking a fine line between heavy-handed interventions for strictly developmental purposes and unfair political or economic exclusion; and it should consider that even the *perception* of a politically biased playing field may deter investors who are not connected to elite circles.

Third, and in our view most importantly, it appears that Ethiopian policymakers overstretch the degree of paternalistic guidance and inter-ference. In Gebreeyesus's (2013, p. 32) words, 'policy makers tend to "patronize" the private sector instead of encouraging competition and innovation'. Likewise, the evaluation of a comprehensive industrial policy programme in 2010 suggested to shift from nurturing preselected subsectors and companies to encouraging private sector led experimenta-tion; to involve the private sector, through business membership organ-isations, more actively in different aspects of policy formulation, implementation and performance assessment; to enable supporting insti-tutions to better understand the demands and speak the language of business; and to increase their customer orientation, which may require changes in the recruitment practices, pay scales and internal systems of reward and penalty (GTZ 2010). The comparison of policy approaches in the leather and cut flower industries supports this view. Moreover, the rigid distinction between developmental and rent-seeking capitalists (with financial service providers and intermediary traders generally being considered as rent-seekers) is misleading as it underestimates the positive functions of market intermediaries and overestimates the public sector's ability to provide such functions more efficiently.

While Ethiopia stands out for its clear development orientation and commitment to structural change, a more entrepreneurial and less patronising type of policymaking would help to realise Ethiopia's big industrial development potential in at least the following three areas:

● Agro-industrial value addition, given the country's varied soil and climatic conditions, the opportunities to increase yields on cultivated and incorporate unused arable land, and the low wage level (Dinh et al. 2012).
● Diversified production of consumer goods and building materials, taking advantage of the rapid increase of purchasing power, the expansion of consuming urban middle classes and the construction boom (Altenburg and Melia 2014). This implies a certain adjustment of the current sectoral priorities and pro-export bias of the industrial development strategy.
● Light manufacturing exports, taking advantage of low wages, 'access to a state-of-the-art and well-located container port in Djibouti, and duty-free access to the U.S. and EU markets' (Dinh et al. 2012, p. 6) for apparel. This would require the establishment of effectively managed industrial zones near Djibouti and adjustment of the currently overvalued real exchange rate.

7.2 MOZAMBIQUE: PERSISTENCE OF ELITE DEALS

Economic Structure and Performance

Mozambique is an almost prototypical case of how history matters and keeps exerting a strong influence on the critical development challenges the country is facing today. For instance, the high transportation costs that severely constrain domestic business are the lasting result of the 19th century partition of the country into a Northern, a Central and a Southern economic zone introduced by Portugal. To date, Mozambique does not have a trunk North–South transport infrastructure. More importantly, Mozambique is still seeking to shake off the repercussions of a long and violent struggle for independence, which later on gave way to a protracted civil war (from 1977 to 1992) that keeps flaring up till today. It was only in August 2014 – following a peace accord more than two decades ago and a renewed armed struggle in recent years – that a truce was signed between the Mozambique Liberation Front (FRELIMO)

Table 7.2   Mozambique – basic data

Surface area (square kilometres)	799,380 (2014)
Population (thousand)	26,473 (2014)
● Share of urban population (per cent)	32 (2014)
● Share of population below national poverty line (per cent)	55 (2009)
● Gini coefficient	0.46 (2009)
GDP (current US$ million)	15,630
GDP per capita (current US$)	610
GDP growth (per cent)	7.4
Average GDP growth 2005–2013 (per cent)	7.1
Competitiveness rank (WEF)*	133 (2014–2015)
Sector composition of GDP (per cent)	
● Agriculture & mining	29
● Industry	21
● (thereof: Manufacturing)	(12) (2011)
● Services	50
Exports/GDP (per cent)	30
Net ODA received (per cent of GNI)	14.0 (2012)
FDI inflow (current US$ million)	5,935
FDI inflow per capita (current US$)	230
Manufactured exports/total exports (per cent)	23.4 (2011)
Medium- and high-tech activities in total MVA (per cent)	10.7 (2011)
Energy consumption per capita (kilograms oil equivalent)	415 (2011)
CO_2 emissions (thousand metric tons and metric tons per capita)	2,882 / 0.1 (2010)

Notes: Unless otherwise specified, data refer to 2013.
* Out of a total of 144 countries covered.

Sources: World Bank (data.worldbank.org/indicator); UNIDO (2013, Annex 3); UNCTAD (unctadstat.unctad.org/wds/ReportFolders/reportFolders.aspx); WEF (2014).

ruling party and the opposition, the Mozambican National Resistance (RENAMO). The relative peace and stability achieved still seems to rest on a fragile foundation.

At the same time, albeit from a very low level, there has been a remarkable macroeconomic performance – in particular, when considered in the broader context of sub-Saharan Africa. GDP growth between 2005 and 2013 averaged 7.1 per cent and displayed a stable pattern with no single annual growth rate below 6 per cent. As a result, poverty levels fell significantly: within the last ten years, the population share in severe poverty was reduced from more than three quarters to less than half.

Serious challenges become apparent, however, when focusing on the country's economic structure. Mozambique's economy is largely dependent on the extractive sector (with fast growing oil, gas and mining activities), while both agriculture (employing 70 per cent of the population) and manufacturing have remained sluggish; the productive base shows little sign of diversification and low levels of domestic value added; capital intensity is high thus generating insufficient new jobs; and the informal sector still accommodates 95 per cent of the population (Braun, Kaufmann and Simons-Kaufmann 2012, p. 7).

Furthermore, the extraordinarily high dependence on foreign resources, both in terms of FDI and ODA, gives rise to concern. With an ODA/GNI ratio of 14 per cent (see Table 7.2), Mozambique has one of the highest levels of aid dependency worldwide.[40] Also, there are massive and fast increasing inflows of FDI, which are mostly targeted at large extractive projects with little linkages to the domestic economy. They neither create significant amounts of employment nor do they trigger any meaningful technology spillovers (see below with regard to the aluminium smelter MOZAL). Productivity levels in the mostly small domestic manufacturing firms have stagnated at best in the last decade (DNEAP 2013).

In a nutshell, Mozambique represents a quintessential case of a natural resource-, foreign investment- and donor-dependent economy with poorly developed domestic capabilities and dynamism. Its performance is largely driven by mega-projects in extractive and energy-related sectors. This pattern is likely to be reinforced in the light of the recent coal and gas boom, based on discoveries of one of the world's largest undeveloped coal reserves and huge offshore gas fields in the country's Northern region. If confirmed in size, these gas reserves would place Mozambique just behind Russia, Iran and Qatar as a global leader (Davis 2013). The implications for adapting current governance systems towards responsible rent management are huge, and time is of the essence in putting transparent mechanisms in place for investing newly generated national savings wisely (World Bank Group 2014).

Economic Governance and Industrial Policy

At this potential watershed moment in the country's economic development, the demands on an effective, long-term and vision-based industrial policy for Mozambique are tremendous, yet the most essential preconditions for this to happen are hardly in place. While both democratic and market-based on paper, the political system is de facto characterised by the strong dominance of a single political party (FRELIMO): 'This "quasi monopoly" has contributed to blurring the distinction between party and Government and has undermined the checks and balances between the country's different branches of government' (Krause and Kaufmann 2011, p. 22). At the same time, there is just an incipient civil society without effective voice, a lack of an independent judiciary and rampant corruption in a variety of forms ranging from patronage and nepotism to administrative bribery in applying or bending regulations. In a recent government survey, 54 per cent of domestic manufacturing firms perceived corruption to have worsened since 2006 – with an average bribe level as high as 10 per cent of their turnover (DNEAP 2013).

A defining element of the country's system of governance is the fact that political and economic interests are densely interwoven. Close ties have persisted between party cadres and leading businesses, largely as a legacy of elite deals clinched during the privatisation phase in the late 1980s when party cadres acquired powerful business groups, attractive land rights and profitable concessions.

The overall impression is one of a reactive industrial policy approach that tends to respond to the interests and expectations of both large investors and donor governments. While the former expect stable investment conditions and reliable investment laws and incentives, the latter have pushed with limited success for reforms of the 'ease of doing business' type – both obviously pulling in the same direction. However, what has been lacking so far, are coherently articulated, long-term policies driving economic diversification, productivity enhancement and linkage creation.

In this context, it is telling that spatial policy measures have largely been customised and limited to the needs of individual investing companies. While numerous SEZs have been created, the most significant ones are essentially designated areas around mega-projects; this applies to MOZAL's aluminium investments, Vale's coal exploration activities, KENMARE's sand exploration project and the gas exploration by SASOL. This seems to have resulted more in protected operating spaces for these companies than in creating a breeding ground for domestic entrepreneurship and learning. As a consequence, the country's SEZs – unlike in the case of many East Asian countries – did not generate any meaningful impact in terms of employment creation nor did they contribute to strengthening domestic capabilities through learning effects (Braun, Kaufmann and Simons-Kaufmann 2012, p. 11).

The salient features of Mozambique's governance system as described above have led some analysts to consider it through the lens of limited access orders, that is, a political system that contains violence and conflicts through the allocation of rents to potentially destabilising groups so as to maintain power and stifle competition (see also Section 6.6). Such limited access orders are often characterised by a dualism consisting of a domestic sector under a tight limited access order regime coupled with international enclaves operated under separate, more liberal rules. In some cases, this may be part of a deliberate strategy to accommodate the demands of donor governments without compromising the domestic sources of policy rents (North et al. 2012).

Against this conceptual backdrop, Mozambique is considered to have moved from a typical case of an exclusionary limited access order during its colonial period to a more open, enlightened type of limited access order today. In describing the contours of what he considers as being a new governance equilibrium, Levy (2012) lists four main elements: the acceptance of multi-party elections; the move towards a market-based economy with more emphasis on private entrepreneurship and a reduction of price controls; the establishment of inclusive Consultative Councils in rural areas; and the changing profile of FRELIMO itself towards more openness and diversity in its membership.

However, he also underlines potential threats, such as FRELIMO's currently uncontested political dominance, which could weaken accountability standards and jeopardise this equilibrium.

Below, we will briefly illustrate the general reflections on economic governance with regard to two sectors: the sugar industry and the aluminium industry. For the former, we draw on the analysis provided by Whitfield et al. (2015), for the latter, on the assessment by Krause and Kaufmann (2011).

Aligning National Elite and Foreign Interests: The Sugar Industry

Mozambique's sugar industry underwent a process of comprehensive rehabilitation within a short time span of about 15 years starting in the mid-1990s. As a result, an industry largely in shambles was lifted to reasonable levels of competitiveness. While between 1998 and 2011 the area under cultivation increased sixfold, the actual production of sugar jumped up by a factor of 32 – clearly indicating massive improvements in productivity. In the entire process of an initial rehabilitation of sugar estates, followed by an upgrading of processing facilities and, later on, an emphasis on more specialised up-market sugar products, foreign investors played a key role. Specifically, the two largest sugar companies from South Africa and a Mauritius-based sugar consortium were brought in with a view to pushing both technological and managerial skill upgrading, and strengthening access to foreign markets. As an essential framework condition, the sugar sector rehabilitation was facilitated by a high degree of political continuity, with not only FRELIMO itself, but even the same faction within the party (around then President Chissano) being in power for almost a decade.

On the one hand, like with many of the country's mega-projects, the development of the sugar industry can be written as a story of missed opportunities. Whereas new jobs were created, 'the creation of further linkages in the economy through outsourcing was relatively limited, exposing the shallowness of the specialized service and supply industries … Neglecting to develop domestic suppliers was called the single biggest mistake by staff at the state sugar institute' (Whitfield et al. 2015). On the other hand, it is also a story of elite enrichment coupled with undeniable developmental impact in several dimensions:

- The regions hosting sugar companies that were targeted for rehabilitation, were chosen on politically motivated grounds – to maximise electoral support through 'stabilizing and transforming rural populations' (Buur, Mondlane Tembe and Baloi 2012, p. 359) – yet they were also profitable locations from an investor's point of view and generated significant domestic employment.[41]
- New formalised sugar business associations were established, which facilitated politically steered rent sharing (given the party-dominated ownership of the industry), but they also made the representation and voice of industry more effective.
- The strengthening of some sugar downstream industries (e.g. beverages), while again benefiting the sector's politicised ownership, also implied at least some progress on economic diversification.
- The guaranteed markets, generous incentives and high profit margins for foreign investors may have been excessive, yet they also led to an – albeit limited – import of technologies and skills that were previously not available domestically.

These are ambiguous effects, which raise intricate issues of elite capitalism and its potential developmental impact. We will revert to this question at the end of this section.

MOZAL – an Isolated Giant?

The aluminium smelter plant MOZAL was started in 2000 and expanded in 2003 and is among the largest smelting facilities worldwide. To date, it is the country's biggest foreign investment project, with a significant impact even in macroeconomic terms. With a cumulative investment of US$2.2 billion, the project accounts for roughly 30 per cent of total exports and consumes almost half of Mozambique's electricity. It is owned by BHP Billiton from Australia (47 per cent), Mitsubishi from Japan (25 per cent), the Industrial Development Corporation of South Africa (20 per cent) and the Government of Mozambique (4 per cent). As part of the negotiations preceding this mega-project, investors were granted tax exemptions for literally half a century, including full exemptions on import duties and value-added tax as well as a cap for corporate taxes at 1 per cent of sales.

The project has been heavily criticised on account of these generous incentives, the massive outflow of profits and interest to foreign (corporate and institutional) investors – estimated to surpass Mozambique's government revenues by a factor of 21 – and the negative environmental and health effects of untreated pollutants (Friends of the Earth Mozambique et al. 2012).

Moreover, the goal of stimulating a variety of linkages to the domestic economy has turned out to be more of a good intention than a reality. From the very beginning, linkage promotion was the stated policy objective of the local investment promotion agency in close cooperation with the International Finance Corporation (IFC). However, numerous challenges have been encountered. These include a weak and dispersed domestic pool of formal industrial enterprises; low levels of experience with modern technologies coupled with a lack of understanding of quality management;[42] the fact that the volume of standard contracts offered by MOZAL exceeded the capacities of SMEs; and a limitation to backward linkages in light of a complete lack of capabilities to process aluminium ingots. No surprise then that the benefits for the domestic economy have remained rather modest. Measured in terms of employment generation, MOZAL – with an investment level above US$2 billion – can be credited with slightly more than 1,000 direct full-time jobs and roughly 2,500 additional jobs through linkages (Krause and Kaufmann 2011, p. 52).

In contrast to the above view that traces the lack of broad-based linkages back to a dearth of required capabilities, explanations of a political economy nature have also been invoked. Based on interviews with local business representatives, it is claimed that emerging economic opportunities were deliberately suppressed: 'Instead of bringing these businesses to the local companies, the politicians would transform these businesses into avenues for private profit' (Nuvunga 2009, p. 29). In this reading, linkage creation under neopatrimonial or limited access conditions is bound to fail as a direct result of political rent diversion.

Main Challenges Ahead

We have seen that Mozambique can boast a stable political system, consistently high growth rates and a rising attractiveness as a location for foreign investors. However, these achievements are driven by a limited number of mega-projects based on exploiting the country's vast natural resources. The bulk of the population has not benefited from these sources of wealth and indeed remained disconnected from a development pattern that is largely enclavistic in nature. Linkage creation is embryonic and not actively pursued. As a result, there are no tangible signs of economic diversification, and the flipside of isolated mega-projects is a vast informal sector that to date is the source of livelihood for most people. A thriving domestic industry has not emerged so far. Moreover, the political system is such that the status quo tends to be perpetuated: in what is essentially a type of crony capitalism, there is massive space for self-serving behaviour of politicians-cum-businessmen, who control key resources and can effectively block access to new profitable economic opportunities.

Ten years ago, the country's formally democratic system was characterised as 'peaceful and stable, but weak and untested' (Carbone 2003, p. 18). The current resource boom will put it to an unprecedented test. In addition to the huge coal and gas reserves already being exploited, there are expectations for large oil discoveries, and the major global energy players (Italy's Eni, Norway's Statoil, Malaysia's Petronas and others) are rushing to Mozambique. In a political system that so far has been lacking full transparency and strongly relied on insider elite deals, the pressure from civil society will increase and demands for an effective and transparent use of the new resource wealth will mount. The government will thus be faced with the dual challenge of responding to these political expectations *and* acquiring the capabilities to deal with complex technical issues of financial and fiscal policy.

Given the exceedingly high aid dependency of Mozambique, donor agencies can obviously play a crucial role in pushing for reform. However, experience over many years of development cooperation in the country has shown that donor influence has suffered from a systemic bias: progress in areas like infrastructure, health or education is coupled with stagnation or even deterioration in areas like governance, transparency, stakeholder participation or the judiciary system, that is, wherever the very foundation of political power is at stake. In this perspective, donor funds may well be in danger of becoming a stabilising factor for the current political order: allowing the government to gain legitimacy on indicators of social progress while stalling a hard core agenda of political reform, accountability and economic diversification. Like Vietnam (see Section 7.5 below), Mozambique was among the first pilot countries for the UN system to move towards a more coherent delivery of development assistance. However, the lion's share of development funds originates from a range of bilateral donors with interests that at best are not harmonised and at worst are at cross-purposes. In some cases, they may also be closely aligned with bilateral investment and business interests.

In the final analysis, the challenge is how to capitalise on the existence of a stable yet corruption-prone party elite and use its power and resources to set in motion a positive development process. Framed in this manner – as very pointedly done by Hanlon and Mosse (2010) – the build-up of national business champions with political connections could be a precondition for effective latecomer industrialisation, like in the East Asian model as exemplified by the Korean *chaebol* corporations. However, for such a model of 'elite developmental capitalism' to succeed, that is, not to act in a predatory but in a developmental manner, some demanding conditions in terms of state support and elements of competition and innovation would need to be fulfilled. Whether or not this is likely to be the case in Mozambique is currently very much an open question.

7.3 NAMIBIA: GOOD GOVERNANCE IS NOT ENOUGH

Economic Structure and Performance[43]

At a GDP per capita level close to US$6,000, Namibia is categorised as an upper-middle-income country. Its economic growth performance has remained strong in recent years, with an annual average growth rate of 4.5 per cent between 2005 and 2013, and is expected to rise over the next couple of years due to substantial investments in new mining projects (uranium, copper, gold) and related infrastructure. The macroeconomic framework is remarkably stable and characterised by low inflation rates, relatively balanced fiscal revenues and expenditure as well as a manageable level of public debt and a moderate current account deficit.

The main sources of growth stem from the extraction and processing of minerals, such as diamonds, uranium, copper and zinc, almost entirely aimed at export markets and generally with limited economic linkages and employment generation (less than 2 per cent of the country's labour

Table 7.3   Namibia – basic data

Surface area (square kilometres)	824,290 (2014)
Population (thousand)	2,348 (2014)
● Share of urban population (per cent)	46 (2014)
● Share of population below national poverty line (per cent)	29 (2009)
● Gini coefficient	0.64 (2004)
GDP (current US$ million)	13,113
GDP per capita (current US$)	5,870
GDP growth (per cent)	5.1
Average GDP growth 2005–2013 (per cent)	4.5
Competitiveness rank (WEF)*	88 (2014–2015)
Sector composition of GDP (per cent)	
● Agriculture	6
● Industry	33
● (thereof: Manufacturing)	(n.a.)
● Services	60
Exports/GDP (per cent)	43
Net ODA received (per cent of GNI)	2.1 (2012)
FDI inflow (current US$ million)	699
FDI inflow per capita (current US$)	304
Manufactured exports/total exports (per cent)	n.a.
Medium- and high-tech activities in total MVA (per cent)	n.a.
Energy consumption per capita (kilograms oil equivalent)	717 (2011)
CO_2 emissions (thousand metric tons and metric tons per capita)	3,176 / 1.5 (2010)

Notes: Unless otherwise specified, data refer to 2013.
* Out of a total of 144 countries covered.

Sources: World Bank (data.worldbank.org/indicator); UNIDO (2013, Annex 3); UNCTAD (unctadstat.unctad.org/wds/ReportFolders/reportFolders.aspx); WEF (2014).

force) due to the use of specialised, capital-intensive technologies. However, in terms of the sectoral composition of GDP, the significance of mining activities has sharply dropped from 19.6 per cent in 1990 to just 11.3 per cent in 2012, while the share of manufacturing has more than doubled from 5.3 to 11.3 per cent in the same period – with key drivers being fish and meat processing and some limited beneficiation of minerals. To date, labour-intensive manufacturing activities are dominated by food and beverage production and fish processing, while other industries, such as textiles, clothing or electronics, have not emerged in

Namibia at any significant scale. In terms of employment, agriculture relies mainly on household subsistence farming – still the main source of income for the vast majority of the country's population – under challenging climatic conditions (Namibia being the driest sub-Saharan African country). Commercial agriculture has seen recent strides into horticulture, including rapidly growing production and export of table grapes.

The country's tourism sector – based on rich biodiversity, wildlife and highly varied landscapes – is a significant economic factor with high potential for further expansion. The medium-term forecast for the next ten years ranks Namibia's growth rate in tourist arrivals among the top five globally. In 2013, based on both direct and indirect effects, the sector already accounted for 15 per cent of GDP and close to 20 per cent of employment (WTTC 2014). Its further development hinges on removing a number of investment bottlenecks related to insecure land tenure in communal areas, insufficiently coordinated land use planning and the non-availability of specialised financial support facilities.

The economic dependence on South Africa (Namibia's colonial power until the country's independence in 1990) is exceedingly high as can be gauged from the regional pattern of trade: in recent years, close to 30 per cent of exports went to South Africa and more than 75 per cent of imports were sourced from South Africa. In Southern Africa, this high level of geographical import concentration is surpassed only by Botswana.

Highly Unequal Non-Inclusive Growth Pattern

Globally, Namibia is among the countries with the highest levels of inequality. The Gini coefficient stood at a value of 0.64 in 2004 (see Table 7.3), with contradictory reports about its more recent development. While national sources claim a slight improvement, other sources point to a further aggravation to around 0.7 in 2011 (Bertelsmann Stiftung 2014a). Be that as it may, there is no doubt that, in all relevant dimensions, the Namibian society is suffering from excessive forms of inequality. This applies equally to massive income gaps between white and black population groups, glaring disparities between urban and rural areas, and a fast growing divide between an emerging middle class and the majority of the population.

At the same time, the country is not creating enough jobs to cater to the needs of its growing population. According to the most recent labour force survey (Namibia Statistics Agency 2014), unemployment has remained worryingly high and rose to 30 per cent of the population in

2013. Whereas the female/male unemployment gap slightly narrowed, youth unemployment (age 15–34) grew further to reach a level of 42 per cent. Moreover, unemployed youth are concentrated in the more densely populated Northern regions and among the economically marginalised black population groups, which adds to the potentially explosive social effects.

On the positive side, it bears mention that Namibia is among just a small number of African countries with a functioning social safety net for vulnerable population groups (elderly and disabled citizens as well as orphaned children) and social security provisions (e.g. sick leave, medical benefits) for employed workers in the formal sector of the economy.

Good Governance and Business Environment Record yet Limited Economic Diversification

An outstanding feature of Namibia's political performance are the relatively positive governance indicators as well as those related to the quality of the institutional and physical infrastructure. In almost all governance dimensions considered in our country studies (and as summarised below in Chapter 8, Table 8.2), the country ranks high among all developing countries and indeed first among the five countries covered here. Specifically, this applies to the following indicators: government effectiveness, voice and accountability, steering capability, consensus building, fundamentals of market-based competition, rule of law, corruption perception, transparency of government policymaking and judicial independence. In general, Namibia features a democratic constitution based on the separation of powers and on guaranteeing fundamental liberties to its citizens.

Moreover, Namibia compares well with other African countries in terms of its business environment and, above all, the quality of its physical infrastructure. Despite some remaining deficiencies related to transport, water and energy supply, the country ranked as high as 4th and 11th in Africa, respectively, in the 2013/14 WEF Global Competitiveness Report and the African Development Bank's (AfDB's) Africa Infrastructure Development Index (AfDB 2014).

In addition, the country's financial system is well developed, boasts a number of well-managed and sufficiently capitalised banks, has shown a remarkable degree of resilience to external shocks and expanded its reach to the country's population and business community. 'Namibia's financial system is flush with investible funds as 35 percent of all pension fund assets must be invested domestically' (AfDB 2014, p. 6). Clearly then, when it comes to all these 'framework conditions', Namibia has the essential ingredients in place that should allow the country to grow its economy and become a role model of successful economic development in Africa. The preconditions exist for enhancing productivity, attracting investment, unleashing entrepreneurship and creating new sources of wealth.

However, despite the existence of such a highly conducive investment environment, economic diversification is not happening in any meaningful way and 'the extraction and processing of minerals for export remains Namibia's main growth driver' (AfDB 2014, p. 2). A home-grown dynamic industrial sector has not emerged; economic linkages have remained embryonic; fragmented and often isolated economic activities persist; and the 'missing middle' of SMEs is a reality to date. The further improvement and refinement of the business environment, as desirable as this may be, will yield low marginal benefits. The focus of industrial policy must move towards measures that contribute to creating new skills and technological capabilities.

Role and Approach of Industrial Policy

At the outset, it is noteworthy that Namibia's independence was gained exactly at the time when the socialist system, as embodied in the Soviet Union and Eastern Europe, reached its economic limits and eventually broke down. This historic collapse not only rendered a socialist economic approach obsolete as a role model but also led to reduced financial support from Soviet ideological sources. This was one important factor for South West Africa People's Organization (SWAPO) to embrace a capitalist, market-based development model. Another driver was the perceived need to send clear signals to the predominantly white business community so as to counter a possible wave of capital flight. Against this backdrop, economic pragmatism and ensured property rights were the order of the day. Also, a dialogue with the business community on planned policy measures was sought from the outset. However, in view of the exceedingly small number of business players in each economic sector, this dialogue took place in an ad hoc manner and involved primarily large enterprises.

There is no dearth of policy declarations and officially adopted documents covering industrial development. Starting back in 1992 with a White Paper on Industrial Development (arguing for enhanced diversification and stimulation of linkages), there has been a sequence of National Development Plans (from NDP 1 in 1995 to the current NDP 4) and a dedicated Policy and Programme on Small Business Development of 1997 (aimed at reducing informality and pushing technological upgrading without, however, expressing clear sectoral priorities). Under the overall umbrella of the government's Vision 2030 (published in 2004), the country's most recent Industrial Policy was formally adopted by cabinet and parliament in 2013[44] and subsequently translated into a 'growth at home' implementation strategy emphasising the creation of domestic value chains. The document basically contains a compilation of guiding principles that are to be complemented with a more specific implementation plan. The ten guiding principles emphasise: alignment with the Vision 2030 objective to become a developed industrialised nation by 2030, macroeconomic stability, openness as a means to foster economies of scale, targeting of priority sectors, integration of markets and infrastructure needs, equitable and broad-based economic empowerment, a predictable and stable regulatory environment, consumer protection through competition policy, flexibility, and 'locking in' the benefits of the current low level of GHG emissions.

While these are appropriate and commendable principles, there is a noticeable lack of directionality in terms of formulating a national transformation project. The document underlines the need to add value to the country's primary commodities, to increase the share of processed exports, to enhance the contribution of SMEs to manufacturing production, to develop service-oriented new products and to promote a knowledge and innovation-based industry – yet exactly how these diverse objectives can be reconciled, what they imply for targeting specific industrial sectors, which type of skills need to be promoted, remains unanswered. Also, as elaborated in greater detail by Rosendahl (2010), various industrial policy programmes in place (illustrated e.g. by the EPZ Act and the Sites and Premises Programme) lack an *ex ante* definition of measurable outcomes, independent monitoring schemes and a separation of regulatory from implementation responsibilities. Furthermore, the multiplicity of policy programmes implemented by various government agencies does not allow a clear attribution of results and thus precludes any effective cost–benefit analyses.

Limited Impact of Incentives for Export Processing

Since the mid-1990s, Namibia has relied on a dedicated incentive regime for export-oriented manufacturing, in addition to a general open door, non-discriminatory approach towards foreign investors. The EPZ Act of 1995 offers two investment tracks in terms of both a 'single factory' concept (enterprises receiving EPZ status in any chosen location in the country) and a 'dedicated space' concept, which promotes investments in specially designated industrial parks. Both types of investment are largely managed by the Offshore Development Company (ODC), which – due to lack of interest on the part of private investors – has remained predominantly under state ownership. The investment incentives offered to foreign and domestic companies with an export share (outside the Southern African Customs Union (SACU) area) of at least 70 per cent are generous and include exemption from a variety of taxes and import duties. The EPZ policy does not, however, feature any sectoral priorities. While the ODC Investor Guide offers examples of potential industrial sectors, these range from textiles to steel, from automotive component to cement industries – thus not exhibiting any clear sense of direction as to which industrial profile the country is trying to establish and promote.

To date, no comprehensive evaluation of Namibia's EPZ programme has been undertaken. However, judging from an early study undertaken by the country's Labour Resource and Research Institute (LaRRI 2000), and more recent interviews conducted by Rosendahl (2010), it is evident that the development impact of the attracted investments has remained insignificant. After slightly more than a decade in operation, some 80 per cent of initially registered companies had either deregistered or ceased operations. Employment creation reached just 20 per cent of the target level of 25,000 stipulated for the programme and was confined mostly to unskilled workers. There was no evidence of any skill upgrading attempts; in fact the envisaged budgetary provisions for training subsidies were never effected. Also, backward linkages to domestic support companies remained limited, largely because sufficiently competitive and reliable local suppliers simply did not exist. On the other hand, the costs of the EPZ programme in terms of forgone tax revenues were quite substantial.

In essence, the Namibian EPZ programme confirms the more general experience that it is not primarily financial incentives that attract foreign investment and generate positive spillovers for the domestic economy. Rather, three other factors are critically important: clear indications from government as to which long-term vision and sectoral priorities guide the process of economic transformation; the size of the domestic or regional market that can potentially be served; and the gradual build-up of local entrepreneurial capacity and basic managerial and technical skills. For the last to happen, an alignment between the promotion of large enterprises and the strengthening of SMEs would be required.[45] While in Namibia an appropriate policy instrument was created in the late 1990s in the form of the Sites and Premises Programme (aimed at providing affordable sites in serviced industrial estates to SMEs), the reality is characterised by a 'total lack of support services offered within the parks and the complete absence of programmes to promote linkages between small and larger enterprises' (Rosendahl 2010, p. 31). The overall conclusion, thus, is that so far the stated policy objective of using foreign investments as a conduit for dynamising and diversifying the domestic economy has failed to materialise. As recently as 2013, the country's Minister for Trade and Industry himself drew the sobering conclusion that 'only a few of these companies have in fact managed to live up to our expectations of building production capacity, transferring skills and job creation' and called for efforts to properly monitor and evaluate the performance of EPZ companies (Namibian Sun 2013).

Regional Cooperation and Integration

Namibia's economic development potential is severely constrained by the miniscule size of its domestic market. With a total population of just above two million and purchasing power held down by high levels of income inequality, the country's market seen in isolation does not offer viable prospects for producing goods at large scale. A broader look at regional integration and its potential to effectively enlarge markets, enhance economies of scale and stimulate investment flows is thus necessary.

Namibia is a member of both the Southern African Development Community (SADC) and – along with Botswana, Lesotho, South Africa and Swaziland – the SACU. Within the 15-member SADC, Namibia has one of the highest export and import ratios within the Community with 35 per cent of exports going just to South Africa and Angola (Mbekeani 2013; data for 2006–2008). Significantly, outside South Africa, Namibia – which is hosting the SACU Secretariat – is the only SACU member with its own harbours, most importantly the Port of Walvis Bay. Through a number of transport corridors, Walvis Bay connects Namibia with other countries in Southern Africa: with Zambia, Zimbabwe, DR Congo and Malawi through the Trans-Caprivi Corridor; with Botswana and the Northern Provinces of South Africa through the Trans-Calahari Corridor; and with Southern Angola through the Trans-Cunene Corridor. Between 2005 and 2012, cargo transport through these corridors more than doubled in volume (AfDB 2014, p. 7).

The Namibian government has recognised the need to further strengthen this critically important infrastructure (including through upgrading container terminals and establishing state-of-the-art storage facilities) and also push for the removal of existing non-tariff barriers to trade. The National Logistics Master Plan (as a component of the Transport Master Plan) aims at turning the country into the regional logistics centre for SADC[46] with a view to capitalising on the expected rapid growth of regional trade, also in light of ongoing tripartite negotiations towards creating a SADC–COMESA–EAC free trade area.

Good Governance is not Sufficient

As emphasised earlier in this section, Namibia boasts an impressive governance record, in particular when measured by regional standards. The country ranks third in the 2014 Ibrahim Index of African Governance (surpassed only by Mauritius and Cape Verde) and even ranks first in the component index covering safety and rule of law.[47] This is a key achievement and must not be underestimated as a starting point on which sustained economic development can build. However, in and by itself, this is a necessary but not a sufficient foundation. The definition of a national vision in terms of a long-term transformation project is critically important to provide signals to the business community where to invest and also to inspire citizens to unite behind clearly expressed goals and targets. For Namibia, there are a number of realistic options ranging from the aforementioned notion of becoming a regional transport and logistics hub to a tourism-centred strategy capitalising on the country's pristine natural environment and rich biodiversity[48] or, with prior investments into technical skill upgrading, attracting labour-intensive manufacturing serving the regional market. Deciding on the course to take, and communicating a transformation path to the country's population, is a matter for a broad-based, national consultative process to pursue.

Presently, important steps in this direction are taken by the government, with support from external partners. Within the broader context of the 'growth at home' framework, the key industrial policy building blocks are put to a critical review by all stakeholders concerned. Specifically, the policy measures aimed at promoting SMEs and foreign investment are being completely overhauled.

7.4 TUNISIA: STRUCTURAL CHANGE UNDER AUTHORITARIAN RULE

Economic Structure and Performance

Tunisia is an upper-middle-income country with a GDP per capita well above US$4,000 and a recent economic growth record of close to 4 per cent annually. The country has a significant industrial sector, which accounts for more than 30 per cent of GDP, with roughly half of industrial output generated by manufacturing activities.

Table 7.4   Tunisia – basic data

Surface area (square kilometres)	163,610 (2014)
Population (thousand)	11,018 (2014)
• Share of urban population (per cent)	67 (2014)
• Share of population below national poverty line	
(per cent)	16 (2010)
• Gini coefficient	0.36 (2010)
GDP (current US$ million)	46,994
GDP per capita (current US$)	4,200
GDP growth (per cent)	2.5
Average GDP growth 2005–2013 (per cent)	3.8
Competitiveness rank (WEF)*	87 (2014–2015)
Sector composition of GDP (per cent)	
• Agriculture & mining	9
• Industry	30
• (thereof: Manufacturing)	(16) (2011)
• Services	61
Exports/GDP (per cent)	47
Net ODA received (per cent of GNI)	2.4 (2012)
FDI inflow (current US$ million)	1,096
FDI inflow per capita (current US$)	100
Manufactured exports/total exports (per cent)	82 (2011)
Medium- and high-tech activities in total MVA (per cent)	9.3 (2011)
Energy consumption per capita (kilograms oil equivalent)	890 (2011)
CO_2 emissions (thousand metric tons and metric tons per capita)	25,878 / 2.5 (2010)

Notes: Unless otherwise specified, data refer to 2013.
* Out of a total of 144 countries covered.

Sources: World Bank (data.worldbank.org/indicator); UNIDO (2013, Annex 3); UNCTAD (unctadstat.unctad.org/wds/ReportFolders/reportFolders.aspx); WEF (2014).

Since gaining independence (following 75 years of French colonial rule from 1881–1956, which ended relatively peacefully through negotiations), the Tunisian economy underwent a process of significant restructuring and diversification. From a heavy dominance of agriculture and some raw materials (oil, gas, phosphate), the economy moved gradually into services (notably tourism) and manufacturing. With the native bourgeoisie initially mostly engaged in trading and the non-existence of a risk-taking indigenous entrepreneurial and business elite (Erdle 2011,

p. 8), this represents a remarkable transition to a relatively advanced industrial economy.

The geographical as well as socio-political proximity to the European market has played a crucial role, further enhanced by the signing of the Association Accord in 1995 and the establishment of a free trade zone for industrial products from 1996–2008. This was accompanied by a national industrial modernisation programme specifically aimed at upgrading the country's key export sectors with a view to enabling them to compete successfully in EU markets. This so-called *mise à niveau* programme is reviewed in greater detail below.

The story of export-driven economic diversification in Tunisia has two sides to it and can be seen as a glass half empty or half full, depending on the emphasis chosen. On the positive side, Tunisia has achieved a remarkably high degree of diversification, which indeed is second to none in the African context. An initial focus on textiles and clothing has given way to a dynamic rise of electrical, engineering and electronics industries (including automotive and aeronautics components), which have recorded an annual export growth of 18 per cent between 2000 and 2012 (AfDB, OECD and UNDP 2014, p. 252). More recently, tradable information and communication services have also emerged, with call centres and accounting services being located in the country. Tunisia has thus been increasingly integrated into a growing number of global value chains. When taking the number of products accounting for more than three quarters of all exports as an indicator, the country displays by far the most diversified export portfolio of all African countries: in 2012, this specific indicator stood at 93 followed by 83 for South Africa and 63 for Morocco (ibid., p. 279). In 2013, the number of enterprises engaged wholly in export activities was slightly above 2,600 and these generated more than 320,000 jobs (ibid., p. 14). Efforts are being undertaken now to move towards more innovation- and knowledge-based industries supported by various dedicated spaces ranging from business incubators to high-technology parks and R&D support programmes.

However, a closer look at the industrial structure reveals a number of critical issues. Most of the product diversification has taken place in just two sectors (textiles and electrical/electronics), which still account for the lion's share of Tunisia's exports. In terms of regional export markets, there is a pronounced dependence on European destinations, which accounted for 73 per cent of all exports – one quarter of total exports going to France alone and another quarter to Italy and Germany together.

Furthermore, the majority of export products is of a low value added nature and exhibits just basic levels of technological sophistication, which have remained unchanged for several decades (AfDB 2014a). Only very recently has there been a tendency for the share of medium- and high-technology manufactured exports to rise. According to UNIDO data, it increased from 32 per cent in 2006 to 46 per cent in 2011 (UNIDO 2013, p. 203) – still significantly below the comparable shares of East Asian countries (e.g. China, Malaysia and Thailand display shares of close to 60 per cent). The low level of export sophistication in turn translates into a strong reliance on unskilled labour and only limited transfer of more advanced technological and managerial skills. In addition, the regional concentration of export-oriented activities along the coast has further sharpened geographical disparities with the result that, to date, Tunisia's industrial fabric has remained highly dualistic in nature (Karray and Driss 2014).

At the same time, despite growing regional development gaps, quite some progress in reducing poverty and inequality has been made. The decade from 2000 to 2010 saw the share of people living in poverty (according to the national definition) being halved to 16 per cent (AfDB 2014a, p. 22), while the Gini coefficient stayed fairly stable at an internationally relatively low value of 0.36 (see Table 7.4). While this is partly due to the robust economic growth during this period, it is also, however, the result of high government expenditures that are unlikely to be sustainable in the long run.

Economic Governance and Industrial Strategies and Policies[49]

Tunisia's dynamic economic development, diversification and upgrading – with a performance clearly outcompeting the other Middle East and North African countries – were achieved under an authoritarian, neo-patrimonial system (Altenburg 2013). Since becoming independent, the country has basically known just two long-term presidents until the unfolding of the 'Jasmine Revolution' of early 2011. Below, we will briefly review the salient features of these successive regimes.

The first regime under Habib Bourguiba was in power for more than three decades (1956–1987). From its inception, it was able to capitalise on a strong and effective bureaucracy, an ethnically and religiously fairly homogeneous population and a well-educated and socially mobile middle class. While party members had preferential access to top positions in business and administration, the system was inclusive in terms of party membership, which was open to all population segments. Among the regime's political priorities, a *dirigiste* industrial policy assumed a central position and moved the country to a mixed economy with elements of both import substitution and export promotion and an early emphasis on textiles as a productive driver and tourism as a services pillar. At the same time, financial transfers to state-owned enterprises (often in monopolistic positions in strategic sectors) occupied a high and growing share of government expenditure, which turned out to become unsustainable in the mid-1980s. Living conditions started to deteriorate, youth unemployment increased and the International Monetary Fund (IMF) had to be called in for a bailout package accompanied by a structural adjustment programme. When social conflicts and riots escalated and the situation seemed to be getting out of hand, Bourguiba was toppled from within by his prime minister, General Ben Ali.

The Ben Ali regime stayed in power for almost a quarter of a century, that is, until 2011, and during this period implemented far-reaching reforms that resulted in a complete institutional overhaul, a radical renewal of the political elite (both party members and government bureaucrats) and a liberalisation of the economy. This led to a transition from the 'heavily regulated and insulated statist economy they had inherited into an increasingly outward-oriented, market-driven economy that would be attuned to the rhythm of globalisation' (Erdle 2011, p. 13). Significantly, Tunisia joined the General Agreement on Tariffs and Trade (GATT) in 1990 (and later the WTO in 1995) and was the first Mediterranean country to sign an association agreement with the EU, which was concluded in 1995 and became fully effective in 2008. This implied an important commitment to a complete phase-out of tariffs for all manufactured goods within a 12-year period and necessitated strong investments into the upgrading of Tunisia's manufacturing sector to be able to gain inroads into European markets and withstand import competition on the domestic market. In this context, the country benefited from a broad range of technical cooperation programmes offered by both the EU and other donors, which also served as domestic financial carrots in support of far-reaching political reforms towards strengthening market mechanisms.

In general, the consensus within the Ben Ali elite circle pointed in the direction of less state control and stronger reliance on private business players within a gradually deregulated environment. Thus, a role reversal took place, with private investment encouraged to drive economic growth while the state took responsibility for 'upholding the regime's "welfarist promise" of both collective advancement and individual improvement' (Erdle 2011, p. 19). At the same time, there was no change in terms of sectoral priorities. The country's main competitive advantages continued to be seen in textiles and in tourism (more recently also in information and communication services), that is, in sectors which could capitalise on the proximity to European markets and the confidence of European investors and consumers in Tunisia's political and economic stability.

In addition to a whole range of policy measures aimed at strengthening the financial sector, deregulating market access, facilitating foreign trade and reducing existing price distortions, three main pillars of industrial policy can be highlighted:

- A sustained *privatisation process* involving first small enterprises in light, largely agro-processing industries; then moving into larger, more profitable manufacturing and transport companies; and finally (after 1998) also covering companies in strategic sectors previously reserved for public ownership. All in all, more than 200 companies were thus privatised within just one decade.
- The establishment of a large number of *industrial zones* offering generous investment incentives. By 2010, more than 120 such zones existed on paper, yet only a minority were fully operational and managed effectively in accordance with relevant international standards, including those related to environmental and waste management. Most of these zones are located in the capital and coastal areas thus contributing to a reinforcement of prevailing regional disparities. In 2009, a programme was launched to create sector-specific industrial clusters (*pôles de compétitivité* based on the French model) mainly around large private lead firms offering also training and research support to enterprises.
- The *National Upgrading Programme* (*programme de mise à niveau*), arguably the most important of all industrial policy programmes in Tunisia (described in greater detail below).

National Upgrading Programme

The National Upgrading Programme (PMN) came into being in 1995 with an initial focus on manufacturing enterprises. Meanwhile, the programme has been broadened to encompass virtually all Tunisian businesses regardless of their sector of operation.[50] The programme is managed by a dedicated government unit (*Bureau de mise à niveau* – BMN) and financed from the Fund for the Development of Industrial Competitiveness (FODEC), which in turn is sourced both domestically (from a 1 per cent tax levied on domestic sales and finished imports) and from a variety of bilateral and multilateral donors. The programme's rationale is the provision of targeted support with a view to enabling domestic enterprises to survive the opening of the economy and compete successfully in global markets, in particular on the main EU markets. Raising productivity, improving product quality and ensuring reliability of delivery are among the main support dimensions covered. In the first

15 years of operation, close to 3,000 manufacturing companies and more than 100 service companies were supported – with official data claiming a turnover increase of 10 per cent and an employment increase of 20 per cent attributable to PMN interventions (Erdle 2011, p. 33).

A number of characteristic features help to explain the programme's remarkable achievements and success. Above all, the defining elements include:

- a comprehensive approach towards industrial modernisation ranging from upgrading of physical infrastructure to emphasis on 'soft' components, such as management and marketing;
- a light and lean eligibility approach making the programme easily accessible for most private companies;
- an integrated management structure under the sole responsibility of the Ministry of Industry and with participation from all relevant stakeholders in the decision-making process;
- a strong national ownership with PMN being placed at the core of the country's development strategy, Tunisian policymakers defining and implementing the programme and a strictly supporting role assigned to foreign donors; and
- explicit recognition of the potential social implications of enhanced competition and industrial restructuring with support facilities available for companies and workers negatively affected.

Successful Industrial Policy?

As recently as 2010, the Tunisian industrial policy approach of market-driven diversification under authoritarian rule was widely considered as extraordinarily successful and portrayed as a role model for other countries to follow (Baliamoune-Lutz 2013). The assessment of Erdle (2011) underlines that the ruling elite was conscious of the need to soften the impact of an open and competitive economy on the population at large and that there was a clear nexus between productivity growth on the one hand and broad-based welfare gains on the other. He further stresses that a strong growth performance went hand in hand with macro-economic stability, that Tunisia was among the limited number of countries able to stay on a growth path even amidst the global financial and economic crisis of 2009 (for a deeper analysis of the reasons see Loewe and Brach 2010) and that – based on an active promotion of prioritised manufacturing sectors and the attraction of foreign investment – the country was on its way to becoming an industrial society with a politically strong and economically well-endowed middle class.

This is not to say that there are no shortcomings and weaknesses. Clearly, a fundamental dualism between coastal and interior regions, between the few large and the many small companies, and between those serving export markets and those oriented towards the domestic market still prevails. Also, the dominance of consumer products and relatively simple assembly operations for intermediary investment goods signals that a full breakthrough into technologically more sophisticated activities has not yet happened. However, the critical challenge has always been the generation of sufficient employment for a growing population, which helps to explain that industrial policy in Tunisia 'is in the first degree about short-term job creation, and only in the second degree about longer-term industrial deepening' (Erdle 2011, p. 43). The government has created a variety of dedicated support schemes and incentives targeting university students, young professionals, redundant workers and business start-ups, with a view to offering employment opportunities.

The 'Jasmine Revolution'

The obvious question (if not the paradox) is why in this context of a stable, active and reasonably successful industrial policy a sudden revolutionary change occurred. The outbreak of the so-called Jasmine Revolution – which turned out to be the alarm bell for the broader Arab spring phenomenon – was not anticipated by political observers and technical experts alike. Different factors can be drawn upon to attempt an explanation.

First, while the Ben Ali regime was able to deliver stable growth, it was also based on a heavy concentration of assets and income within a small group of people closely connected to the ruling elite clans and especially to the extended presidential family. Among the population at large, the perception was widespread 'that it was difficult, if not impossible, to do business in Tunisia without consent from the president's family' (Rijkers, Freund and Nucifora 2014, p. 4). Indeed, the country's investment laws and incentives were one of the key mechanisms for rent capture. In a statistical analysis of more than 200 firms owned by the Ben Ali family, Rijkers, Freund and Nucifora (2014) provide evidence that their superior performance (inter alia in terms of market share and profits) can largely be explained by favourable regulations that both restricted foreign investment and made business expansion contingent upon prior government approval. Arguably, the resulting unfair treatment of domestic entrepreneurs – and, more generally, the perceived loss of dignity by ordinary citizens vis-à-vis a state bureaucracy seen as acting arbitrarily – was a key trigger of the civil uprising.

At the same time, the existence of a broad, well-educated middle class oriented towards European values constituted a strong multiplier.

Second, in addition to the stark regional disparities, Tunisia was suffering from a high unemployment rate of around 15 per cent, which was (and remains) structurally distorted to the disadvantage of educated youth. Paradoxically, there is a strong positive correlation between the rate of unemployment and the level of education. While the share of university graduates among the unemployed rose from 4 per cent in 1995 to 10 per cent in 2004 and almost 25 per cent in 2012, the share of uneducated persons among all job seekers declined from 17 per cent in 1995 to 12 per cent in 2004 and 5 per cent in 2012 (Karray and Driss 2014). However, the unemployment rate as an indicator of social disparities needs to be put into perspective: In the Middle East and North Africa (MENA) context, Tunisia has a relatively advanced social security system that recognises and supports registered unemployed people. This contributes to a comparatively high official unemployment rate. What it does not reveal though is the high rate of people that are underemployed.

Unfinished Business

Where does this leave Tunisia today? The new government – formed after remarkably peaceful democratic elections, which took place between October and December 2014 – has inherited some fundamental challenges on a policy agenda that can at best be called unfinished. Foremost among these is the political imperative to reintegrate disenfranchised youth into society; it is noteworthy that as much as 80 per cent of voters in the 18–25 age bracket boycotted the parliamentary election. Confidence in a future without corruption can only come from a radical overhaul and possibly break up of existing business empires and a transparent process and accountability in applying regulations and granting incentives. To date, the investment code of the Ben Ali regime has remained unchanged, thus contributing to a continued sense of suspicion and frustration among the population.

Above all, the unfinished agenda of industrial restructuring needs to be addressed. Whereas the short-term increase in unemployment one year after the revolution (moving up to 17 per cent as a result of falling investment according to Achy 2011) could have been expected, the long-term trend needs to be reversed. This will require skilful policies that overhaul the country's education system and push diversification into high value added and knowledge-intensive sectors that can absorb the growing supply of university graduates. Concurrently, in the coastal regions the tourism sector should be able to provide large numbers of jobs at lower education and skill levels once tourist arrivals pick up after renewed confidence in the country's political system. Also, the past reliance on easily accessible European markets should be challenged and complemented by a broader, more open assessment that looks at the potential for Tunisia's economy to tap into global markets, also within a South–South perspective.

Finally, the potential of solar energy as a source of export revenues and technological development has remained largely untapped so far. Despite Tunisia's 'plan solaire' (adopted in 2009) and the big expectations initially pinned on the now aborted Desertec Project, progress in building large-scale solar installations has been slow. Currently, a new project aimed at supplying Tunisian solar energy to the UK is in an advanced stage of preparation. A fresh look at the economic case for enhanced Tunisia–EU energy integration (also in the broader MENA context) is called for, in particular in light of the strong emphasis on renewables within the long-term EU decarbonisation strategy. If well planned and integrated into a comprehensive industrial policy framework, there could also be significant spillovers in terms of building up domestic capacity for component manufacturing.

7.5   VIETNAM: ESCAPING THE MIDDLE-INCOME TRAP?

Economic Structure and Performance

The economic rise of Vietnam in recent decades has been nothing short of spectacular. The country represents an extraordinary success story of rapid and sustained growth. Just little more than two decades ago, Vietnam was among the poorest economies worldwide. In 1990, its GDP per capita stood at less than US$100 – significantly lower than that of Tanzania, less than half of Ethiopia's and less than one third of Rwanda's per capita income. Severe poverty was rampant, much of the country's physical infrastructure in need of rehabilitation and economic activity largely confined to agriculture and inefficient state-owned enterprises – all in all a country that, just like South Korea a few decades earlier, was widely considered as a hopeless case of economic stagnation if not decline.

Today, Vietnam is a lower-middle-income country with a GDP per capita above US$1,700 (2013) and boasts one of the most impressive poverty reduction records in recent history. The share of the population living in severe poverty has become almost insignificant and a strong

Table 7.5   Vietnam – basic data

Surface area (square kilometres)	330,951 (2014)
Population (thousand)	90,179 (2014)
● Share of urban population (per cent)	33 (2014)
● Share of population below national poverty line (per cent)	17 (2012)
● Gini coefficient	0.36 (2012)
GDP (current US$ million)	171,393
GDP per capita (current US$)	1,740
GDP growth (per cent)	5.4
Average GDP growth 2005–2013 (per cent)	6.2
Competitiveness rank (WEF)*	68 (2014–2015)
Sector composition of GDP (per cent)	
● Agriculture & mining	18
● Industry	38
● (thereof: Manufacturing)	(24) (2011)
● Services	43
Exports/GDP (per cent)	84
Net ODA received (per cent of GNI)	2.8 (2012)
FDI inflow (current US$ million)	8,900
FDI inflow per capita (current US$)	97
Manufactured exports/total exports (per cent)	70 (2011)
Medium- and high-tech activities in total MVA (per cent)	20.3 (2011)
Energy consumption per capita (kilograms oil equivalent)	697 (2011)
CO_2 emissions (thousand metric tons and metric tons per capita)	150,230 / 1.7 (2010)

Notes: Unless otherwise specified, data refer to 2013.
* Out of a total of 144 countries covered.

Sources: World Bank (data.worldbank.org/indicator); UNIDO (2013, Annex 3); UNCTAD (unctadstat.unctad.org/wds/ReportFolders/reportFolders.aspx); WEF (2014).

middle class has emerged in particular in and around the country's main cities, Ho Chi Minh City and Hanoi.

Economic success was largely propelled by a growing industrial sector, which accounts for close to 40 per cent of GDP (38 per cent in 2013). Within the industrial sector, manufacturing industry has exhibited a particularly pronounced dynamism generating 88 per cent of gross industrial output in 2012 (General Statistics Office of Vietnam 2014). From 2000 to 2009, Vietnam's average annual growth rate of MVA was as high as 11 per cent, thus even surpassing that of China. This is also true for manufactured exports, which in the same period grew at 21 per cent annually compared to 20 per cent in China (MoIT and UNIDO 2011, pp. 28f.). In short, the country provides a distinct example of an industry-based, export-oriented development strategy (with an export/ GDP ratio of close to 60 per cent) and a strong contribution coming from FDI. Measured in terms of the Competitive Industrial Performance Index (UNIDO 2013a), it ranked 54th among 135 countries in 2010 – up from rank 72 ten years earlier.

A couple of remarkable sectoral success stories have underpinned this strong economic performance. Vietnam has built up a coffee production base virtually from scratch and has become the world's second important coffee exporter (after Brazil) with a market share close to 20 per cent and employment of around 2.5 million. Similarly, in shrimps farming, the country is now third ranking in global exports; close to 50 per cent of its entire seafood exports are accounted for just by shrimps. In textiles and apparel exports, Vietnam ranks fifth worldwide with a labour force of more than two million. While the value chain has remained limited so far (90 per cent of enterprises in the sector produce garments), there are plans of moving also into spinning and weaving/knitting operations.

The Role of Industrial Policy

How can this remarkable performance be explained? Clearly, a deliberate and active industrial policy has played a decisive role. Let us thus take a look at the general policy approach and the main policy instruments applied over time (for more detailed accounts see Perkins and Vu Thanh 2010; Rama 2008; MoIT and UNIDO 2011; ODI 2011).

In the years up to the mid-1980s, the main emphasis of Vietnam's industrial strategy and policy was placed on strengthening basic and heavy industries (initially metallurgy, mechanical engineering and chemicals; followed by energy, machinery, shipbuilding and transportation equipment) and selected light industries (consumption goods and agricultural equipment) behind high protective walls and relying primarily on state-owned enterprises and cooperatives. In accordance with the Communist Party ideology prevailing in those years, there was no private sector to speak of and the comprehensive central planning of economic activity remained largely unchallenged. Physical production targets were given priority over efficiency considerations, while in terms of international exposure, the country was firmly integrated into the COMECON trading system.

After some unsuccessful tinkering with limited reforms, the Sixth Party Congress held in 1986 embarked on a fundamental reform process and launched the transformation towards a 'socialist-oriented market economy' (known in Vietnamese as 'doi moi' meaning 'renovation'). One of the triggers for this policy shift was the huge and growing trade deficit coupled with a massive decrease in Soviet aid, which necessitated a push towards building up an export-oriented sector. While the main spirit and many building blocks of 'doi moi' were borrowed from the reforms implemented earlier in neighbouring China, there were also distinct differences, for example in terms of much less emphasis on rural development and an initial neglect of domestic non-state enterprises, such as the collective township and village enterprises in China.

In the years between 1986 and the decade of the1990s, the main contours of Vietnam's new industrial policy were put in place and have remained in force to date. These include:

- a principal decision in favour of export-oriented industrialisation focusing on producing consumer goods (e.g. textiles, footwear, seafood) for international markets;
- a gradually expanding autonomy for state-owned enterprises in conjunction with decreasing subsidy levels;
- an opening up of the economy to foreign investors primarily in export-oriented manufacturing (with inward FDI jumping up from almost zero in 1989 to US$2.4 billion in 1996); and
- a legal recognition and economic encouragement of domestic private businesses.

This principal reorientation towards market-oriented development was reinforced in the first decade of the 21st century. Among the notable milestone events were the accession to WTO in 2007 and the adoption by the National Assembly of Enterprise Laws in 2000 and 2005. The importance of these laws cannot be overestimated and must be seen against the backdrop of a minuscule private sector existing before. While the 2000 Enterprise Law brought with it the legal recognition and formalisation of private enterprises as well as simplified registration procedures, the 2005 Enterprise Law was aimed at creating a level playing field for all types of enterprises regardless of their ownership structure.

In particular, the 2005 Enterprise Law triggered a massive wave of new private business operations being established.[51] As a result, the ownership pattern of industrial production changed from being dominated by state-owned enterprises to one overwhelmingly driven by private business: in 2012 (General Statistics Office of Vietnam 2014; preliminary data), the share of state-owned enterprises was down to 16.4 per cent, while that of the domestic non-state sector stood at 37.3 per cent and that of foreign investment at 46.3 per cent. Thus, a previously highly dualistic structure (state-owned and foreign) has been converted into a productive system based on three distinct pillars. At the same time (indeed also in 2005), eight broad groups of state-owned conglomerates were formed, including among others the National Shipbuilding Corporation, National Textiles and Garments Corporation and National Electricity Corporation. While these *chaebol*-type operations may be inefficient judged by world standards, they have allowed Vietnam, unlike in most African countries, to maintain a national industrial and energy base and build competencies in capital and scale-intensive industrial sectors.

However, economic fragmentation has not been overcome. Linkages between state-owned enterprises, foreign-invested enterprises and the domestic business sector are limited and most local firms have remained small, are operating at low productivity levels and are in urgent need of technological and managerial upgrading.

Challenges Ahead

From the above summary perspective, it is evident that the development trajectory of Vietnam has been exceptionally dynamic and successful and has catapulted the country from a poor economy into middle-income status in record time. However, a linear continuation of past trends is by no means guaranteed. Among the critical challenges to be addressed by the country's industrial policymakers in the years to come are: (1) the middle-income country trap, (2) rising inequality, (3) environmental sustainability and (4) the persistence of corruption.

(1) The middle-income country trap
So far, Vietnam has fairly easily progressed to higher income levels and a more diversified industrial sector. The country has captured growing shares of world markets for labour-intensive consumer goods and attracted sizable amounts of foreign investment. It is generally considered as having successfully emulated the Chinese model. The crucial question is whether and how this path can be continued. At higher income levels, the sources and drivers of growth differ from those that enable a country to move out of conditions of poverty. Competitive pressures are intensifying: not yet able to fully compete with more sophisticated producers in mature industrial economies, and no longer able to compete against low-cost producers from poorer countries, such a precarious 'sandwich' position can stifle and ultimately trap further development efforts.

Vietnam now faces the critical challenge of moving from a development phase highly dependent on foreign inputs towards a new phase that will have to rely more strongly on creating domestic internal value (Ohno 2010). Specifically for countries like Vietnam with an exceedingly high dependence on both exports and foreign investment, further industrial upgrading becomes imperative and requires an active industrial policy in various fields:

- Presently, Vietnam's export portfolio displays a high concentration on low-technology products. They account for as much as 62 per cent of total exports (almost twice as high as in China with 32 per cent) while high-technology exports contribute just 12 per cent (MoIT and UNIDO 2011, p. 33; data for 2009). This implies a strong exposure to slow-growing market segments; a pronounced vulnerability to existing and newly entering low-cost producers; and limited technological spillover effects for the domestic economy. Policy measures targeting new high-technology industrial sectors and aimed at making productivity enhancements rather than capital investments the main source of growth will have to focus on removing critical shortages of technical skills, inter alia through linking vocational training centres with business clients (World Bank 2013).
- Strengthening specialised technical skills could also go a long way in maintaining Vietnam's status as an attractive location for foreign investment. Here again, a more targeted approach is necessary. Recently, the country has attracted rising amounts of speculative real-estate investments and is in danger of losing out on investments into productive manufacturing. In this context, targeting high-quality FDI (in terms of employment effects, technology spillovers and linkages with domestic private business) is essential yet would require both enhanced production and quality capabilities on the part of local suppliers, and a modernisation of the country's investment promotion approach and the related government agencies. A recent empirical study concludes that 'Vietnam is unable to take full advantage of FDI inflows because: (i) its financial market is insufficiently developed, (ii) spending on education and training is insufficient, and (iii) technology gap between the foreign and local firms is too large' (Anwar and Nguyen 2010, p. 198).
- Ultimately, the country's entire innovation system calls for an overhaul. Currently, dedicated funding schemes for technology upgrading and innovation are lacking and so are incentives for

importing new technology. At the same time, existing R&D institutions are not geared towards pushing for productive application and commercialisation of research programmes.

(2) Keeping inequality in check

Economic growth is never spreading equitably. Also, in Vietnam, there are signs pointing to a widening rural–urban poverty gap – with rural poverty being concentrated primarily in the Northeast and North Central Coast and there being a high incidence of poverty among ethnic minorities (ODI 2011, p. 9). The country's Communist Party establishment is acutely aware of the risks faced. At a regular meeting of the Central Committee in October 2013, Communist Party chief Nguyen Phu Trong referred to the rich-poor divide as getting worse and warned of the potentially severe implications for social stability.[52]

In general, Vietnam has effectively managed to keep economic inequality in check. While poverty has been reduced at record pace, the increase in equality has remained at modest levels. According to the World Bank database, Vietnam's Gini coefficient actually remained *constant* between 1993 and 2012 (at 0.36) whereas in the same period China's Gini coefficient rose sharply from 0.36 to 0.42. This evidence for Vietnam is corroborated by a stable ratio of income held by the richest and the poorest population quintile (data available up to 2008).

It would seem that this story of growth with equity is not easily explained by structural economic determinants, such as employment creation and productivity growth in sectors with low entry barriers or the deregulation of agricultural markets. In comparison with China, there are indeed more similarities than differences; Vietnam broadly emulates the Chinese development strategy, with a time lag and at lower scale. One interesting explanatory approach thus relies on the political economy of power dynamics and accountability systems in single-party regimes. Vietnam's spending on equalisation transfers (as a share of GDP) is over three times higher than China's, which may be due to the more diffused leadership pattern and parallel constituencies of political leaders (Abrami, Malesky and Zheng 2008).

A key challenge for the future will be to maintain the current relatively low levels of inequality while moving towards more skill and knowledge-intensive comparative advantages.

(3) Environmental sustainability

In Chapter 4 and Section 6.5 above, we have drawn attention to emerging resource-efficiency challenges, the looming risks of climate change and the need, also for developing countries, to consider strategies of gradually decoupling economic growth from the consumption of natural resources. Vietnam has every reason to be concerned. In both its Southern and Northern urban agglomerations, the country's population and productive capacities are highly vulnerable to rising sea levels. Indeed, in terms of the Long-Term Climate Risk Index published by Germanwatch (Harmeling and Eckstein 2013),[53] Vietnam is ranked as the sixth most vulnerable country worldwide. Furthermore, there are serious issues of deforestation (both through burning and illegal logging), losses of mangroves due to rapidly expanding coastal shrimp farming as well as a massive build-up of untreated waste from both household and industrial sources.[54] Clearly, the country's current growth dynamics are outstripping its incipient resource management capabilities.

Without doubt, the country's government is in the process of responding to these challenges and has added a National Green Growth Strategy to its industrial policy portfolio. This strategy was approved in September 2012 and sets goals to promote green, resource-efficient production; to reduce GHG emission intensity by 8–10 per cent (compared to 2010 levels); and to stimulate sustainable consumption. The strategy comes with a roadmap for action and, in terms of institutional management, establishes an Inter-Ministerial Coordinating Board chaired by the deputy prime minister (Asia LEDS Partnership 2013). While it is too early to assess progress in implementation, the sense of urgency and commitment is noteworthy. The Vietnamese government is sending strong policy signals that economic growth at the expense of environmental destruction can no longer be a viable strategy.

(4) Corruption

There is general evidence that sustained economic growth is among the factors that tend to reduce the share of enterprise revenues extracted by bribes. This is also the result of a recent study for Vietnam (Bai et al. 2014). However, the same study reports that, still in 2011, 23 per cent and 70 per cent of businesses, respectively, had to pay a bribe to either expedite registration procedures or move through customs. It does not come as a surprise then that Vietnam performs poorly in terms of the Corruption Perception Index (Transparency International 2014), where it ranks 119th. Clearly, for a country eager to be globally recognised as an increasingly sophisticated investment location, this is causing a high reputational damage over and above the direct economic losses. New government service systems combining deregulation with transparency[55] will be needed to counter stubbornly high corruption levels. One positive example in this direction is the National Business Registration System in effect since 2011, which offers single-point registration services performed uniformly across the country's 63 provinces and linked to a computerised national system (UNIDO 2011).

Key Features of Approaching Industrial Policy

While industrial policy in Vietnam is suffering from a proliferation of national, regional and sectoral economic development strategies – mostly under the label of various 'Masterplans' of which around 80 were formulated in the period 1995–2010 alone – and would thus benefit from enhanced coordination efforts, there are a number of positive elements in how industrial policy is approached in the country.

First, great emphasis is being placed by policymakers in Vietnam on a process of *strategic consensus building*. This may be time-consuming yet, once completed, provides a strong foundation for consistent implementation along an agreed trajectory. Specifically, this is how the principles behind the 'doi moi' transformation were adopted, combined with limited 'accountability mechanisms arising from decentralized power structures and an educated and politically aware population' (ODI 2011, p. 13). To date, the emphasis on land reform, investments into health and education, and a strong reliance on foreign investment and export markets have remained largely unchallenged.

Second, there has been a distinct *propensity to innovate and experiment*. Party cadres in charge have often proven to be pragmatic and willing to throw dogma overboard. The home-grown variation of this approach in Vietnam has been called 'fence breaking'. Facilitated by special transitional provisions for the South, which were in place after the country's reunification, local experiments with market price-based agricultural production were tolerated. Whatever proved to be working well was later endorsed and scaled up by the party leadership (Rama 2008).[56]

Third, key industrial policy *reforms were implemented gradually* and with a view not to jeopardise domestic capacities and structures. For instance, following its accession to WTO in 2007, Vietnam had to open up its retail sector to foreign investors, yet did so in a highly conditional approach that subjected foreign retail investments to prior economic needs tests. In April 2013, after six years of trial, this provision was relaxed (not abolished altogether) by exempting smaller foreign-owned retail operations (below 500 square metres) in approved areas with complete infrastructure from the economic needs tests.[57]

Finally, Vietnamese authorities and policymakers have been exceedingly wary of becoming dependent on donor priorities. It bears mention that the 'doi moi' transformation was initiated even before most international and bilateral donor organisations became active in Vietnam. In subsequent years, when the country turned into a 'donors darling', the government clearly remained in the driver's seat and exercised effective leadership in terms of seeking to ensure coherence among the interventions of a multitude of donors. The example of Vietnam volunteering to be one of the initial pilot countries of the so-called One UN process holds many lessons in this respect.

All in all, Vietnam presents a puzzling case of a socialist economic system with Communist Party cadres taking key decisions, a limited role of the private sector in consultative policy mechanisms,[58] a high incidence of corruption and yet a strong growth record coupled with low levels of inequality.

NOTES

38. http://www.theeastafrican.co.ke/news/Ethiopian-leather-finding-markets-globally–but-little-to-show/-/2558/2454130/-/item/1/-/6xqfdl/-/index.html (accessed 6 May 2015).
39. http://ethiopianflowerexport.com/ (accessed 6 May 2015).
40. Higher ratios are reported mostly for a number of small island states and special cases like Afghanistan and Haiti, based on security and/or humanitarian factors.
41. According to Whitfield et al. (2015), in 2010 the sugar industry accounted for almost 250,000 jobs (including various support functions), which made it Mozambique's largest formal employer.
42. A survey of local enterprises revealed that '99% had serious problems with product quality; 95% did not have the required profile, experience and portfolio of projects; 92% operated with old, worn-out and outdated equipment and technology; 90% suffered from serious management deficiencies and inadequate financial structure and capabilities; and 85% had serious deficiencies with respect to marketing capabilities and business attitude' (Krause and Kaufmann 2011, p. 49; in turn quoted from a Mozambican language paper).
43. Data and analysis in this section are based on AfDB (2014) and Rosendahl (2010).
44. The document published by the Ministry of Trade and Industry under the title Namibia's Industrial Policy is not dated.
45. At a more fundamental level, there are serious deficiencies in Namibia's education system that is characterised by skill mismatches between supply and demand as well as poor teaching and learning performance and high dropout rates in public schools. A long-term Education and Training Sector Improvement Programme was adopted in 2005 yet took a long time to become operational so that its impact has remained uncertain (Bertelsmann Stiftung 2014).
46. www.npc.gov.na/?news=development-of-an-international-logistics-hub-for-sadc-in-namibia (accessed 6 May 2015).
47. The Index is regularly published by the Mo Ibrahim Foundation and can be found at: http://www.moibrahimfoundation.org/iiag/ (accessed 6 May 2015).
48. Namibia was the first country explicitly anchoring the notion of environmentally sustainable development in its constitution.
49. This section and the following sections draw heavily on Erdle (2011).
50. A distinction was introduced into special technology support for priority investments and general support for enterprises in sectors considered as important for the overall success of PMN, including also business services, educational institutions and banking.

51. 'Between 2000 and 2005, more than 160,000 new domestic private firms were formed ... Moreover, during the same period, private enterprises created three million new jobs and invested VND 323 trillion, which is more than the total FDI for the same period' (Perkins and Vu Thanh 2010, p. 19).
52. http://www.thanhniennews.com/society/vietnams-party-chief-warns-against-growing-economic-divide-again-966.html (accessed 6 May 2015).
53. The Index combines indicators quantifying the impact of extreme weather events in terms of death toll, deaths per 100,000 inhabitants, total economic losses and losses per unit of GDP.
54. More than 60 per cent of rural household waste, 16 per cent of urban household waste and more than 60 per cent of waste originating from the country's industrial parks are damaging the environment without any prior treatment (http://tuoitrenews.vn/society/10390/vn-faces-great-environmental-problems-deputy-pm, accessed 6 May 2015).
55. This will be particularly important regarding the establishment in 2006 of eight large, state-owned conglomerates in strategic sectors, which continue to enjoy privileges in receiving financial support (Perkins and Vu Thanh 2010, pp. 31 ff.; MoIT and UNIDO 2011, p. 21).
56. 'In the end, innovative local leaders who could have been whistled out were entrusted to hold the whistle, and to build upon their "fence breaking" experiments. They were invited to Hanoi, not to be thrown into jail, but to take upon bigger responsibilities' (Rama 2008, p. 19).
57. For details see http://www.allens.com.au/pubs/asia/foasia15may13.htm (accessed 6 May 2015).
58. However, research by Schmitz et al. (2012) has shown that active participation by private sector organisations and firms has had a positive impact on successful economic reform in some of the country's provinces.

8. Comparative insights into success and failure

In this chapter, we expand on the country studies presented in Chapter 7 and provide a complementary comparative perspective. Whereas the earlier country-specific sections were geared at developing the main national storylines in terms of the evolution and characteristic approach of industrial policy management, we now adopt more of a bird's eye view, compare key elements of country policy performance, distil some common denominators and seek to gain insights into what exactly determines success or failure. In doing so, we will draw on illustrative examples of policy instruments applied, which to some extent go beyond the more general narratives of Chapter 7.

After a synoptic view at the mixed economic performance of the countries reviewed in this book (Section 8.1), the following sections focus on specific elements of industrial policy that – in various forms and degrees – remain to be addressed in all countries. We group these challenges around the questions of business fragmentation as a constraint for inclusive growth; interaction between the government and the private sector; the pursuit of a national transformation project; mainstreaming of green growth; the balance between planning and search processes; and the requirements of effective policy implementation.

8.1 MIXED PERFORMANCE

In Table 8.1 below, we compare the performance of the countries reviewed in Chapter 7 with regard to GDP growth, share of MVA, and overall competitiveness. The data underline the big differences in terms of competitiveness – ranging from rank 80 for Tunisia to 137 for Mozambique – and industrialisation – with shares of MVA in GDP between 4.2 per cent for Ethiopia and 23.6 per cent for Vietnam.

Table 8.1   Economic performance indicators

	Average GDP growth 2005–2013	MVA/ GDP 2006	MVA/ GDP 2011	Competitiveness (WEF)*		
				Score 2006/07	Score 2014/15	Rank 2014/15
Ethiopia	10.7	4.4	4.2	3.0	3.6	118
Mozambique	7.1	13.6	11.7	2.9	3.2	133
Namibia	4.5	13.6	13.0	3.7	4.0	88
Tunisia	3.8	15.3	16.4	4.7	4.0	87
Vietnam	6.2	21.4	23.6	3.9	4.2	68

Note: * Score: 1 (least competitive) to 7. Rank: N = 144 countries.

Sources: World Bank (data.worldbank.org/indicator); WEF (2014); UNIDO (2013).

Changes in growth and competitiveness, and even in industrial development, depend on many factors beyond industrial policy, including political and macroeconomic stability, commodity prices and international demand conditions. Moreover, industrial policy, as defined in this study, may also target non-manufacturing activities. Table 8.1 thus does not reveal much about the effectiveness of industrial policy. Nevertheless, it helps to put the subsequent qualitative analysis of industrial policies into perspective.

During the period 2005–2013, all five countries benefited from high rates of economic growth. Growth was especially impressive in Ethiopia, Vietnam and Mozambique, although starting from very low levels. For Ethiopia and Mozambique, the last decade was a period of recovery from previous civil wars and failed socialist policies. Against this backdrop, high growth rates reflect a return to normalisation. However, despite its growth, Mozambique hardly increased its competitiveness, indicating that growth was based on singular events – such as the big investment in the MOZAL aluminium smelter – rather than systematic improvement of the policy environment. Ethiopia, in contrast, made a step forward in terms of competitiveness, though this did not lead to significant industrialisation. Competitiveness increased due to progress in construction and commercial agriculture, whereas manufacturing activities grew at a lower rate than overall GDP. Vietnam had the most impressive performance in terms of economic growth based on increased competitiveness and industrialisation. Increased export competitiveness in labour-intensive manufactures and primary products including oil, coffee and seafood mainly explain Vietnam's success. The country study (see Section 7.5) concludes, however, that Vietnam may not yet be fully prepared to make the transition from labour-cost to more knowledge-based advantages, which is crucial for escaping the middle-income trap.

The other countries grew moderately. Following the political turmoil of the Arab spring revolutions, competitiveness fell significantly in Tunisia from a quite high level. The country study (see Section 7.4) describes how Tunisia managed to shift from a largely rent-based to a private sector and export-driven economy.

8.2 FRAGMENTATION OF BUSINESS

Production systems in all countries of our sample are fragmented along different lines. The most conspicuous gap exists between micro/small and large firms. These are not only differentiated by size, but also display enormous productivity gaps, different degrees of formality, different regulatory barriers and different institutional arrangements for business transactions. But fragmentation can also be observed between state-owned and private enterprises. State-owned enterprises still play an important role in all five countries. While the general trend is towards privatisation, in several cases state-owned enterprises are promoted as backbones of the development of the respective sector. Further divisions exist within the private sector. One important division relates to national vs foreign-invested firms, which is often exacerbated by differentiated incentive systems for both groups. Some incentives to attract foreign investors – such as fiscal and tax breaks for companies that import prefabricated goods, assemble and re-export them – deliberately encourage companies *not* to trade with local companies. The division between national and foreign offshore companies is most pronounced in export-oriented Vietnam and Tunisia. In some countries (such as Namibia), the partition of the business community is also due to differences between ethnic minority-owned and other domestic firms. Finally, special business networks exist in relation to national institutions, such as the party-affiliated endowment funds in Ethiopia. Interactions *within* these groups – in terms of shareholding, trade relations and informal ties – are much more common than interactions *between* groups, suggesting that business communities are indeed highly fragmented.

Such fragmentation is harmful. It hampers the evolution of inter-connected ecosystems of small and large firms with all their virtues of mutual specialisation (as elaborated in Section 3.2):

- Firms in integrated production systems can focus on their core competences and buy all necessary parts and services from equally specialised partners. All firms thus benefit from the advantages of specialisation, thereby raising overall productivity.
- When firms interact, factor mobility between them increases. Workers and capital can be reallocated more easily from less efficient to more efficient firms. Specifically, interaction lowers the entry barriers to move from the informal into the formal labour market.
- Linkages also spur knowledge spillovers. For example, when traditional small enterprises become suppliers to modern companies, they have to learn how to meet international standards; quite often, customers train and audit their suppliers.

Linkage creation thus contributes to pro-poor growth. It raises overall productivity *and* helps to reduce the existing large productivity gaps, thus making industrial development more socially inclusive.

Interestingly, industrial policies in the countries reviewed largely neglect the problem of fragmentation. Although some policy documents do mention the need for better linkages, we found hardly any tangible programmes to create linkages and knowledge spillovers. Ethiopia, for example, supports (or even pushes) some of the largest companies to improve their business processes with the help of heavily subsidised consultants. The government expects that once the leading companies are internationally competitive, small companies will benefit from their progress, directly via business linkages or indirectly by emulating their business practices. However, there is little indication of such spontaneous spillovers, and there are no programmes to accelerate them. The few examples of business linkage programmes we found in other countries – including a supplier development programme for Mozambique's large aluminium smelter MOZAL – were limited to specific sectors and hardly involved any micro and small firms.

Most countries have created special ministries and supporting agencies and drafted development plans for *SMEs*, on the one hand, and for *industry*, on the other. As a consequence, policy formulation and implementation for SMEs is not harmonised with the overall industrial policy strategies. This situation creates institutional barriers to knowledge diffusion and forgoes opportunities for the productive integration of SMEs, such as by combining investment promotion with programmes for the development of local SME suppliers. Furthermore, it may distort incentives. For example, subsidies for SMEs and exemptions from (or non-enforcement of) tax and labour rules induce companies to remain small, thus shifting the average enterprise size away from the optimum and reducing aggregate productivity (Pagés-Serra 2010, p. 219). Finally, lack of policy alignment may lead to situations where foreign large-scale investors are attracted and supported without consideration of their impact on local SMEs, which may lead to net job losses.

This outcome is in strong contrast to some successful late industrialising countries, like Singapore, Malaysia and Ireland, which made linkage building a pivotal point of their industrialisation strategies (Battat, Frank and Shen 1996). Here, linkage creation covers a range of activities, from subcontracting exchange schemes, franchising and supplier development programmes to industry clubs and electronic platforms for knowledge-sharing.[59] SME policies are thus well aligned with the overall industrial development strategy.

8.3   GOVERNMENT AND THE PRIVATE SECTOR: PARTNERS IN DEVELOPMENT?

Increasing Recognition of the Private Sector as the Engine of Growth …

All of the countries of our sample went through phases of state-driven development and heavy-handed regulation of private businesses. Vietnam, Mozambique and Ethiopia were part of the socialist bloc aligned with the Soviet Union and pursued centrally planned economic policies until the collapse of the Soviet Union. In Ethiopia, the pro-Soviet regime was ousted by a guerrilla movement, which formed a new government in 1991, but even that movement built on a Marxist ideological background. In Namibia, a guerrilla movement supported by the Soviet Union, Libya and Cuba – SWAPO – took office after defeating the South African apartheid regime and ending its administration of Namibia in 1988. However, the incoming governments in Ethiopia and Namibia pragmatically shifted towards market economies. Tunisia applied central planning during the 1970s and built up large state-owned enterprise sectors, but has incrementally liberalised its economy since.

All countries strongly felt the limitations of centrally planned economies. For instance, Vietnam was at the brink of bankruptcy in the late 1980s; Mozambique suffered from a combination of inefficient central planning (which ended in the late 1980s), civil war and sabotage (until 1992); in Ethiopia, the situation was similar until 1991. When Namibia became independent, the Eastern bloc was already in full decay, so that SWAPO had already abandoned some of its socialist rhetoric before independence. In the MENA region, the economic crises were less severe, but the inefficiency of the state-led economy had become very evident. Moreover, the collapse of the Soviet Union obligated countries to rethink their trade relations.

Today, all five countries embrace the principles of the market economy and regard the private sector as the main driver of productivity enhancement and economic growth. All have engaged in significant programmes of privatising state enterprises. According to the World Bank Privatisation Database,[60] privatisation transactions between 2000 and 2008 amounted to US$ 3.6 billion in Tunisia and US$ 0.9 billion in Vietnam. Transactions in the other countries were much smaller, but, in some cases, the number of privatised small companies was considerable. Also, trade and investment regimes have gradually been liberalised. Simultaneously, macroeconomic management has improved; for instance, fiscal deficits and inflation have been reduced below the level of previous decades.

... but State–Business Relationships are Rarely Collaborative and Governments are Unwilling to Soften Control of 'Strategic' Sectors

While there is a remarkable consensus about the centrality of the private sector, the attitude of most governments towards the private sector remains ambivalent. In all countries, certain consultative processes with business associations are in place, but governments still tend to have a paternalistic and 'command and control' attitude towards the business sector, rather than adopting a facilitating role. Bureaucratic procedures still hamper private sector development considerably. Only Tunisia (ranking 60th from a total of 189 countries) ranks fairly high on the Doing Business Index. Namibia and Vietnam already perform considerably worse (ranking 88th and 78th, respectively) while Ethiopia and Mozambique fall far behind, occupying ranks 132nd and 127th, respectively (World Bank Group 2014).

Decision-making with regard to industrial policy is still mostly top-down, that is, neither local governments nor non-governmental actors, such as business associations, have significant influence. Mistrust towards the private sector is often deep-seated. In Ethiopia, for example, following political conflicts related to the 2005 national elections, the government intervened in the Ethiopian Chamber of Commerce in order to change its management. Subsequently, entrepreneurs perceived the Chamber and most sector associations as organisations through which the government communicates its industrial policies rather than as independent institutions for lobbying or policy dialogue. In single-party systems, like Vietnam, decision-making power is even more centralised in the Communist Party and the central government.

As the number of large national companies tends to be fairly small, they often have direct access to high levels of government and therefore have little incentive to engage in an open and broad-based dialogue (see also Brautigam 2000, p. 15). The government in turn usually depends on these businesses, which are important contributors to the national GDP and export earnings, and is thus responsive to their interests. The interests of the large majority of small and medium-sized businesses, in contrast, are only weakly organised and represented and therefore not capable of effecting a more open and inclusive public–private dialogue.

Moreover, all governments in our sample of countries have established clear limits to economic liberalisation. First, they are unwilling to relax direct control of 'strategic' or sensitive industries, such as telecommunications, mining, energy and banking. In Ethiopia, the government's unwillingness to soften control of telecommunications and banking is the main obstacle for its WTO accession. Even in Tunisia – together with Vietnam the most competitive country of the sample – many enterprises remain under state control, and private investment in construction, infrastructure, transport, communication, culture, education, publishing and food processing is still dependent on the express authorisation of the public authorities. Vietnam's privatisation policy (called 'equitisation') is an illustrative example of the ambiguity of governments towards privatisation. On the one hand, state-owned enterprises are notoriously uncompetitive and account for the lion's share of bad loans in the banking system; on the other, authorities are often 'reluctant to promote equitisation lest they would be criticised as deviating from socialism' (Dinh 2003, p. 12). Recently, as elaborated in Section 7.5, the government privatised many small state-owned enterprises but, at the same time, created large state-owned industry groups, such as in textiles and shipbuilding, as politically controlled vehicles to push the development of the respective sectors, exploit economies of scale and establish internationally competitive brands – following the South Korean *chaebol* model. As Perkins and Vu Thanh (2009, p. 4) state, 'the relevant ministries see the main task of industrial policy as one of protecting and promoting the state owned sector'.

Second, governments are hesitant when it comes to deregulating factor markets for labour, land and capital. Especially in the case of land and labour markets, governments need to strike a careful balance between the need to abolish regulations that might hold back investments and the desire to maintain social peace and political stability. Hence there is a tendency to encourage commercial investments by offering generous land lease rights without fully privatising land markets. Likewise, governments tend to eliminate overly rigid labour regulations (which had often proven to be dysfunctional and prompted employers to bypass legal contracts) but still maintain fairly high levels of protection in the formal labour market.

As a result, hybrid regimes have emerged which rely on the private business as the driver of economic growth but only marginally involve private sector organisations in policy formulation and continue to interfere heavily in investment decisions in a number of ways – ranging from regulations to indirect control of the management and even direct ownership.

Understanding the Political Economy

The reluctance to further privatise state-owned enterprises and deregulate factor markets has social as well as political reasons, some of which cannot be easily dismissed. First, there are concerns about the *social costs* of liberal market reforms. For example, rapid privatisation typically lays off large quantities of redundant workers. In the same vein, fully liberalised land markets are likely to spur the concentration of land ownership, which may threaten the livelihood of those displaced in the process.

Second, *political considerations* play an important role – although they are usually not openly debated. All countries reviewed are still undergoing major system transitions. The political balances among different political or ethnic power groups are often still fragile, and political institutions are therefore vulnerable. Major system changes are possible when power relations change, which might challenge current elites much more fundamentally than in mature democracies and might even result in major social and political crises.

To consolidate political stability, all countries in our sample build on systems of strongly centralised decision-making (such as strong presidentialism and the party-state) and patronage (see also Section 6.6 on the characteristics and implications of limited access orders). Governments are sustained by *inner circles of power* (mostly defined by party membership, but also certain executive organs, such as top bureaucrats and/or the security apparatus) and *outer circles of clientelist networks*, which benefit particular groups in society, including those employed in state-owned or other protected enterprises (parastatals, party-affiliated or military-owned enterprises), the state bureaucracy and politically affiliated organisations, such as the SWAPO-affiliated trade union in Namibia or the Vietnamese Women's Union and Peasant Union. The civil service is often part of the patronage system, which makes it difficult to reform the system in order to make it more performance-based and customer-oriented.

Governments are often strongly interlocked with leading national enterprises. The connections may be direct, as in the case of state ownership; they may be indirect via ownership links, as in the case of party-owned enterprises, enterprises owned and managed by the army, politically controlled endowment funds, or shares of leading politicians in companies; and there may be other forms of indirect links, through informal relationships on the basis of family or kinship ties, or just traditions of favouritism. Influential entrepreneurs are often invited to assume leading positions in government. Also, business associations are quite often politically dependent on governments or dominated by a small group of powerful entrepreneurs, thus not representing sector-wide interests. Some mainly serve the purpose of transmitting messages from government to the business community, rather than lobbying for the interests of the latter.

Strategic policy decisions are to a large extent adopted within closed circles of top decision-makers, mostly members of the ruling parties who also control the upper ranks of the state bureaucracy, state-owned enterprises and parastatals. As a result, lines of accountability are often blurred, and it is difficult to disentangle when government officials influence resource allocation to pursue strategic policy targets and when they favour personal or political friends.

While these systems are politically exclusive, they often seek to enhance their political legitimacy via redistributive measures. As Erdle (2011, p. 15) states for the case of Tunisia, the government approach is to be 'inclusive on the distributive ("output") side, while remaining exclusive on the participatory ("input") side'. Namibia's Black Economic Empowerment programme and Ethiopia's strong emphasis on poverty reduction and outstanding achievements towards the Millennium Development Goals are typical examples. In Vietnam, members of the Communist Party concede that their legitimacy depends on their ability to ensure increasing living standards for the ordinary citizens and social security schemes, which primarily focus on state officials and public sector workers as a way of keeping supporters aligned. Labour market regulations that strongly favour the workforce in the formalised segment of the economy play a similarly stabilising role. In addition, legitimacy is often sought through a nationalist discourse, especially by leaders who gained authority from their successful struggle against colonial powers.

The constituencies on which governments and politico-economic elites rely vary from country to country, but the ways resources are used to favour political supporters are similar. Typically, those employed in the public sector, state-owned and other protected enterprises receive a range of benefits – high wages, subsidies, pension and insurance schemes, severance payments, public holidays, and so on – not granted to other citizens. Patronage relations may also be defined along ethnic lines, either officially (such as in the case of Black Economic Empowerment in Namibia) or informally. In Ethiopia, it is claimed that Tigray people have better access to politics than other ethnicities, although it is not easy to find evidence for these allegations.

Patronage systems are meant to secure the loyalty of key political and economic groups. The strong tendency to keep control of state-owned enterprises and policy areas that provide patronage resources – from state banks to telecom companies and pension funds – must be interpreted from a political power perspective rather than a narrow angle on economic efficiency. Such a perspective also explains why all countries are fairly risk-averse when it comes to market reforms that might provoke political resistance, such as radical labour market reforms or privatisation programmes.

8.4 NATIONAL PROJECTS OF INDUSTRIAL TRANSFORMATION AND SELECTIVE POLICIES

Throughout this book, we have stressed the importance of channelling development efforts towards a national project of industrial transformation that builds on a broad social consensus and gives direction to government entities and private investors alike. All of the countries considered have laid down their visions and goals in plans, including Five-Year Plans, Industrial Development Strategies and specific 'vision' documents that outline medium-term targets for 2020 or 2025. The case studies, however, revealed that, in practice, the willingness and capability for building consensus on a long-term national project of industrial transformation varies greatly among the five countries.

Some governments are highly committed to an agenda of industrial development and upgrading of competitive advantages and make great efforts to invest in human capital and specialised supporting institutions. Such vision and determination is clearly discernible in Ethiopia and Tunisia – even if one may not always agree with their routes to implementation. Here, governments put great emphasis on human resource development and invest considerably in industrial upgrading. Ethiopia clearly recognised the lack of competitive industries as a key obstacle for its development and therefore engaged in an exceptional programme of building up technical universities and a vocational training system, establishing a national system of quality management, and setting up technological institutes for the most important industries (such as leather; textiles; meat and dairy).[61] In addition, Ethiopia embarked on an industrial upgrading programme aimed at increasing the productivity and export performance of large and medium-sized firms. Likewise, Tunisia's leadership defined a strategy to develop manufacturing industries catering for the European market. It was the first country on the southern rim of the Mediterranean to implement a free trade zone with the EU. In parallel, Tunisia launched an industrial upgrading programme that heavily subsidised investments of manufacturing firms.

Vietnam has some elements of a national transformation strategy. The Vietnamese government has strongly supported the successful establishment of new export activities including coffee, shrimp and fish (pangasius) farming. Also, it has set up two modern science parks to facilitate the transition from labour-cost based assembly operations for export to knowledge-based activities. At the same time, the country does not have a clear roadmap for industrialisation and no concrete sector-specific action plans. 'As a result, many important policy questions remain unanswered, including the future roles of SOEs [state-owned enterprises], private firms and FDI, respectively; the choice between export orientation and import substitution under deepening integration; and the scope and extent of official support to emerging as well as declining industries' (Ohno 2009, p. 73). Likewise, the country has underestimated the necessary investments for the next stage of industrial development, such as in higher education.

The other governments mostly confine themselves to incremental reforms of the investment climate or initiating discrete investment projects without having a clear strategy for the future. Although some 'vision' documents are usually drafted by the central governments, there is no clear perspective on the *direction of change* in terms of priority sectors, untapped potentials and latent comparative advantages, and no *specific strategy* to identify next steps, specific constraints and ways to overcome them. Likewise, there is no strong, centralised and systematic process for agreeing on a national transformation project and to mobilise stakeholder support.

In Namibia, a detailed strategy for industrial development and productivity growth is even less discernible. As Rosendahl (2010) summarises in her country study, 'there is a "policy void" when it comes to policies and strategies for private sector development and industrial transformation'. While a few industrial development projects have been pursued (such as to establish industrial parks) – in most cases with rather limited success – they are not embedded in a long-term strategy. However, there are encouraging signs of recent new policy initiatives (see Section 7.3). In a similar vein, Mozambique has a (poorly implemented) strategy to develop suppliers to the large aluminium smelter MOZAL, but lacks a convincing overall strategy for economic diversification and upgrading.

The lack of an ambitious and coherent national transformation project does not, however, prevent countries from applying selective policies in favour of specific industries and groups of firms. Industrial development plans identify economic sectors (such as agro-industries) that should receive special support – even if the selection is often rather unspecific and not derived from a systematic upgrading strategy (see above); specific programmes are implemented to improve the efficiency of particular clusters or value chains (such as for the textile and garment industries); export industries are in some cases favoured over producers for domestic markets; SME programmes offer incentives depending on firm size, and so on. While the theoretical debate about the advantages and disadvantages of selective, that is, sectorally targeted (and thus market-distorting), policies still continues, policymakers in all countries have clearly made their choice in favour of selective interventions.

Grand projects – aimed at building up big state-led investments in key industries or completely new activities for which the country currently has no comparative advantage – are only exceptionally pursued. Vietnam's support for building up a national shipbuilding industry on the basis of a large state-owned conglomerate is one of the few exceptions. Instead, industrial development strategies mostly focus on incremental improvement of existing comparative advantages, such as trying to increase the value added of their agricultural products.

8.5 GREEN GROWTH AND CLIMATE CHANGE: NOT YET MAINSTREAMED

In general, objectives and measures related to promoting green growth and responding to climate change (both in terms of mitigation and adaptation) are not yet coherently incorporated in industrial policies. As we have argued above (see Section 6.5), climate change will have an important influence on the direction of structural change in developing countries. First, there will be mounting global pressure to reduce the consumption of fossil fuels and change the energy mix in favour of renewable sources. Reduced demand will compel oil and gas exporting countries in particular to diversify their economies. Second, countries need to adapt production systems to changing climate conditions. In agriculture, crop varieties and technologies need to be adapted to different temperature and rainfall patterns; for instance, new irrigation systems may be needed where rainfalls become less regular. Third, carbon taxes and carbon pricing policies will increasingly affect production costs. Even if developing countries do not tax energy consumption themselves and do not participate in emissions trading systems, they will be affected by policy changes in industrialised countries. The emergence of carbon markets is already stimulating investments in new energy sources in developing countries. Also, the Kyoto Protocol allows industrialised countries to meet part of their commitments by developing CDM emission reduction projects in developing countries. Furthermore, carbon taxes and markets in the North will affect the relative competitiveness of economic activities that depend on energy and carbon prices, such as long-distance tourism.

These new opportunities and risks are of course perceived in the five countries of our sample. In the Maghreb countries, large European industry initiatives are underway to exploit solar and wind energy with a view to providing much of Europe's energy from the North African desert.[62] Sub-Saharan Africa is starting to receive major investments in biofuel projects. At the same time, climate-related risks increasingly receive public attention; for example, the negative impacts of rising sea levels are expected to threaten Vietnam's thriving aquaculture in coastal areas.

In most countries, however, these insights are not yet adequately reflected in industrial development strategies. On the one hand, pricing policies are not yet adapted in a way to internalise environmental costs. Energy costs in particular remain heavily subsidised, reflecting the fact that universal access to energy is much higher on the political agenda than emissions reduction (as demonstrated by Vidican 2014 for the Middle East and North African countries). At the same time, subsidies for renewable energy are mainly financed from international sources, such as the Global Environment Facility.

On the other hand, there are only a few activities to systematically explore new opportunities related to the international climate agenda and to assess the related economic risks. Although some of the countries have published official documents outlining their climate change policies – such as Nationally Appropriate Mitigation Action (NAMA) and National Adaptation Programme of Action (NAPA) plans or reports to the UN Framework Convention on Climate Change – these are not yet integral parts of the economic planning systems. Hence they are neither mainstreamed in national policies nor translated into concrete roadmaps for implementation (see Ellis, Baker and Lemma 2009).

Only a few initiatives have been identified that aim to exploit the opportunities for diversification related to climate change. Tunisia has drafted a 'Solar Plan' comprising numerous projects related to renewable energies and energy efficiency. These cover solar energy, wind energy, energy efficiency, electric interconnection with Italy and manufacture of photovoltaic solar panels. Whether the country will be content to attract foreign investment in renewables or whether it will proactively try to build up domestic technological capabilities is not yet clear.

8.6 PLANNING VS SEARCHING

An overall impression is that industrial development plans and pro-grammes are not very creative in identifying opportunities for upgrading and diversification – neither in the choice of priority sectors nor in the way policies are designed.

With regard to *choice of priority sectors*, most priorities are derived from the desire to develop linkages from existing industries or resource bases. Most policies aim to increase *forward linkages*. In Namibia, industrialisation through beneficiation of raw materials is the core of industrial policy. The country provides incentives for the beneficiation of diamonds, semi-precious stones and minerals and encourages meat and fish processing; for instance, it obligated the Namdeb Diamond Corpor-ation to process a certain share of its high-quality diamonds locally, thereby giving rise to the establishment of several cutting and polishing companies in Namibia. Mozambique taxes raw cashew exporters to encourage investments in domestic processing industries. Ethiopia has created technology institutes for leather processing and meat and dairy industries. In the leather industry, the country imposed a new tariff on exports of raw hides and skins in order to force exporters to add value locally. With regard to *backward linkages*, most countries of the sample have fairly strong garment industries and support the establishment of textile and yarn industries in order to complement the value chain within their own national boundaries.

This focus reflects a widely held assumption that the domestic value chains should be as complete as possible. This, however, need not always be the case. In some cases it may be better to concentrate on upgrading options that are more in line with existing comparative advantages than to try building up complementary value chain functions for which there are no comparative advantages. In the garment and textile industry, for example, it may be better to increase added value by offering full package supply, reducing the time to market, or targeting fashion markets *within the garment industry* and to import textiles, yarns and accessories. Attempts to produce textiles in small countries have often failed as these industries are highly capital-intensive and require large economies of scale and scope. For example, Namibia's only textile company had to shut down for lack of competitiveness. Even for Vietnam, where garment assembly is the number one export activity, analysts are highly sceptical about whether the government strategy of backward integration (driven mainly by the large state-owned textile and garment conglomerate Vinatex) can be successful in an open economy and given the proximity to China. Goto (2007) suggests focusing on product and process upgrading within the garment industry rather than vertical integration. In the case of leather, Ethiopia's policy to tax exports of raw hides and skins led to an export drop that could not yet be compensated for by increases in exports of *processed* leather.

This is not an argument against incentives for vertical integration; rather, governments need to assess carefully whether the new activities they want to induce are viable in terms of factor endowment, scale economies and complementary assets. However, we did not come across many systematic appraisals of this type. Although it is not always easy to recapitulate how priority sectors were chosen, not many examples of detailed master plans for specific industries are based on thorough research and national consultations.

While systematic analytical work supported by stakeholder consultation is one way to identify upgrading opportunities, governments should also encourage decentralised entrepreneurial search processes and localised policy experiments (for the latter see Section 7.5 on Vietnam). In fact, we identified a few successful cases of such policies, such as the promotion of indigenous plant products for export in Namibia. In 1999, the government provided several million Namibian dollars for research and promotion on indigenous plant products, which indirectly led to the formation of an Indigenous Plant Task Team (IPTT), a multi-stakeholder coordinating body mainly driven by non-governmental organisations (NGOs) and donors. The IPTT promotes the search for new products that have an export market and can be cultivated in a socially inclusive way. The IPTT has successfully developed markets for high-value plants for the cosmetics and pharmaceutical industries.

Another example is the Ethiopian cut flower industry. As described in Section 7.1, the initiative to export flowers was fully private sector driven. The government, however, was highly supportive in providing tax incentives, permitting low-cost access to suitable land, negotiating competitive freight tariffs with the national airline and establishing a National Horticulture Development Agency to respond to industry needs. Hence the government supported a comparative advantage where it had spontaneously emerged, rather than defining a priority area and creating support structures in a top-down manner.

Regarding the way programmes are designed, we identified a certain neglect of instruments aiming to unleash entrepreneurial creativity and encourage experimentation. Typically, governments offer some sort of support to make *established firms* more competitive, including highly subsidised consultancy services aimed at improving process organisation at the factory level. Beneficiaries are typically selected on the basis of company characteristics (size, subsector, etc.) rather than an assessment of the viability of their investment projects. Furthermore, all countries have a range of instruments to offer physical infrastructure – such as industrial parks, business incubators and individual factory buildings. In contrast, there are not many programmes that encourage the search for new market opportunities and business models. While most countries have some technology centres that aim to encourage the use of innovative technologies, their outreach is very limited.

Above, we argued that latecomer countries typically have too few entrepreneurs able to detect new markets or business models (even if they are 'new to the country' rather than 'new to the world' innovations) and thereby create new opportunities for followers. One reason is that potential entrepreneurs are often locked into information-scarce environments (e.g. characterised by low educational attainment, few demanding customers and lack of entrepreneurial role models); also, innovations that are only 'new to the country' do not benefit from intellectual property protection, even though developing them may be costly for the local pioneer. Hence, there are good reasons to encourage the search for new markets and business models. Appropriate tools range from time-bound subsidies for non-traditional exports to business plan competitions, venture capital funds, coaching of innovative start-up companies, curricula that focus on entrepreneurship development in vocational training and universities, incentives to lure the diaspora into new business activities, and so on. Such tools, however, are rarely used in the five countries.

8.7 ENSURING EFFECTIVE POLICY IMPLEMENTATION

Government failure stems either from lacking technical and institutional capabilities or political unwillingness to adopt coherent and rational industrial policies (see sections 5.2 and 5.3). As far as capabilities are concerned, many basic principles of good industrial policy are well known (see Section 5.4) and can thus be learned. Government agencies can be trained – in the case of low- and lower-middle income countries possibly with the help of donors – to practise such principles. Moreover, systematic learning routines can be built into these agencies. It should also be recalled that governments may choose among more and less sophisticated policy instruments (see Table 5.1). Thus agencies can start with policies that are simple and imply little risk and gradually move towards more differentiated approaches or riskier interventions as they increase their management capabilities.

It is much more difficult to increase policy effectiveness when the core of the problem is lack of political willingness, such as when lobby groups gain special treatment and politicians depend on backing from interest groups. It is obviously hard to introduce checks and balances in any political system when they jeopardise the interests of firmly established rent-seeking groups. However, change is possible. Some of the countries reviewed in Chapter 7 (such as Vietnam and Ethiopia) evolved from socialist planning to market economies and now implement modern competitiveness-enhancing policies. Change may come from different sources, and it may be radical or incremental.

Some countries, such as many developing countries that switched from socialist planning to market economies, underwent *radical* system transitions. Radical changes were also introduced during the structural adjustment programmes of the 1980s and 1990s, triggered by a combination of unsustainable fiscal and trade deficits and external pressure. In both cases, the previously pursued industrial policy packages were largely discredited.

But even if countries do not experience major system transitions and crises, *gradual* changes may be introduced by development-oriented political leaders, often with support from development agencies. As Ohno (2009) shows, the likelihood of success increases greatly with a visionary political leadership that ensures that reforms are implemented against the resistance of interest groups that benefit from the status quo. Many countries have embarked on civil service reform programmes that reform the incentive structure of public services in order to make them more effective and transparent and hold service providers accountable. Incremental improvement at the level of meso-institutions and specific policies and instruments, in turn, *may*, in some cases, have a positive impact on the underlying politics (Bräutigam 2000, pp. 5 f.) because:

- if economic institutions are improved, such as by introducing compulsory performance measurement of economic programmes or by institutionalising feedback mechanisms from the target group back to public service providers, the cost of bad policies becomes more transparent, which may mobilise the business community, civil society and reform groups within the government to sustain and deepen reforms;

- if a considerable number of indigenous businesses start to grow as a result of reforms, the constituency for these reforms may grow; and
- more exchange with private sector organisations and professional service providers is likely to improve the government's understanding of the importance of a growing private sector and the need for effective industrial policies.

Decisions regarding industrial policy should thus take the possibility of *policy learning* into account. Hence industrial policies should not be easily dismissed on the grounds of weak *present* industrial policy management capabilities. However, learning routines should be built into the policy process.

In Section 5.4, we summarised principles of successful industrial policy implementation. While our empirical studies indicate that in all five countries reviewed industrial policy processes deviate strongly from these good practices, there are notable differences among countries. This is what one would have expected from the countries' different ranking on governance indicators. Table 8.2 shows how the five countries rank on selected indicators related to industrial policy, including measures of government effectiveness and steering capability, transparency of policy-making, favouritism and corruption, judicial independence, and the like. Overall, in terms of government effectiveness, the data paint a fairly favourable picture for Namibia and Tunisia and a very unfavourable one for Mozambique.

For the particular field of *industrial policy*, however, a more differentiated picture emerges, which in some cases, diverges from our own country assessment. For instance, Namibia, which ranks first with regard to 'government effectiveness' and 'steering capability', in fact revealed lesser capabilities for managing industrial policy processes than lower-ranking Ethiopia. This holds for several dimensions of *industrial policy management capability*, including the capabilities to identify opportunities for industrial development and define incremental steps towards their achievement; to build consensus around this strategy; and to deliver services cost-effectively. As we have seen, Ethiopia has been able to launch a highly ambitious national transformation project to make the economy competitive, involving big investments in export-related infrastructure, higher education, vocational training, technology institutes and firm-level programmes. Namibia and Mozambique, in contrast, both lack comprehensive industrial development strategies.[63] It should be noted, however, that we also encountered significant differences in terms of industrial policy effectiveness among sectors or policy areas *within* countries.

Let us now look at several dimensions of policy implementation in detail.

Overall implementing capacity of the state bureaucracy. Across the five countries, considerable differences exist with regard to the attitude and effectiveness of the national bureaucracies. Those countries that effectively manage their industrial policies invested in their central state bureaucracy at an early state. In Tunisia, for example, the central state bureaucracy had already been created by the Husaynid reformers in the 19th century and was further strengthened by the French colonial authorities. Likewise, Ethiopia started relatively early to build sovereign national institutions. Already in 1909, Emperor Menelik II appointed nine ministers and started to build up a modern civil service (Taffesse 2008, p. 373), thereby giving the country an advantage vis-à-vis many other sub-Saharan countries. Vietnam's administration also builds on well-educated administrative cadres, which enables the government to provide fairly good public services covering the whole national territory. For example, the availability of extension services for coffee farming and aquaculture was decisive for the rapid take-off of these activities.

Checks and balances. Compared to mature democracies, policies in all five countries are subjected to few democratic checks and balances, as is reflected in their low scores, with the exception of Namibia, on the 'voice and accountability' indicator (which measures the extent to which citizens are able to participate in selecting their government, enjoy freedom of expression, freedom of association, and free media). For instance, Ethiopia has passed a law that restricts the activities of NGOs and independent research centres, thereby further reducing opportunities to disclose incidences of corruption or highlight risks involved in particular institutional arrangements. Moreover, there is very little monitoring and evaluation of industrial policies, and virtually no independent third party monitoring (except for some donor-financed programmes). Implementing agencies generally report to ministries, but reporting is mainly limited to *activities* and does not provide much information on *outcomes* or even *impact*. Vietnam and Ethiopia stand out for their quite detailed Five-Year Plans, which define detailed policy targets and indicators and are subjected to critical mid-term reviews. Even these reports, however, are biased towards *activities*.

Evidence-based policymaking. As impact monitoring is weak, there is little hard evidence of policy effectiveness on which policymakers can build. Also, we found very few signs of systematic reflection on policies.

Table 8.2 Selected governance indicators related to industrial policy

Indicator	What it measures	Range of scores	Ethiopia	Mozambique	Namibia	Tunisia	Vietnam
Government effectiveness (WGI)	Quality of public services, quality of civil service and degree of its independence from political pressures; quality of policy formulation and implementation; credibility of government's commitment to such policies	-2.5 (low) to 2.5 (high)	-0.5	-0.7	0.2	0.0	-0.3
Voice and accountability (WGI)	Extent to which country's citizens are able to participate in selecting their government; freedom of expression; freedom of association; free media	-2.5 (low) to 2.5 (high)	-1.3	-0.3	0.4	-0.1	-1.3
Steering Capability (BTI)	How far political leadership sets and maintains strategic priorities, how effective it is in implementing reform programmes, how flexible and innovative it is to learn from past experiences	1 (low) to 10 (high)	4.3	6.3	7.3	5	5
Consensus building (BTI)	Ability of political leadership to establish a broad consensus on reform with other actors in society without sacrificing its reform goals	1 (low) to 10 (high)	2.8	4.8	7	4.6	4.4
Fundamentals of market-based competition (BTI)	Freedom of pricing; currency convertibility; freedom to participate in the market and set up a business; free use and transfer of profits; non-discrimination among various forms of companies and sizes of businesses	1 (low) to 10 (high)	3	4	7	6	4
Safeguards against monopolies & cartels (BTI)	Extent of existing safeguards to prevent the development of economic monopolies and cartels	1 (low) to 10 (high)	3	2	6	5	6

Rule of law (BTI)	Extent to which state powers check and balance each other and ensure civil rights. Includes separation of powers; independence of the judiciary; penalties for officeholders who abuse their powers	1 (low) to 10 (high)	3	4.5	7.3	5	2.5
Corruption Perception Index (CPI)	Overall extent of corruption (frequency and/or size of bribes) in the public and political sectors.	1 (low) to 10 (high)	3.3	3.1	4.9	4	3.1
Favouritism in decisions of government officials (GCI)	Extent to which government officials, when deciding upon policies and contracts, ensure that well-connected firms and individuals are not favoured	1 (low) to 7 (high)	2.8	2.5	2.9	3.2	3
Transparency of government policymaking (GCI)	Extent to which firms are usually informed by government of changes in policies and regulations affecting their industry	1 (low) to 7 (high)	3.3	3.6	3.9	3.8	3.5
Judicial independence (GCI)	Extent to which judiciary is independent from political influences of members of government, citizens or firms	1 (low) to 7 (high)	2.9	2.5	4.7	3.6	3.4
Wastefulness of government spending (GCI)	Extent to which the composition of public spending efficiently provides necessary goods and services not provided by the market	1 (low) to 7 (high)	3.4	2.7	3.2	3.3	2.9
Legal enforcement of contracts (DBI)	Procedures, time and cost to resolve a commercial dispute	1 (high) to 181 (low)	44	145	69	78	46

Sources: World Bank (2013b); Bertelsmann Stiftung (2014); Transparency International (2014); WEF (2014); World Bank Group (2014).

Although our cases studies revealed a range of different *policy styles* even within countries – for example Ethiopia's sector policy for leather is government-driven, whereas the policy for the flower industry is industry-led – these cases are not compared with a view to policy learning. With the exception of Vietnam, where several think tanks closely collaborate with policymakers,[64] the countries have no policy think tanks that are regularly invited to review policies and inform policymaking.

Quality of service provision. Business development services – such as trade and investment promotion; consultancies for process organisation, technology development or marketing; lab testing services; and certification of products and processes – are mainly provided by state agencies, which are fully subjected to the rules of public administration. Hence, they find it difficult to operate in a business-like manner, that is, to 'speak the language' of business people and respond rapidly to their needs, which explains the poor performance of many government institutions, including the EPZs in Namibia and Ethiopia's Investment Promotion Agency. None of the countries systematically delegates such services to private service providers or develops semi-autonomous economic promotion agencies. Moreover, services are often highly, or even fully, subsidised, leading to substantial deadweight effects.

Significant subsidies are offered by the Industry Upgrading Programmes in Tunisia – including to fairly large enterprises – and the factory benchmarking programme in Ethiopia. However, exit strategies for these subsidies are often not well defined. While some international donors undertake efforts to trigger markets for private service providers, governments mostly consider these services a state responsibility.[65] In other cases, particularly where many foreign investors call for effective responses, fairly flexible institutional arrangements have been established. For instance, the Investment Promotion Agency in Ho Chi Minh City, Vietnam, and Ethiopia's Horticulture Development Agency have a relatively high degree of autonomy in responding to the needs of their customers.

Policy coordination. Industrial policies are generally not well coordinated with other related policies, in particular SME policies, investment promotion and trade policies, science and technology policies, education and training policies, and infrastructure development and agricultural policies. The ministries in charge tend to draft stand-alone policy documents and establish incentive systems that are not harmonised with the rest. Although the lack of policy coordination is frequently recognised by governments, there are obviously political reasons that work against policy harmonisation; for instance, ministries are assigned to different political factions in the government. This policy fragmentation exacerbates the difficulty to agree on a national transformation project.

NOTES

59. See also Altenburg (2000) for an overview of best practice linkage policies.
60. http://data.worldbank.org/data-catalog/privatization-database (accessed 15 May 2015).
61. In only four years, the number of students in undergraduate programmes of public universities more than doubled, reaching more than 250,000 in 2009. In parallel, a technical and vocational training system was established, enrolling 815,000 students in 2010 and aiming at 1,130,000 in 2015 (Trah et al. 2010).
62. See Desertec and Erdle (2010) (http://www.desertec.org/de?gclid=CLnn_4KK2KUCFQa GDgod42HajQ, accessed 6 May 2015). However, at the time of writing the future of the Desertec project is highly doubtful as the consortium of business players seems to be falling apart.
63. In Mozambique, efforts to create a class of national entrepreneurs or capitalists by offering privatised assets to politically connected persons and supporting them with subsidised credits largely failed, and large parts of the credits were never paid back (Hanlon and Smart 2008, p. 106). Likewise, programmes to support SMEs – including the *Fundo de Fomento a Pequena Industria* and the *Instituto de Desenvolvimento da Industria Local* – failed to achieve any discernible impact and are now being closed down. Namibia's programme to promote investments in EPZ is another example of policy failure. To date, EPZ employ only about 5,000 workers (20 per cent of the envisaged target) and only have minimal impact in terms of technology transfer and skill development (Rosendahl 2010).
64. These include the Central Institute for Economic Management (CIEM), the National Institute for Science and Technology Policy and Strategic Studies (NISTPASS) and the Institute for Industry Policy and Strategy (IPSI).
65. For example, GTZ dropped its activities to develop partly private business development services for lack of interest on the Ethiopian side.

9. Rethinking industrial policy in developing countries

9.1 FAILING MARKETS AND WEAK STATES: STRIKING THE RIGHT BALANCE

Throughout our analysis, we have highlighted a central dilemma of industrial policymaking in most developing countries. On the one hand, there are good reasons to cast doubt on many governments' ability to manage industrial policies effectively. Financial and administrative resources are scarce, and the democratic institutions that hold governments accountable are often rather weak. Many scholars therefore hold that countries at early levels of institutional development should avoid selective policies and focus instead on reforming the overall investment climate. Even Lall (2004, p. 101), a strong supporter of industrial policy, argues that 'in general, the lower the capabilities, accountability and commitment of the government the lower the degree of selectivity it can safely be entrusted with'.

On the other hand, market failure is pervasive, especially in poor countries where the development of entrepreneurship and market institutions is relatively recent. In Chapter 2, we argued that industrial policy involves far more than correcting market failures and externalities, that it is essentially about supporting societal goals and hence must be framed in a genuinely normative perspective. As we also stressed, this does not, however, detract from the relevance of market failures as a determinant of industrial policy and as one of the building blocks of its *raison d'être*. In Box 9.1, we thus recall the most important market failures and illustrate what they imply specifically in poor countries that are caught in poverty traps, with mutually reinforcing constraints on the supply and the demand side. In many poor countries, 'a viable capitalist class has not yet emerged' (Khan 2004, p. 182). The main part of the private sector consists of micro and small entrepreneurs who do not meet the most basic preconditions for confronting international competitors – in terms of overall education, technical and managerial skills, market information, finance, mobility, and so on. Moreover, market transactions are embedded in manifold non-market customs and rules that hamper competitiveness-based resource allocation. For all these reasons, the productivity gap separating today's developing countries from the top industrial countries is much larger than the gap that the now developed industrial latecomers had to overcome in the 19th century to catch up with Britain and other frontrunners (Chang 2003, p. 27).

BOX 9.1 THE MOST IMPORTANT MARKET FAILURES IN POOR COUNTRIES

Informational externalities arise because information about new markets and viable business ideas are not freely available, and those who bear the risks of exploring new products and markets are unable to fully appropriate the benefits. In low- and lower-middle-income countries, we can assume that the relevant information is even harder to come by than it is in rich countries. It is quite clear that there are fewer and less reliable statistics and commercial providers of market analysis. Even if entrepreneurs have access to certain *codified* information, they mostly operate in less diversified social environments, where they are rarely able to experience how other entrepreneurs have developed innovative business models, such as how they have anticipated trends, networked with related entrepreneurs, observed the success and failure of similar product launches, tested options, received feedback from customers, and so on. Such tacit knowledge is key to innovative entrepreneurship, and it requires embeddedness in a learning environment with very dense information flows, which is why large global cities are entrepreneurial hotspots. The environment in poor countries tends to be information-scarce, with fewer entrepreneurial role models, less product diversity, less-demanding customers, fewer specialised business media, and so on, especially for micro and small enterprises and rural environments.

A similar argument applies for *dynamic scale economies* and *knowledge spillovers*. When economic structures are hardly diversified and the policy environment discourages experimenting with new business ideas, firms are more likely to miss out on future competitive advantages.

Coordination failure is also extremely relevant for latecomer development and is likely to occur when investment projects require simultaneous investments in related activities to become viable. Take the example of a country with promising locational and agro-ecological conditions for horticulture exports. Even if a country offers an excellent investment climate and investors recognise its potential, it will typically start off with a lack of irrigation; bad roads; no cooling chain facilities in place; no high-quality inputs and specialised technical support services available; inefficient port and airport facilities; high freight rates due to low trade volumes; and so on. Developing all the necessary infrastructure facilities and services simultaneously far exceeds the possibilities of most individual investors. Unless a major coordinated effort is organised to develop complementary assets – either by a very big corporate investor or an ambitious

developmental state – the potential for horticultural exports will remain unexploited. In addition, latecomer countries face competition from early movers
who have, over decades, gradually built the necessary cluster synergies and
therefore benefit from economies of specialisation and scale.

Source: Authors.

Despite the limitations of the public sector, it is therefore hard to imagine
ways to unleash a virtuous circle of productivity development without a
government that builds consensus on a national project of industrial
transformation, encourages investment in human capital, accelerates the
emergence of an entrepreneurial class, builds trust and helps to organise
producers, and reforms a range of other formal and informal institutions.
At early stages of development, the size of the productivity gap between
rich and poor countries, the lack of entrepreneurial competences and
manifold market failures call for a particularly interventionist role of
industrial policy. As countries move up the income ladder, more and
more government functions can, and should, be transferred to market
actors.

At early stages of latecomer development, rising entry barriers and
increased competition may easily overburden the learning capacity of
domestic firms and thus frustrate the incipient processes of entrepreneurship development. To avoid this outcome and exploit the opportunities of open markets, local externalities, such as specialised
infrastructure and complementary financial and business development
services, need to be strengthened. Yet, this is where we find a classic case
of coordination failure. Commercial providers are unlikely to take the
risk of investing in specialised facilities as long as demand for them is
not well established, and vice versa. Strong collective efforts may be
required to develop local cluster synergies at the necessary scale before
the respective activity takes off.

It should also be noted that anticipating the broad directions of
structural change is not as difficult and risky for developing economies as
it is in advanced economies. Critics of industrial policy rightly argue that
bureaucrats are unlikely to anticipate new market opportunities better
than entrepreneurs (Pack and Saggi 2006), especially with regard to
cutting-edge, 'new to the world' innovations. In poor developing countries, however, the main challenge of structural change is not to push the
technological frontier but to adopt patterns of specialisation already well
established elsewhere. For instance, it is obvious that traditional retail
systems are increasingly being replaced by global retail chains; as a
result, there is a need for economies of scale and increasing quality and

reliability standards on the part of all their suppliers. In such a situation, governments can adopt selective measures that help to bring about the necessary changes to the national retail system – such as by regulating the market entry of foreign chains to encourage supplier development and franchise systems, improve quality assurance among potential suppliers, and so on. In general terms, the development of comparative advantages is incremental and based on initial factor conditions, which limits the range of available options. For instance, in a country with appropriate agro-ecological conditions and proximity to major OECD markets, it is not very risky to adopt selective policies in favour of horticultural production.

On balance, it is plausible to assume that the risks of political capture, waste of scarce public resources, and market distortion are greater in less developed political and administrative systems; also, it clearly becomes more and more difficult for latecomers to produce tradable goods (whether for exports or domestic consumption) in the presence of enormous international asymmetries in productivity, scales, knowledge and other externalities. Collective action, including selective promotional activities for particularly promising sectors, is needed to cope with this latecomer challenge. The question is not whether developing countries should apply industrial policies or not, but what can be done to improve their effectiveness and avoid political capture. This problem, however, is anything but trivial.

9.2   WAYS FORWARD: KEY ELEMENTS OF FUTURE INDUSTRIAL POLICY

It is now widely accepted that the countries that managed to catch up with the old industrialised and high-income countries are the ones whose governments proactively promoted structural change, encouraging the search for new business models and markets, and channelling resources into promising and socially desirable new activities. Evidence of failed industrial policy experiments, however, is also abundant. Hence, while market failure justifies public intervention in markets in principle, inappropriate policies may have worse results than non-intervention. The question is thus not whether industrial policies should be adopted or not, but how they can be implemented more effectively – an especially challenging question for latecomer economies, where market failure is particularly common and government action is required to form even the most basic market institutions, such as creating a national entrepreneurial class and encouraging the formation of business associations. At the same time, the effectiveness of the state is typically low, and the risks of political capture are considerable as the political systems often build on favouritism and lack political checks and balances.

Our study of industrial policy in selected low- and middle-income countries revealed examples of success and failure. It confirmed that industrial policies may be implemented successfully even in low-income countries with weak institutions, but it also identified many programmes that failed to generate the desired outcome or at least raised doubts about cost-effectiveness. Generally, most policies deviated considerably from the good practice principles described in Section 5.4. Both the positive and negative observations, however, allow us to extract seven key **lessons** for industrial policy.

First, the political leaders must have the firm will to pursue a **national project of productive transformation** aimed at diversifying their economies and developing new competitive advantages in higher-value activities. As such activities usually require a range of assets unavailable in poor countries, they are unlikely to emerge spontaneously without a coordinating agent (or they only materialise slowly compared to international competitors who pursue a proactive strategy). Governments must therefore provide direction to, and coordinate, competent ministries and implementing agencies, public and private actors, central and local governments as well as the support of international donors.

Second, these transformation projects need to **build on existing or anticipated comparative advantages and define upgrading pathways** that are manageable for the relevant national actors. Overly ambitious targets may overestimate the learning capacity of the domestic private sector – and/or the supporting institutions – and thus waste government resources. It should be noted, however, that the opposite of industrial policy – wholesale liberalisation – may also overburden domestic entrepreneurs, with the effect that importers and foreign investors destroy the embryonic technological capabilities that exist. The key is to increase competition and apply non-market incentives in a way that induces the private sector to upgrade without overstraining its capacities and without creating unproductive rents.

Third, the transformation process needs to **balance economic, social and environmental objectives**. A lopsided focus on purely economic growth targets without due regard to their distributional implications and their impact on environmental assets and boundaries will generate opposition from civil society and affected population groups and undermine its own long-term sustainability.

Specifically, low-income countries are typically characterised by deep and even widening productivity gaps. The lack of productive integration of large parts of the workforce perpetuates poverty and forgoes opportunities for inter-firm specialisation that would make the whole economy more competitive. Unless productive integration is proactively supported, competition on an uneven playing field typically crowds out large numbers of less efficient producers and destroys traditional jobs without being able to create a comparable number of employment opportunities in the emerging, more efficient activities. The desirable effect of creative destruction then tips over, leading to a detrimental increase of necessity entrepreneurship and informality. Liberalisation must therefore go hand in hand with targeted and temporary protection as well as proactive policies for knowledge transfer and capacity building. Again, the challenge is to encourage productivity growth at a pace that allows for integration of local producer groups and protection of the most vulnerable groups.

Likewise, environmental sustainability needs to be built into industrial development strategies and mainstreamed in the implementation process. As the world will increasingly shift towards a low-carbon economy, even countries with low per capita emissions will be affected. Governments are therefore well advised to anticipate these changes, to avoid being locked into unsustainable techno-institutional systems and to try to exploit early mover advantages.

Fourth, optimal upgrading pathways – in terms of productivity increases, social inclusion and environmental sustainability – can only be identified if industrial policy is devised as a **collaborative process of experimental learning**, involving stakeholders and ensuring feedback loops between planning, implementation and impact measurement. Policies need to be agreed upon in a collaborative manner, inviting the private sector, public entities and civil service organisations to bring in their expertise. Public funds should usually be matched with private contributions to make sure that beneficiaries assume ownership for the respective programmes. Implementing agencies should operate in a business-like, customer-oriented manner, and hence be authorised to recruit and promote personnel based on performance criteria. Service providers, both public and private, should be subject to as much competition as possible, and there should be mechanisms for customers to hold them accountable. Performance should be measured regularly and independently, and results should be fed back into the process of policy formulation in order to adapt policies. To safeguard impartiality, the different roles of government – policy formulation, financing, implementation, evaluation, and so on – need to be unbundled. Independent policy think tanks may further ensure that policy decisions are evidence-based and rent-seeking behaviour is avoided.

Fifth, the focus of industrial policy should shift from promoting established firms in traditional industries to **supporting innovative ideas and encouraging experimentation**. There is a strong case for subsidising the search costs of innovators, because testing a new business concept involves costs and risks of failure. When the concept is successful, however, competitors will usually copy it and thus dissipate the rents that can be obtained from the business innovation. Due to this non-appropriability, market-enhancing entrepreneurship will typically be undersupplied – unless governments encourage the search process. This problem is particularly severe in poor countries, where information diffuses slowly – for instance, because entrepreneurs lack access to demanding export or urban markets where new niche markets usually emerge, and because some countries have institutional disincentives for risk-taking entrepreneurs.

Sixth, the **strengthening of linkages** between firms and segments of the business community is crucial. Poor developing countries are typic-ally characterised by segmented enterprise structures, with few linkages between different groups of enterprises, such as foreign-invested firms, large national firms, and micro and small firms. Large productivity gaps impede integration of micro and small firms in specialised business networks. In order to exploit economies of specialisation and stimulate knowledge spillovers, efforts are needed to integrate these groups through supplier development programmes, incentives for technology transfer, encouragement of joint ventures, franchising arrangements, and the like.

Seventh, **international and regional trade and investment links** should be promoted and gradually increased. In global competition, economies of scale become more and more important. This tends to reduce the competitiveness of firms operating in small national markets. Creating larger markets is therefore particularly important for firms in many low- and middle-income countries. Regional economic integration is one way of improving trade and investment opportunities in an environment that is often not as challenging as the world market. Regional integration calls for a greater emphasis on common infrastruc-ture projects and regulatory reforms aimed at reducing the costs of trading across borders. Insertion of producers from developing countries in value chains governed by global lead firms can be another promising option. If properly managed, it allows domestic firms to adopt product and process innovations, access large markets and thereby overcome the limitations of small-scale production.

In conclusion, developing countries – in particular those at early stages of economic development – need to pursue active industrial policies to surmount the many disadvantages of latecomer development.

If governments bear the above lessons in mind, they can significantly accelerate upgrading and diversification of their economies. Beyond these general lessons, a good deal of trial-and-error learning is needed to find the most appropriate industrialisation pathway for each particular country. Some countries have embarked on promising, albeit different, pathways despite relatively low levels of government effectiveness and weak political checks and balances. More research is needed to fully understand the political economy behind these processes, that is, what motivates political leaders or growth coalitions to embark on national projects of transformation and what explains their different willingness and ability to manage the risks of political capture.

In the ultimate analysis, the choice open to policymakers is between passively reacting to changing external realities on the one hand and proactively setting in motion a goal-based political management process on the other. To be sure, in the face of uncertainty, experimentation and uncharted policy territory, the latter is no guarantee for *not* making mistakes along the way. But then, as James Joyce has pointed out, mistakes can turn into portals of discovery.

References

Abrami, R., E. Malesky and Y. Zheng (2008), 'Accountability and inequality in single-party regimes: a comparative analysis of Vietnam and China', Cambridge, MA: Harvard Business School, HBS Working Paper 08-099.

Achy, L. (2011), 'Tunisia's economy one year after the jasmine resolution', Carnegie Middle East Center, available at http://carnegie-mec.org/2011/12/27/tunisia-s-economy-one-year-after-jasmine-revolution (accessed 16 January 2015).

AfDB (2014), 'Namibia: country strategy paper 2014–2018', Tunis: African Development Bank, available at http://www.afdb.org/fileadmin/uploads/afdb/Documents/Project-and-Operations/2014-2018_-_Namibia_Country_Strategy_Paper.pdf (accessed 16 January 2015).

AfDB (2014a), 'Tunisia: interim country strategy paper 2014–2015', Tunis: African Development Bank, available at http://www.afdb.org/fileadmin/uploads/afdb/Documents/Project-and-Operations/2014-2015_-_Tunisia_Interim_Country_Strategy_Paper.pdf (accessed 16 January 2015).

AfDB, OECD and UNDP (2014), *African Economic Outlook 2014: global value chains and Africa's industrialization*, Tunis: African Development Bank, Paris: Organisation for Economic Co-operation and Development, New York: United Nations Development Programme.

Agence Francaise de Développement and The World Bank (2014), *Youth employment in Sub-Saharan Africa*, Washington, DC: World Bank.

Aiginger, K. (2007), 'Industrial policy: a dying breed or a re-emerging phoenix', *Journal of Industry, Competition and Trade*, **7**, pp. 297–323.

Aldrick, P. (2011), 'Davos WEF 2011: wealth inequality is the "most serious challenge for the world"', *The Telegraph*, 26 January.

Altenburg, T. (1998), 'Malaysia: Industriepolitik zwischen Asienkrise und politischer Patronage', Bonn: Friedrich Ebert Foundation, FES-Analyse.

Altenburg, T. (2000), 'Linkages and spillovers between transnational corporations and small and medium sized enterprises in developing countries: opportunities and policies', in UNCTAD (ed.), *TNC-SME linkages for development: issues – experiences – best practices*, New

York and Geneva: United Nations Conference on Trade and Development, pp. 3–61.

Altenburg, T. (2010), 'Industrial policy in Ethiopia', Bonn: Deutsches Institut für Entwicklungspolitik/German Development Institute (DIE), Discussion Paper.

Altenburg, T. (2013), 'Can industrial policy work under neopatrimonial rule?', Helsinki: United Nations University World Institute for Development Economics Research (UNU/WIDER), Working Paper 41.

Altenburg, T. et al. (2008), 'Industrial policy – a key element of the social and ecological market economy', in C. Kuesel, U. Maenner and R. Meissner (eds), *The social and ecological market economy – a model for Asian development?* Eschborn, Germany: Deutsche Gesellschaft für Technische Zusammenarbeit (GTZ), pp. 134–53.

Altenburg, T. and U. Eckhardt (2006), *Productivity enhancement and equitable development: challenges for SME development*, Vienna: United Nations Industrial Development Organization.

Altenburg, T. and E. Melia (2014), 'Kick-starting industrial transformation in Sub-Saharan Africa', in J.M. Salazar-Xirinachs, I. Nübler and R. Kozul-Wright (eds), *Transforming economies: making industrial policy work for growth, jobs and development*, Geneva: International Labour Office, pp. 355–78.

Altenburg, T. and A. Stamm (2004), 'Towards a more effective provision of business services', Bonn: Deutsches Institut für Entwicklungspolitik/ German Development Institute (DIE), Discussion Paper.

Altenburg, T. and C. Von Drachenfels (2006), 'The "new minimalist approach" to private-sector development: a critical assessment', *Development Policy Review*, **24** (4), pp. 387–411.

Amsden, A. (1989), *Asia's next giant: South Korea and late industrialization*, New York: Oxford University Press.

Amsden, A. (2001), *The rise of 'The Rest': challenges to the West from late-industrializing economies*, New York: Oxford University Press.

Anwar, J. and L. Nguyen (2010), 'Foreign direct investment and economic growth in Vietnam', *Asia Pacific Business Review*, **16** (1–2), pp. 183–202.

Arndt, C. and C. Oman (2006), *Uses and abuses of governance indicators*, Paris: OECD (Development Centre Study).

Asia LEDS Partnership (2013), 'Case study: Vietnam's green growth strategy', available at http://asialeds.org/resources/case-study-vietnams-green-growth-strategy?search=true&name=451 (accessed 16 January 2015).

Athreye, S. and M. Hobday (2010), 'Overcoming development adversity: how entrepreneurs led software development in India', *International Journal of Technological Learning, Innovation and Development*, **3** (1), pp. 36–46.

Auty, R.M. (1993), *Sustaining development in mineral economies: the resource curse thesis*, London, New York: Routledge.

Bai, J. et al. (2014), 'Does economic growth reduce corruption? Theory and evidence from Vietnam', Cambridge, MA: National Bureau of Economic Research, NBER Working Paper No. 19483.

Baliamoune-Lutz, M. (2013), 'Tunisia's development experience: a success story?', in A. Fosu (ed.), *Achieving development success: strategies and lessons from the developing world*, Oxford: Oxford University Press, pp. 457–80.

Battat, J., I. Frank and X. Shen (1996), 'Suppliers to multinationals: linkage programs to strengthen local companies in developing countries', Washington, DC: Foreign Investment Advisory Service, Occasional Paper 6.

Bazan, L. and L. Navas-Alemán (2004), 'The underground revolution in the Sinos Valey: a comparison of up-grading in global and national value chains', reprinted in H. Schmitz (ed.), *Local enterprises in the global economy*, Cheltenham, UK and Northampton, MA, USA: Edward Elgar, pp. 110–39.

Bell, D. (1974), *The coming of post-industrial society*, New York: Harper Colophon Books.

Bell, M. (2007), 'Technological learning and the development of production and innovative capacities in the industry and infrastructure sectors of the least developed countries: what role for ODA?', a paper prepared for UNCTAD, Sussex: SPRU Science and Technology Policy Research.

Bertelsmann Stiftung (2014), 'Transformation Index BTI 2014', available at www.bti-project.org/atlas (accessed 12 February 2015).

Bertelsmann Stiftung (2014a), 'Namibia country report', Gütersloh: Bertelsmann Stiftung.

Bhagwati, J. (1958), 'Immiserizing growth: a geometrical note', *Review of Economic Studies*, **25** (3), pp. 201–5.

Biesebroeck, J. van (2005), 'Firm size matters: growth and productivity growth in African manufacturing', *Economic Development and Cultural Change*, **53** (3), pp. 545–83.

Bigsten, A. and M. Söderbom (2006), 'What have we learned from a decade of manufacturing enterprise surveys in Africa?', *World Bank Research Observer*, **21** (2), pp. 241–65.

Birdsall, N. (2007), 'Do no harm: aid, weak institutions, and the missing middle in Africa', Washington, DC: Center for Global Development, Working Paper 113.

BMU (2008), *Ecological industrial policy: sustainable policy for innovation, growth and employment*, Berlin: Federal Ministry for the Environment, Nature Conservation, Building and Nuclear Safety/ Bundesministerium für Umwelt, Naturschutz, Bau und Reaktorsicherheit.

Boehm, F. (2007), 'Regulatory capture revisited – lessons from economics of corruption', Passau: Internet Center for Corruption Research (ICGG), Working Paper, available at www.icgg.org/downloads/Boehm %20-%20Regulatory%20Capture%20Revisited.pdf (accessed 16 January 2015).

Boulding, K. (1969), 'Economics as a moral science', *American Economic Review*, **59** (1), pp. 1–12.

Bowen, A. and S. Fankhauser, S. (2011), 'Low-carbon development for the least developed countries', *World Economics*, **12** (1), pp. 145–62.

Bown, C.P. and B. Hoekman (2008), 'Developing countries and enforcement of trade agreements: why dispute settlement is not enough', *Journal of World Trade*, **42** (1), pp. 177–203.

Boyle, J. et al. (2013), 'Exploring trends in low-carbon, climate-resilient development', Winnipeg: International Institute for Sustainable Development (IISD), available at http://www.iisd.org/pdf/2013/exploring_trends_low_climate.pdf (accessed 16 January 2015).

Bratton, M. and N. van de Walle (1997), *Democratic experiments in Africa: regime transitions in comparative perspective*, Cambridge: Cambridge University Press.

Braun, K., F. Kaufmann and C. Simons-Kaufmann (2012), 'Social market economy as a vision for Mozambique?', IESE Conference Paper No.4, available at http://www.iese.ac.mz/lib/publication/III_Conf2012/IESE_IIIConf_Paper4.pdf (accessed 16 January 2015).

Bräutigam, D. (2000), 'Interest groups, economic policy, and growth in Sub-Saharan Africa', Washington, DC: United States Agency for International Development (USAID), African Economic Policy Discussion Paper 40.

Broome, J. (2008), 'The ethics of climate change', *Scientific American*, June 2008, pp. 69–73.

Brynjolfsson, E. and A. McAfee (2014), *The second machine age: work, progress, and prosperity in a time of brilliant technologies*, New York and London: W.W. Norton.

Brynjolfsson, E., A. McAfee and M. Spence (2014), 'New world order: labor, capital, and ideas in the power law economy', available at http://www.foreignaffairs.com/articles/141531/erik-brynjolfsson-andrew-mcafee-and-michael-spence/new-world-order (accessed 16 January 2015).

Buur, L., C. Mondlane Tembe and O. Baloi (2012), 'The white gold: the role of government and state in rehabilitating the sugar industry in Mozambique', *Journal of Development Studies*, **48** (3), pp. 349–62.

Byrne, R., H. de Coninck and A. Sagar (2014), 'Low-carbon innovation for industrial sectors in developing countries', Amsterdam: Energy Research Centre of the Netherlands (ECN), Climate & Development Knowledge Network, Policy Brief.

Carbon Tracker Initiative (2012), 'Unburnable carbon: are the world's financial markets carrying a carbon bubble?', available at http://www.carbontracker.org/wp-content/uploads/2014/09/Unburnable-Carbon-Full-rev2-1.pdf (accessed 16 January 2015).

Carbon Tracker Initiative (2013), 'Unburnable carbon 2013: wasted capital and stranded assets', available at http://carbontracker.live.kiln.it/Unburnable-Carbon-2-Web-Version.pdf (accessed 16 January 2015).

Carbone, G. (2003), 'Emerging pluralist politics in Mozambique: the Frelimo–Renamo party system', London: Development Research Centre, Crisis States Programme Working Paper No. 23.

Chang, H.-J. (1996), *The political economy of industrial policy*, Houndmills: Macmillan, 2nd edn.

Chang, H.-J. (2001), 'Breaking the mould: an institutionalist political economy alternative to the neoliberal theory of the market and the state', Geneva: United Nations Research Institute for Social Development (UNRISD), Social Policy and Development Programme Paper No. 6.

Chang, H.-J. (2003), 'Kicking away the ladder: infant industry promotion in historical perspective', *Oxford Development Studies*, **31** (1), pp. 21–32.

Chang, H.-J. (2006), 'How important were the "Initial Conditions" for economic development – East Asia vs. Sub- Saharan Africa', reprinted in H.-J. Chang, *The East Asian development experience: the miracle, the crisis, and the future*, London: Cornell University Press, Chapter 4.

Chang, H.-J. (2009), 'Industrial policy: can we go beyond an unproductive confrontation? A plenary paper for ABCDE', Seoul: Annual World Bank Conference on Development Economics, 22–24 June.

Chang, H.-J. (2010), *23 things they don't tell you about capitalism*, London: Penguin Books.

Chang, H.-J. and I. Grabel (2014), *Reclaiming development: an alternative economic policy manual*, London and New York: Zed Books.

Chenery, H. et al. (1974), *Redistribution with growth*, London: Oxford University Press.

Chiu, S.W.K. (1996), 'Unravelling Hong Kong's exceptionalism: the politics of laissez-faire in the industrial takeoff', *Political Power and Social Theory*, **10**, pp. 229–56.

Chowdhury, A. (2009), 'Microfinance as a poverty reduction tool – a critical assessment', New York: United Nations Department of Economic and Social Affairs (UN DESA), DESA Working Paper 89.

Cimoli, M. (2005), 'Heterogeneidad estructural, asimetrías tecnológicas y crecimiento en América Latina', Santiago de Chile: United Nations Economic Commission for Latin America and the Caribbean (UN ECLAC).

Cimoli, M. et al. (2006), 'Institutions and policies shaping industrial development: an introductory note', New York: Columbia University, Paper prepared for the Task Force on 'Industrial Policies and Development' within the Initiative for Policy Dialogue, directed by Joseph Stiglitz.

Cimoli, M., G. Dosi and J.E. Stiglitz (eds) (2009), *Industrial policy and development: the political economy of capabilities accumulation*, Oxford: Oxford University Press.

Collier, P. (2007), 'Accountability in the provision of services: a framework for Africa research', Oxford: Oxford University, Centre for the Study of African Economies, Department of Economics (mimeo).

Collier, P. (2007a), *The bottom billion: why the poorest countries are failing and what can be done about it*, Oxford: Oxford University Press.

Collier, P., G. Conway and T. Venables (2008), 'Climate change and Africa', *Oxford Review of Economic Policy*, **24** (2), pp. 337–53.

Collier, P. and A.J. Venables (2007), 'Rethinking trade preferences to help diversify African exports', Oxford: Centre for Economic Policy Research, CEPR Policy Insight 2.

Commission on Growth and Development (2008), *The growth report: strategies for sustained growth and inclusive development*, Washington, DC: World Bank.

Committee of Donor Agencies for Small Enterprise Development (2001), 'Business development services for small enterprises: guiding principles for donor intervention', Washington, DC: World Bank Group.

Crespo, R. (1998), 'Is economics a moral science?', *Journal of Markets and Morality*, **1** (2), pp. 201–11.

Cunningham, S. and J. Meyer-Stamer (2005), 'Planning or doing local economic development? Problems with the orthodox approach to local economic development', *Africa Insight*, **3** (4), pp. 4–14.

Curzon Price, V. (1981), *Industrial policies in the European community*, New York: St. Martin's Press.

Daly, H. (1977), *Steady-state economics: the economics of biophysical equilibrium and moral growth*, San Francisco: Freeman.

Davis, K. (2013), 'What does oil and gas discoveries mean for Mozambique?', available at http://www.ventures-africa.com/2013/04/what-does-oil-and-gas-discoveries-mean-for-mozambique/ (accessed 16 January 2015).

Deichmann, U. et al. (2008), 'Industrial location in developing countries', *World Bank Research Observer*, **23** (2), pp. 219–46.

Dewar, M.E. (1998), 'Why state and local economic development programs cause so little economic development', *Economic Development Quarterly*, **12**, pp. 68–87.

Di Maio, M. (2009), 'Industrial policies in developing countries: history and perspectives', in M. Cimoli, G. Dosi and J.E. Stiglitz (eds), *Industrial policy and development*, Oxford: Oxford University Press, pp. 107–43.

Dinh, H. et al. (2012), *Light manufacturing in Africa: targeted policies to enhance private investment and create jobs*, Washington, DC: World Bank.

Dinh Van, A. (2003), 'Developing the socialist-oriented market economy in Vietnam', Hanoi: Central Institute for Economic Management.

Djankov, S. et al. (2002), 'The regulation of entry', *Quarterly Journal of Economics*, **117** (1), pp. 1–37.

DNEAP (2013), '2012 survey of Mozambican manufacturing firms: descriptive report', Maputo, Mozambique: National Directorate of Studies and Policy Analysis.

Dossani, R. (2005), 'Origins and growth of the software industry in India', Stanford, Asia-Pacific Research Center, available at http://aparc.fsi.stanford.edu/publications/origins_and_growth_of_the_software_industry_in_india (accessed 16 January 2015).

EBRD (2008), *Transition Report 2008: growth in transition*, London: European Bank for Reconstruction and Development.

Eifert, B., A. Gelb and V. Ramachandran (2005), 'Business environment and comparative advantage in Africa: evidence from the investment climate data', Washington, DC: Center for Global Development, CGD Working Paper 56.

Ellis, K., B. Baker and A. Lemma (2009), 'Policies for low carbon growth', London: Overseas Development Institute (ODI), Research Report.

Erdle, S. (2010), 'The DESERTEC Initiative powering the development perspectives of Southern Mediterranean countries?', Bonn: Deutsches Institut für Entwicklungspolitik / German Development Institute (DIE), Discussion Paper.

Erdle, S. (2011), 'Industrial policy in Tunisia', Bonn: Deutsches Institut für Entwicklungspolitik / German Development Institute (DIE), Discussion Paper.

Esser, K. (1993), 'América Latina. Industrialización sin vision', *Nueva Sociedad*, no. 125, Mayo–Junio, pp. 27–46.

Esser, K. et al. (1996), *Systemic competitiveness: new governance patterns for industrial development*, London: Frank Cass, GDI Book Series 5.

Evans, P. (1995), *Embedded autonomy: states and industrial transformation*, Princeton, NJ: Princeton University Press.

Fagerberg J. and Srholec M. (2005), 'Catching up: What are the critical factors for success?' *Industrial Development Report 2005*, Background Paper Series, UNIDO, Vienna.

Freeman, C. (2008), *Systems of innovation: selected essays in evolutionary economics*, Cheltenham, UK and Northampton, MA, USA: Edward Elgar.

Friends of the Earth Mozambique, Jubilee Debt Campaign, and Tax Justice Network (2012), 'Whose development is it? Investigating the Mozal aluminium smelter in Mozambique', London: Jubilee Debt Campaign.

Gebre-Egziabher, T. (2007), 'Impacts of Chinese imports and coping strategies of local producers: the case of small-scale footwear enterprises in Ethiopia', *Journal of Modern African Studies*, **45** (4), December, pp. 647–79.

Gebreeyesus, M. (2013), 'Industrial policy and development in Ethiopia: evolution and present experimentation', Helsinki, Finland: United Nations University World Institute for Development Economics Research (UNU-WIDER), Working Paper 125.

Geden, O. and S. Fischer (2014), 'Moving targets: Die Verhandlungen über die Energie- und Klimapolitik der EU nach 2020', Berlin: Stiftung Wissenschaft und Politik (SWP), Studie S1.

General Statistics Office of Vietnam (2014), 'Monthly statistical information', available at http://www.gso.gov.vn/default_en.aspx?tabid= 470&idmid=3&ItemID=14450 (accessed 16 January 2015).

Gereffi, G. (1999), 'International trade and industrial upgrading in the apparel commodity chain', *Journal of International Economics*, **48** (1), pp. 37–70.

Ghani, E. and S. O'Connell (2014), 'Can service be a growth escalator in low income countries?', Washington, DC: World Bank, Policy Research Working Paper 6971.

Goel, V.K., C. Dahlman and M.A. Dutz (2007), 'Diffusing and absorbing knowledge', in M.A. Dutz (ed.), *Unleashing India's innovation:*

towards sustainable and inclusive growth, Washington, DC: World Bank, pp. 83–103.

Goldstein, A. and S. McGuire (2004), 'The political economy of strategic trade policy and the Brazil–Canada export subsidies saga', *World Economy*, **27** (4), pp. 541–66.

González, A. and R. Rosenberg (2006), 'The state of microfinance: outreach, profitability and poverty', Washington, DC: Consultative Group to Assist the Poor, CGAP Working Paper.

Goto, K. (2007), 'The development strategy of the Vietnamese export oriented garment industry: vertical integration or product and process upgrading?', *Asian Profile*, **35** (6), pp. 521–29.

Green, F. (2014), '"This time is different": the prospects for an effective climate agreement in Paris 2015', London: School of Economics and Political Science (LSE), Centre for Climate Change Economics and Policy, Policy Paper.

GTZ (2010), *Engineering Capacity Building Programme: Ethiopia Project Progress Review (PPR) 2010*, Eschborn, Germany: unpublished.

Guruswamy, L. (2011), 'Energy poverty', *Annual Review of Environment and Resources*, **36**, pp. 139–61, DOI: 10.1146/annurev-environ-040610-090118.

Hallegatte, S., M. Fay and A. Vogt-Schilb (2013), 'Green industrial policies: when and how', Washington, DC: World Bank, Policy Research Working Paper 6677.

Hampel-Milagrosa, A., M. Loewe and C. Reeg (2015), 'The entrepreneur makes a difference: evidence on MSE upgrading factors from Egypt, India, and the Philippines', *World Development*, **66**, pp. 118–30.

Hanlon, J. and M. Mosse (2010), 'Mozambique's elite – finding its way in a globalized world and returning to old development models', Helsinki, Finland: United Nations University World Institute for Development Economics Research (UNU-WIDER), Working Paper No. 2010/105.

Hanlon, J. and T. Smart (2008), *Do bicycles equal development in Mozambique?*, Woodbridge, UK: James Currey.

Harmeling, S. and D. Eckstein (2013), 'Global Climate Risk Index 2013: who suffers most from extreme weather events? Weather-related loss events in 2011 and 1992 to 2011', Bonn: Germanwatch.

Harper, M. (2009), *Inclusive value chains in India: linking the smallest producers to modern markets*, Singapore: World Scientific Publishers.

Hausman, D. and M. McPherson (1993), 'Taking ethics seriously: economics and contemporary moral philosophy', *Journal of Economic Literature*, **31**, pp. 671–731.

Hausmann, R. and D. Rodrik (2002), 'Economic development as self-discovery', Cambridge, MA: National Bureau of Economic Research, NBER Working Paper 8952.

Hausmann, R., D. Rodrik and A. Velasco (2008), 'Growth diagnostics', in N. Serra and J.E. Stiglitz (eds), *The Washington consensus reconsidered: towards a new global governance*, New York: Oxford University Press, pp. 324–54.

Hewitt, A. and I. Gillson (2003), 'Review of the trade and poverty content in PRSPs and loan-related documents: report commissioned by Christian Aid', London: Overseas Development Institute (ODI).

Hirschman, A.O. (1958), *The strategy of economic development*, New Haven, CT: Yale University Press.

Hobday, M. and F. Perini (2009), 'Latecomer entrepreneurship: a policy perspective', in M. Cimoli, G. Dosi and J.E. Stiglitz (eds), *Industrial policy and development*, Oxford: Oxford University Press, pp. 470–505.

Hout, W. (2013), 'Néopatrimonialisme et développement: le rôle de pilote des poches d'éfficacité', *Revue Internationale de Politique Comparée*, **20** (3), pp. 76–96.

IEA (2010), *Reviewing existing and proposed emissions trading systems*, Paris: Organisation for Economic Co-operation and Development/International Energy Agency.

IEA (2011), *World energy outlook 2011*, Paris: Organisation for Economic Co-operation and Development/International Energy Agency.

IEA (2013), 'World energy outlook 2012 factsheet', Paris: International Energy Agency, available at http://www.worldenergyoutlook.org/media/weowebsite/2012/factsheets.pdf (accessed 16 January 2015).

Ikiara, G.K., J. Olewe-Nyunya and W. Odhiambo (2004), 'Kenya: formulation and implementation of strategic trade and industrial policies', in C. Soludo, O. Ogbu and H.-J. Chang (eds), *The politics of trade and industrial policy in Africa: forced consensus?*, Trenton, NJ and Asmara, Eritrea: Africa World Press, pp. 205–24.

Ikpeze, N.I., C.C. Soludo and N.N. Elekwa (2004), 'Nigeria: the political economy of the policy process, policy choice and implementation', in C. Soludo, O. Ogbu and H.-J. Chang (eds), *The politics of trade and industrial policy in Africa: forced consensus?*, Trenton, NJ and Asmara, Eritrea: Africa World Press, pp. 341–67.

Johnson, O., T. Altenburg and H. Schmitz (2014), 'Rent management capabilities for the green transformation', in A. Pegels (ed.), *Green industrial policy in emerging economies*, London: Routledge, pp. 9–38.

Kanagawa, M. and T. Nakata (2008), 'Assessment of access to electricity and the socio-economic impacts in rural areas of developing countries', *Energy Policy*, **36**, pp. 2016–29.

Kaplinsky, R. (1993), 'Export-processing zones in the Dominican Republic: transforming manufactures into commodities', *World Development*, **21** (11), pp. 1851–65.

Kaplinsky, R. and M. Morris (2008), 'Do the Asian Drivers undermine export-oriented industrialization in SSA?', *World Development*, **36** (2), pp. 254–73.

Karray, Z. and S. Driss (2014), 'Industrial policy at the service of balanced territorial development in Tunisia', Tunis: African Development Bank, AfDB Economic Brief.

Kelsall, T. and D. Booth, with D. Cammack and F. Golooba-Mutebi (2010), 'Developmental patrimonialism? Questioning the orthodoxy on political governance and economic progress in Africa', London: Overseas Development Institute (ODI), Africa Power and Politics Programme, Working Paper No. 9.

Khan, M. (2004), 'State failure in developing countries and institutional reform strategies', in B. Tungodden, N. Stern and I. Kolstad (eds), *Toward pro-poor policies: aid, institutions, and globalization, Annual World Bank Conference on Development Economics, Europe (2003)*, Oxford University Press and World Bank, pp. 165–95.

Khan, M.H. (2010), 'Political settlements and the governance of growth-enhancing institutions', London: University of London, School of Oriental and African Studies, Research Paper Series on Governance for Growth.

Khan, M.H. and K.S. Jomo (eds) (2000), *Rents, rent-seeking and economic development: theory and evidence in Asia*, Cambridge: Cambridge University Press.

Kim, L. and R.R. Nelson (2000), 'Introduction', in L. Kim and R. Nelson (eds), *Technology, learning and innovation: the experiences of newly industrialising economies*, Cambridge: Cambridge University Press, pp. 1–9.

Klasen, S. (2006), 'Pro-poor growth and gender inequality', in L. Menkhoff (ed.), *Pro-poor growth: policy and evidence*, Berlin: Duncker & Humblot, pp. 151–79.

Klein, M. and B. Hadjimichael (2003), 'The private sector in development: entrepreneurship, regulation and competitive disciplines', Washington, DC: World Bank.

Knack, S. and A. Rahman (2004), 'Donor fragmentation and bureaucratic quality in aid recipients', Washington, DC: World Bank, Policy Research Paper 3186.

Kramer, G.J. and M. Haigh (2009), 'No quick switch to low-carbon energy', *Nature*, **462**, pp. 568–9.

Krause, M. and F. Kaufmann (2011), 'Industrial policy in Mozambique', Bonn: Deutsches Institut für Entwicklungspolitik/German Development Institute (DIE), Discussion Paper.

Krishnan, P. and I. Shaorshadze (2013), 'Technical and vocational education and training in Ethiopia', London: International Growth Centre, IGC Working Paper.

Krueger, A.O. (1974), 'The political economy of the rent-seeking society', *American Economic Review*, **64** (3), pp. 291–303.

Kurtz, M. (2001), 'State developmentalism without a developmental state: the public foundations of the "free market miracle" in Chile', *Latin American Politics and Society*, **43** (2), pp. 1–25.

Laffont, J. and J. Tirole (1991), 'The politics of government decision-making: a theory of regulatory capture', *Quarterly Journal of Economics*, **106** (4), pp. 1089–127.

Lagarde, C. (2014), 'The road to sustainable global growth', speech delivered at the School of Advanced International Studies, Washington, DC: 2 April 2014, available at http://www.imf.org/external/np/speeches/2014/040214.htm (accessed 12 February 2015).

Lall, S. (1995), 'Industrial strategy and policies on foreign direct investment in East Asia', *Transnational Corporations*, **4** (3), pp. 1–26.

Lall, S. (2003), 'Reinventing industrial strategy: the role of government policy in building industrial competitiveness', Oxford: Oxford Department of International Development, QEH Working Paper 111.

Lall, S. (2004), 'Selective industrial and trade policies in developing countries: theoretical and empirical issues', in C. Soludo, O. Ogbu and H.-J. Chang (eds), *The politics of trade and industrial policy in Africa: forced consensus?*, Trenton, NJ and Asmara, Eritrea: Africa World Press, pp. 75–109.

LaRRI (2000), 'Export processing zones in Namibia: taking a closer look', Windhoek: Labour Resource and Research Institute.

Levy, B. (2012), 'Seeking the elusive developmental knife-edge: Zambia and Mozambique – a tale of two countries', in D. North et al. (eds), *In the shadow of violence: the problem of development in limited access order societies*, New York: Cambridge University Press.

Liedholm, C. (2002), 'Small firm dynamics: evidence from Africa and Latin America', *Small Business Economics*, **18** (1–3), pp. 227–42.

Liedholm, C. and D. Mead (1999), *Small enterprises and economic development: the dynamics of micro and small enterprises*, Abingdon, UK and New York: Routledge.

Lin, J. (2011), 'From flying geese to leading dragons. New opportunities and strategies for structural transformation in developing countries', Washington, DC: World Bank, Policy Research Working Paper 5702.

Lin, J. (2012), *Demystifying the Chinese economy*, Cambridge: Cambridge University Press.

Lin, J. (2012a), *The quest for prosperity: how developing economies can take off*, Princeton, NJ: Princeton University Press.

Lin, J. and H.-J. Chang (2009), 'Should industrial policy in developing countries conform to comparative advantage or defy it? A debate between Justin Lin and Ha-Joon Chang', *Development Policy Review*, **27** (5), pp. 483–502.

Lin, J. and C. Monga (2010), 'Growth identification and facilitation: the role of the state in the dynamics of structural change', Washington, DC: World Bank, Policy Research Working Paper 5313.

Liu, X. and C. Shu (2001), 'Determinants of export performance: evidence from Chinese industries', available at https://www.cb.cityu.edu.hk/EF/getFileWorkingPaper.cfm?&id=254 (accessed 16 January 2015).

Loewe, M. et al. (2007), 'The impact of favouritism on the business climate: a study of *Wasta* in Jordan', Bonn: Deutsches Institut für Entwicklungspolitik / German Development Institute (DIE), Studies 30.

Loewe, M. and J. Brach (2010), 'The global financial crisis and the Arab world: impact, reactions and consequences', *Mediterranean Politics*, **15** (1), pp. 45–71.

Lütkenhorst, W. (2004), 'Corporate social responsibility and the development agenda. The case for actively involving small and medium enterprises', *Intereconomics*, **39**, pp. 157–66.

Lütkenhorst, W., T. Altenburg, A. Pegels and G. Vidican (2014), 'Green industrial policy: managing transformation under uncertainty', Bonn: Deutsches Institut für Entwicklungspolitik/German Development Institute (DIE), Discussion Paper.

Lütkenhorst, W. and A. Pegels (2014), 'Stable policies – turbulent markets: Germany's green industrial policy: the costs and benefits of promoting solar PV and wind energy', Winnipeg: International Institute for Sustainable Development (IISD).

Mazzucato, M. (2014), *The entrepreneurial state: debunking public vs. private sector myths*, London and New York: Anthem Press, rev. edn.

Mbekeani, K. (2013), 'Intra-regional trade in Southern Africa: structure, performance and challenges', Tunis: African Development Bank Group, Regional Integration Policy Papers 2.

McGlade, C. and P. Ekins (2014), 'Unburnable oil: an examination of oil resource utilization in a decarbonized energy system', *Energy Policy*, **64**, pp. 102–12.

McMillan, M. and D. Rodrik (2012), 'Globalization, structural change, and productivity growth', Washington, DC: International Food Policy Research Institute, IFPRI Discussion Paper 01160.

Mead, D.C. (1994), 'The contribution of small enterprises to employment growth in Southern and Eastern Africa', *World Development*, **22** (12), pp. 1881–94.

Meadows, D.H. et al. (1972), *The limits to growth*, New York: Universe Books.

Meinshausen, M. et al. (2009), 'Greenhouse-gas emission targets for limiting global warming to 2°C', *Nature*, **458**, pp. 1158–62.

Mendoza, R.U. (2008), 'Why do the poor pay more? Exploring the poverty penalty concept', *Journal of International Development*, **23**, pp. 1–28.

Meyer-Stamer, J. (2009), *Moderne Industriepolitik oder postmoderne Industriepolitiken?*, Bonn: Friedrich-Ebert-Stiftung, Schriftenreihe Moderne Industriepolitik.

Miroudot, S. et al. (2009), *Trade in Intermediate Goods and Services*, Paris: Organisation for Economic Co-operation and Development, OECD Trade Policy Working Paper No. 93, TAD/TC/WP(2009)1/ FINAL.

Mo Ibrahim Foundation (2014), 'Ibrahim Index of African Governance', available at http://www.moibrahimfoundation.org/iiag/ (accessed 16 January 2015).

MoIT and UNIDO (2011), 'Viet Nam industrial competitiveness report 2011', Hanoi, Vietnam: Ministry of Industry and Trade, Government of Vietnam, Vienna: United Nations Industrial Development Organization.

Moran, T.H. (1999), 'Foreign direct investment and development: the new policy agenda for developing countries and economies in transition', Washington, DC: The Institute for International Economics.

Morch von der Fehr, N.-H. (2005), 'The African entrepreneur: evidence on entrepreneurial activity and firm formation in Zambia', Washington, DC: World Bank, PPED Discussion Paper.

Morris, M., R. Kaplinsky and D. Kaplan (2012), '"One thing leads to another" – commodities, linkages and industrial development: a conceptual overview', published free online, available at http://www.prism. uct.ac.za/Papers/MMCP%20Paper%2012_1.pdf (accessed 6 May 2015).

Nadvi, K. and H. Schmitz (1994), 'Industrial clusters in less developed countries: review of experiences and research agenda', Brighton, UK: Institute of Development Studies, Discussion Paper 339.

Nadvi, K. and F. Wältring (2002), 'Making sense of global standards', Duisburg, Germany: Institute of Development and Peace, INEF Report 58.

Namibia Statistics Agency (2014), 'The Namibia Labour Force Survey 2013 Report', Windhoek, Namibia.

Namibian Sun (2013), 'EPZ companies not performing as expected', available at http://www.namibiansun.com/business/epz-companies-not-performing-expected.57212 (accessed 16 January 2015).

Nelson, R.R. (1994), 'The co-evolution of technology, industrial structure, and supporting institutions', *Industrial and Corporate Change*, **3** (1), pp. 47–63.

Nordhaus, W. (1994), *Managing the global commons: the economics of climate change*, Cambridge, MA: MIT Press.

Nordhaus, W. (2013), *The climate casino: risk, uncertainty and economics for a warming world*, New Haven, CT and London: Yale University Press.

North, D. et al. (2012), 'Limited access orders: rethinking the problems of development and violence', available at https://web.stanford.edu/group/mcnollgast/cgi-bin/wordpress/wp-content/uploads/2013/10/Limited_Access_Orders_in_DW_-II_-2012.0310.print-version.13.1220.pdf (accessed 16 January 2015).

North, D.C., J.J. Wallis and B.R. Weingast (2009), *Violence and social orders: a conceptual framework for interpreting recorded human history*, Cambridge: Cambridge University Press.

Nuvunga, M. (2009), 'Understanding state-society linkages for poverty reduction: the relationship between the state and domestic non-state actors in poverty reduction processes', IESE Conference Paper No. 38, available at http://www.iese.ac.mz/lib/publication/II_conf/CP38_2009_Nuvunga.pdf (accessed 16 January 2015).

ODI (2011), 'Viet Nam's progress on economic growth and poverty reduction: impressive improvements', London: Overseas Development Institute.

OECD (2009), 'Is informal normal? Towards more and better jobs in developing countries', Paris: Organisation for Economic Co-operation and Development.

OECD (2010), *Perspectives on global development 2010: shifting wealth*, Paris: Organisation for Economic Co-operation and Development.

OECD (2011), *Divided we stand: why inequality keeps rising*, Paris: Organisation for Economic Co-operation and Development.

Ohno, K. (2009), 'The middle income trap: implications for industrialization strategies in East Asia and Africa', Tokyo: GRIPS Development Forum.

Ohno, K. (2010), 'Avoiding the middle income trap: renovating industrial policy formulation in Vietnam', Hanoi and Tokyo: Vietnam Development Forum and National Graduate Institute for Policy Studies.

References 199

Olukoshi, A.O. (2004), 'Democratisation, globalisation and effective policy making in Africa', in C. Soludo, O. Ogbu and H.-J. Chang (eds), *The politics of trade and industrial policy in Africa: forced consensus?*, Trenton, NJ and Asmara, Eritrea: Africa World Press, pp. 43–73.

Ortiz, I. and M. Cummins (2011), 'Global inequality: beyond the bottom line: a rapid review of income distribution in 141 countries', New York: United Nations International Children's Emergency Fund, UNICEF Social and Economic Policy Working Paper.

Oxfam (2014), *Even it up: time to end extreme inequality*, Oxford: Oxfam International.

Pack, H. and K. Saggi (2006), 'The case for industrial policy: a critical survey', Washington, DC: World Bank, Policy Research Working Paper 3839.

Pagés-Serra, C. (ed.) (2010), *The age of productivity: transforming economies from the bottom up*, Washington, DC: Inter-American Development Bank.

Paraskevopoulou, E. (2013), 'Conquering unknown waters: smart specialization and the evolution of the Chilean salmon industry', Washington, DC: World Bank, Innovation Policy Platform Case Study, available at https://innovationpolicyplatform.org/sites/default/files/rdf_imported_documents/Conquering%20Unknown%20Waters.pdf (accessed 16 January 2015).

Pegels, A. (ed.) (2014), *Green industrial policy in emerging countries*, London: Routledge.

Perkins, D. and T. Vu Thanh (2009), 'Viet Nam's industrial policy: designing policies for sustainable development', Cambridge, MA: Harvard Policy Dialogue Papers, Series on Vietnam's WTO Accession and International Competitiveness Research, Policy Dialogue Paper Number 1.

Perkins, D. and T. Vu Thanh (2010), 'Vietnam's industrial policy: designing policies for sustainable development', Ho Chi Minh City, Vietnam: Harvard Kennedy School and UNDP.

Piketty, T. (2014), *Capital in the twenty-first century*, Cambridge, MA: Harvard University Press.

Polanyi, K. (1944), *The great transformation*, New York: Farrar & Rinehart.

Porter, M.E. (1990), *The competitive advantage of nations*, New York: Free Press.

Porter, M.E. and C. van der Linde (1995), 'Green and competitive: ending the stalemate', *Harvard Business Review*, **73** (5), pp. 120–34.

Pratt, J. and R. Zeckhauser (eds) (1985), *Principals and agents: the structure of business*, Boston, MA: Harvard University Press.

Rama, M. (2008), 'Making difficult choices: Vietnam in transition', Washington, DC: World Bank, Commission on Growth, Development Working Paper 40.

Ranis, G. (2004), 'The evolution of development thinking: theory and policy', New Haven, CT: Yale University Press, Economic Growth Center Discussion Paper No. 886, available at http://www.yale.edu/ leitner/resources/docs/ssrn-id551645.pdf (accessed 16 January 2015).

Rasiah, R. (1994), 'Flexible production systems and local machine tool subcontracting: electronics component transnationals', *Cambridge Journal of Economics*, **18** (3), pp. 279–98.

Ravallion, M. (2001), 'Growth, inequality and poverty: looking beyond averages', *World Development*, **29** (11), pp. 1803–15.

Ravallion, M. (2010), 'Mashup indices of development', Washington, DC: World Bank, Policy Research Working Paper 5432.

Reardon, T. et al. (2000), 'Effects of non-farm employment on rural income inequality in developing countries: an investment perspective', *Journal of Agricultural Economics*, **51** (2), pp. 266–88.

Reardon, T. et al. (2003), 'The rise of supermarkets in Africa, Asia, and Latin America', *American Journal of Agricultural Economics*, **85** (5), pp. 1140–46.

Reinhardt, G. et al. (2007), 'Screening lifecycle assessment Jatropha biodiesel', Heidelberg, Germany: Institute for Energy and Environmental Research.

Rijkers, B., C. Freund and A. Nucifora (2014), 'The perils of industrial policy: evidence from Tunisia', (mimeo), available at http://site resources.worldbank.org/FINANCIALSECTOR/Resources/Perilsof IndustrialPolicy_Tunisia.pdf (accessed 16 January 2015).

Rockström, J. et al. (2009), 'Planetary boundaries: exploring the safe operating space of humanity', *Ecology and Society*, **14** (2), Art. 32, available at www.ecologyandsociety.org/vol14/iss2/art32/ (accessed 16 January 2015).

Rodríguez-Clare, A. (2001), 'Costa Rica's development strategy based on human capital and technology: how it got there, the impact of Intel, and lessons for other countries', *Journal of Human Development*, **2**, pp. 311–24.

Rodrik, D. (1995), 'Getting interventions right: how South Korea and Taiwan grew rich', *Economic Policy*, **20**, pp. 53–97.

Rodrik, D. (2004), 'Industrial policy for the twenty-first century', London: Centre for Economic Policy Research. CEPR Discussion Paper 4767.

Rodrik, D. (2013), 'Green industrial policy', Draft, available at http:// www.sss.ias.edu/files/pdfs/Rodrik/Research/Green-growth-and-industrial-policy.pdf (accessed 16 January 2015).

Rodrik, D. (2015), 'Premature deindustrialisation', Draft, available at https://ipl.econ.duke.edu/bread/system/files/bread_wpapers/439.pdf (accessed 8 June 2015).

Rosendahl, C. (2010), 'Industrial policy in Namibia', Bonn: Deutsches Institut für Entwicklungspolitik / German Development Institute (DIE), Discussion Paper.

Rosser, A. (2006), 'The political economy of the resource curse: a literature survey', Brighton, UK: Institute of Development Studies (IDS), Working Paper 268.

Rozenberg, J., A. Vogt-Schilb and S. Hallegatte (2013), 'How capital-based instruments facilitate the transition toward a low-carbon economy: a tradeoff between optimality and acceptability', Washington, DC: World Bank, Policy Research Working Paper 6609.

Rücker, A. and G. Trah (2007), 'Local and regional economic development: towards a common framework for GTZ's LRED interventions in South Africa', Eschborn, Germany: Deutsche Gesellschaft für Technische Zusammenarbeit (GTZ).

Salazar-Xirinachs, J., I. Nübler and R. Kozul-Wright (eds) (2014), *Transforming economies: making industrial policy work for growth, jobs and development*, Geneva: International Labour Organization (ILO).

Sandel, M. (2012), *What money can't buy: the moral limits of markets*, London: Penguin Books.

Scharpf, F.W. (1993), 'Coordination in networks and hierarchies', in F.W. Scharpf (ed.), *Games in hierarchies and networks*, Frankfurt: Campus, pp. 65–123.

Schmitz, H. (1999), 'Collective efficiency and increasing returns', *Cambridge Journal of Economics*, **23** (4), pp. 465–83.

Schmitz, H. (2006), 'Learning and earning in global garment and footwear chains', *European Journal of Development Research*, **18** (4), pp. 546–71.

Schmitz, H. et al. (2012), 'Who drives economic reform in Vietnam's provinces?', Brighton, UK: Institute of Development Studies (IDS), Research Report Vol. 2012, No. 76.

Schmitz, H. and P. Knorringa (2000), 'Learning from global buyers', *Journal of Development Studies*, **37** (2), pp. 177–205.

Schröder, S. (2007), *Vergleichende Energiebilanzierung der regionalen und überregionalen Produktion von Wein und Äpfeln*, Gießen: Justus-Liebig-Universiät, Dissertation im FB Agrarwissenschaften.

Schumpeter, J.A. (1962), *Capitalism, socialism, and democracy*, New York: Harper and Row, 3rd edn.

Schwarzer, J. (2013), 'Industrial policy for a green economy', Winnipeg: International Institute for Sustainable Development (IISD).

Singh, A. (2009), 'The past, present and future of industrial policy in India: adapting to the changing domestic and international environment', in M. Cimoli, G. Dosi and J.E. Stiglitz (eds), *Industrial policy and development: the political economy of capabilities accumulation*, Oxford: Oxford University Press, pp. 277–302.

Sleuwaegen, L. and M. Goedhuys (2003), 'Technical efficiency, market share and profitability of manufacturing firms in Côte d'Ivoire: the technology trap', *Cambridge Journal of Economics*, **27** (6), pp. 851–66.

Smith, A. (2013), *The climate bonus: co-benefits of climate policy*, London: Earthscan/Routledge.

Snodgrass, D. and T. Biggs (1996), *Industrialization and the small firm: patterns and policies*, San Francisco: International Center for Economic Growth.

Soludo, C., O. Ogbu and H.-J. Chang (eds) (2004), *The politics of trade and industrial policy in Africa: forced consensus?*, Trenton, NJ and Asmara, Eritrea: Africa World Press.

Stern, N. et al. (2007), *Stern review on the economics of climate change*, Cambridge: Cambridge University Press.

Stiglitz, J.E. (1996), 'Some lessons from the East Asian miracle', *World Bank Research Observer*, **11** (2), pp. 151–77.

Stiglitz, J., J. Lin and C. Monga (2013), 'Introduction: the rejuvenation of industrial policy', in J. Stiglitz and J. Lin, *The industrial policy revolution I: the role of government beyond ideology*, Basingstoke, UK and New York: Palgrave Macmillan, pp. 1–15.

Streeten, P. (1981), *First things first: meeting basic human needs in the developing countries*, Oxford: Oxford University Press.

Taffesse, M. (2008), 'The Ethiopian civil service reform program', in T. Assefa (ed.), *Digest of Ethiopia's national policies, strategies and programs*, Addis Ababa, Ethiopia: Forum for Social Studies, pp. 373–417.

Taleb, N. (2008), *The black swan: the impact of the highly improbable*, London: Penguin Books.

Taylor, A.M. (1998), 'On the costs of inward-looking development: price distortions, growth, and divergence in Latin America', *Journal of Economic History*, **58** (1), pp. 1–28.

Tban, C. and L. Fung-Yee Ng (1995), 'Manufacturing evolution under passive industrial policy and cross-border operations in China: the case of Hong Kong', *Journal of Asian Economics*, **6** (1), pp. 71–88.

Tendler, J. and M.A. Amorim (1996), 'Small firms and their helpers: lessons on demand', *World Development*, **24** (3), pp. 407–26.

Tirole, J. (1996), 'A theory of collective reputations (with applications to the persistence of corruption and to firm quality)', *Review of Economic Studies*, **1**, pp. 1–22.

Trah, G. et al. (2010), 'Programme progress report: engineering capacity building programme', Eschborn, Germany, (mimeo).

Transparency International (2014), 'Corruption Perception Index 2014', available at www.transparency.org/cpi2014 (accessed 12 February 2015).

Tybout, J.R. (2000), 'Manufacturing firms in developing countries: how well do they do, and why?', *Journal of Economic Literature*, **38**, pp. 11–44.

UNCSD (2012), 'Outcome document A/Conf.216/L.1', UN Conference on Sustainable Development, Rio de Janeiro.

UNCTAD (2007), *The least developed countries report: knowledge, technological learning and innovation for development*, New York and Geneva: United Nations Conference on Trade and Development.

UNCTAD (2009), *Trade and environment review 2008/2009: promoting poles of clean growth to foster the transition to a more sustainable economy*, New York and Geneva: United Nations Conference on Trade and Development.

UNDP (2011), *Towards human resilience: sustaining MDG progress in an age of economic uncertainty*, New York: United Nations Development Programme.

UNDP (2013), 'Human Development Report 2013: the rise of the South: human progress in a diverse world', New York: United Nations Development Programme, available at http://hdr.undp.org/sites/default/files/Country-Profiles/ETH.pdf (accessed 22 February 2015).

UNECA (2014), *Economic report on Africa 2014. Dynamic industrial policy in Africa: innovative institutions, effective processes and flexible mechanisms*, Addis Ababa, Ethiopia: United Nations Economic Commission for Africa.

UNGA (2005), 'Document A/Res/60/1', New York: United Nations General Assembly.

UNIDO (2009), *Industrial Development Report 2009. Breaking in and moving up: new industrial challenges for the bottom billion and the middle-income countries*, Vienna: United Nations Industrial Development Organization.

UNIDO (2011), 'Business registration reform in Vietnam: a situation analysis of the reform and of UNIDO support', Vienna: United Nations Industrial Development Organization.

UNIDO (2013), *Industrial Development Report 2013. Sustaining employment growth: the role of manufacturing and structural change*, Vienna: United Nations Industrial Development Organization.

UNIDO (2013a), *The industrial competitiveness of nations: looking back, forging ahead*, Vienna: United Nations Industrial Development Organization.

UNIDO (2014), *Statistical outlook on world manufacturing*, Vienna: United Nations Industrial Development Organization.

UNIDO (2014a), *International yearbook of industrial statistics 2014*, Vienna: United Nations Industrial Development Organization.

Unruh, G. (2000), 'Understanding carbon lock-in', *Energy Policy*, **28**, pp. 817–30.

Utz, A. and C. Dahlman (2007), 'Promoting inclusive innovation in India', in M.A. Dutz (ed.), *Unleashing India's innovation: toward sustainable and inclusive growth*, Washington, DC: World Bank, pp. 105–28.

Vidican, G. (2014), 'Reforming fossil fuel subsidies in the MENA countries', in A. Pegels (ed.), *Green industrial policy in emerging economies*, London: Routledge, Routledge Studies in Ecological Economics.

Wade, R.H. (1990), *Governing the market: economic theory and the role of government in East Asian industrialization*, Princeton, NJ: Princeton University Press.

Wade, R.H. (2007), 'Rethinking industrial policy for low income countries', Paper presented at the African Economic Conference, 15–17 Nov., Addis Ababa, Ethiopia: African Development Bank/UNECA.

Walker, I. (1995), 'Mercados regionales de trabajo y localización de las Zonas Industriales de Procesamiento en Honduras', in T. Altenburg and H. Nuhn (eds), *Apertura comercial en Centroamérica: nuevos retos para la industria*, San José, Costa Rica: Departamento Ecuménico de Investigaciones (DEI), pp. 165–89.

WBGU (2009), 'Solving the climate dilemma: the budget approach', Berlin: Wissenschaftlicher Beirat der Bundesregierung Globale Umweltveränderungen/German Advisory Council on Global Change.

WB-IEG (2008), 'Doing Business: an independent evaluation: taking the measure of the World Bank-IFC Doing Business Indicators', Washington, DC: World Bank Independent Evaluation Group.

WEF (2009), *The Global Competitiveness Report 2009–2010*, Geneva: World Economic Forum.

WEF (2013), *Global Risks 2013: eighth edition*, Cologne and Geneva: World Economic Forum.

WEF (2014), *The Global Competitiveness Report 2014–2015*, Geneva: World Economic Forum.

Weisbach, D. and C. Sunstein (2008), 'Climate change and discounting the future: a guide for the perplexed', Chicago, IL: University of Chicago, Harvard Law School Program on Risk Regulation, Research

Paper No. 08-12, available at papers.ssrn.com/sol3/papers.cfm? abstract_id=1223448 (accessed 16 January 2015).

Westphal, L. and H. Pack (2000), 'Industrialization meets globalization: uncertain reflections on East Asian experience', Maastricht: UNU-Institute for New Technologies (UNU/INTECH), Discussion Papers 8.

Whitfield, L. et al. (2015), *The politics of African industrial policy: a comparative perspective*, Cambridge: Cambridge University Press (forthcoming).

Wilkinson, R. and K. Pickett (2009), *The spirit level: why greater equality makes societies stronger*, New York: Bloomsbury Press.

World Bank (2004), 'A review of rural development aspects of PRSPs and PRSCs 2004–2004: agriculture and rural development internal report', Washington, DC: World Bank.

World Bank (2004a), *World Development Report 2005: a better investment climate for everyone*, Washington, DC: World Bank.

World Bank (2006), 'India: inclusive growth and service delivery: building on India's success', Washington, DC: World Bank, Development Policy Review, Report 34580-IN.

World Bank (2008), *World Development Report 2009: reshaping economic geography*, Washington, DC: World Bank.

World Bank (2012), *Inclusive green growth: the pathway to sustainable development*, Washington, DC: World Bank.

World Bank (2013), 'Vietnam Development Report 2014 – skilling up Vietnam: preparing the workforce for a modern market economy', Washington, DC: World Bank.

World Bank (2013a): 'Africa's pulse, vol. 7', Washington, DC: World Bank.

World Bank (2013b), 'Worldwide Governance Indicators', available at info.worldbank.org/governance/wgi/ (accessed 12 February 2015).

World Bank Group (2014), *Doing Business 2015: going beyond efficiency*, Washington, DC: World Bank.

World Bank Group (2014a): 'Third Ethiopia economic update: strengthening export performance through improved competitiveness', Washington, DC: World Bank.

World Bank and IFC (2005), *Doing Business in 2005: removing obstacles to growth*, Washington, DC: World Bank.

World Commission on Environment and Development (1987), *Our common future*, Oxford: Oxford University Press.

WTO and IDE-JETRO (Institute of Developing Economies – Japan External Trade Organization) (2011), *Trade patterns and global value chains in East Asia: from trade in goods to trade in tasks*, Geneva: World Trade Organization.

WTTC (2014), 'Economic Impact 2014', Namibia and London: World Travel & Tourism Council.

Yeo, H.-K. and G. Akinci (2011), 'Low-carbon, green special economic zones', in T. Farole and G. Akinci (eds), *Special economic zones: progress, emerging challenges, and future directions*, Washington, DC: World Bank, pp. 283–308.

Zoellick, R. (2010), 'The end of the third world', *International Economy*, pp. 40–43.

Zwizwai, B., A. Kambudzi and B. Mauwa (2004), 'Zimbabwe: economic policy-making and implementation: a study of strategic trade and selective industrial policies', in C. Soludo, O. Ogbu and H.-J. Chang (eds), *The politics of trade and industrial policy in Africa: forced consensus?*, Trenton, NJ and Asmara, Eritrea: Africa World Press, pp. 225–52.

Index

and rising inequality 19
and spatial redistribution 26
in Vietnam 148–9
see also carbon efficiency; solar
    installations

Taffesse, M. 171
Taiwan 44, 57, 96
Taleb, N. 34
targeted interventions 46, 57–8, 83, 102,
    119, 122, 138, 147
taxes
    carbon tax 29–31, 36, 88, 165
    on exports 166–7
    tax breaks 24
Tban, C. 39
technology
    and automation 20, 71–2
    and competitiveness 69
    and green policies 28, 30–32, 35–6
    information technology 20, 40, 97
    and learning 25, 31, 32, 55, 58–9, 89,
        95
    and SMEs 20–21
    and societal acceptance 10
    Vietnam innovations 147–8
Tendler, J. and M.A. Amorim 82
Tirole, J. 47, 92
tourism sector
    in Namibia 127, 133
    in Tunisia 134, 137, 141–2
trade policies
    export subsidies 101, 103
    import restrictions 102
Trah, G. 24
transport 26, 29, 70, 73, 119
    electric 35, 36
    and regional cooperation 132–3
Tunisia 171, 174
    economic structure 133–6
    future challenges 141–2
    governance and policies 136–8
    and green policies 165–6
    industrial policy 139–40
    'Jasmine Revolution' 140–41
    national projects 163
    National Upgrading Programme
        138–9

performance indicators 154, 155
and privatisation 157–9
Tybout, J.R. 75

UNCSD (United Nations Conference
    on Sustainable Development)
    15
UNGA (United Nations General
    Assembly) 15
UNIDO (United Nations Industrial
    Development Organization) 26,
    66, 144
United States, incentives 38–40
Utz, A. and C. Dahlman 85

value chains 25, 30, 67, 69, 84, 89,
    166
    and ODA inflows 101
    in Tunisia 135
    in Vietnam 144
Venables, T. 68
Vietnam 167, 171
    economic structure 142–4
    and equitisation 157–9
    future challenges 146–51
    industrial policy 144–6
    national projects 163, 164
    ODA inflows 101
    performance indicators 154–5
Vogt-Schilb, A. 31, 36

Wade, R.H. 40, 44
Walker, I. 81
WBGU 31, 86
Weisbach, D. and C. Sunstein 12
welfare economics 12–13
    and state intervention 47, 50–51
Whitfield, L. 97, 98, 122
Wilkinson, R. and K. Pickett 18
women entrepreneurship 81, 160
World Bank 51, 58, 61, 73, 82, 85, 92,
    99, 147
    and green policies 30
    income-based classification 63,
        107
    and spatial redistribution 23–4
    Worldwide Governance Indicators
        (WGI) 93, 94, 172